Childhood Studies

Childhood Studies

Making Young Subjects

Karen Wells

polity

First published in 2018 by Polity Press

Polity Press
65 Bridge Street
Cambridge CB2 1UR, UK

Polity Press
101 Station Landing
Suite 300,
Medford, MA 02155
USA

ISBN-13: 978-0-7456-7023-2
ISBN-13: 978-0-7456-7024-9 (pb)

Library of Congress Cataloging-in-Publication Data

Names: Wells, Karen, 1961- author.
Title: Childhood studies : making young subjects / Karen Wells.
Description: Cambridge, UK; Malden, MA, USA : Polity, 2017. | Series: Short introductions | Includes bibliographical references and index.
Identifiers: LCCN 2017013931 (print) | LCCN 2017032973 (ebook) | ISBN 9781509525348 (Mobi) | ISBN 9781509525355 (Epub) | ISBN 9780745670232 (hardback) | ISBN 9780745670249 (pbk.)
Subjects: LCSH: Child development. | Children--Social conditions. | Child psychology.
Classification: LCC HQ767.85 (ebook) | LCC HQ767.85 .W45 2017 (print) | DDC 305.23--dc23
LC record available at https://lccn.loc.gov/2017013931

A catalogue record for this book is available from the British Library.

Typeset in 10 on 12 pt Sabon by Toppan Best-set Premedia Limited
Printed and bound in Great Britain by CPI Group (UK) Ltd, Croydon

For further information on Polity, visit our website: politybooks.com

For my daughter Devan Carey Wells

Contents

1

Making Young Subjects

Introduction

This book is about how Childhood Studies has conceptualized the figure
of the child, the social field of childhood, and the relationship between
age as a category of subjectivity and other categories of subjectivity,
including race, class and gender. The book is interested in understanding
how subjects are formed, how children come to understand themselves
as particular kinds of people through the ways that the structures of
class, racism and sexism are pressed upon them by different social, political and cultural forces.

Childhood Studies

Childhood Studies is a multidisciplinary and interdisciplinary field with
a shared focus on childhood as a social category or structure and children
as social agents or actors. The 'old' social studies of childhood developed
out of the child-study movement and the psy-sciences that made the child
an object (rather than a subject) of investigation. Their core concern was
the education and appropriate development of the child that were central
to the disciplines of pedagogy and psychology. Children mainly figured,
if at all, as an (often silent) part of the sociology of the family. Sociology
connected with psychology and pedagogy in its interest in normal
socialization.

What is widely called the 'new social studies of childhood' rejected
this interest in children as emergent or developing subjects and focused

instead on children and childhood in their own right. Children are conceptualized within Childhood Studies as agents who are constrained by
the social structures that they are situated within but who do not pas-
sively succumb to these structures; they are agents or actors and they
make society as much as society makes them. From this perspective the
expert is no longer the psychologist, the teacher or the sociologist, but
children themselves. This shift in the epistemology of childhood (in how
we can claim to know what childhood is or who children are) privileges
first person accounts and participatory research over experiments,
surveys and observation.

Conceptualizing the child as agential marshalled a particular view of
children's capacities and competencies. Largely it deployed an argument
that children are as rational, self-knowing and independent as adults.
The fact that in most cultures children are understood to be irrational,
ignorant and dependent was, Childhood Studies suggested, an effect of
discrimination against children. This discrimination paralleled other
social exclusions, for example those structured by racism and sexism.

The insistence on children being rational, self-knowing and independent left little room for a distinctive child subject – in effect it suggests
that children are like small adults. This view has been criticized in recent
work for embracing a modern, stable, self-knowing subject just when
many of the rest of the social sciences and humanities were rejecting this
way of conceptualizing subjectivity. Furthermore, there was some criticism that the baby (the child's body) had literally been thrown out with
the bathwater (socialization theories) and that it was time to bring the
body back in and to acknowledge the effect on their place in the social
world of the distinctiveness of children's bodies and (relatedly) their
imaginations.

Childhood Studies established some important theoretical and meth-
odological frames for thinking about children as subjects. It is now an
established discipline and some of the gaps in its framing of children and
childhood have become apparent. Childhood Studies needs new theoretical tools and empirical focus if it is to continue to have explanatory
power in relation to understanding what it means to be a child in the
contemporary world.

In response to these concerns scholars in Childhood Studies have
begun to look for new social theories for theorizing childhood in more
complex ways. Whilst poststructuralism certainly has not taken over
Childhood Studies, Foucault's governmentality theory, Butler's gender
performativity, Agamben's state of exception, Latour's actor network
theory and other critical social theories, are starting to appear in Childhood Studies. This critical work has been particularly useful for understanding how childhood intersects with other social positions.

My central argument in this book is that childhood is a profoundly unequal space. Childhood Studies frames this inequality primarily as generational inequality between adults and children. I want to suggest that this does not capture the complex ways in which age, as one category of subordinate social status, intersects with others such as race, gender, class and disability. Although the concept of multiple childhoods has been in the discipline since its inception, it has tended to understand multiplicity in spatial and temporal ways: there is childhood there and childhood here; childhood then and childhood now. What has been less explored under this rubric of multiple childhoods is the multiplicity of childhood within a time-space; how racism, sexism and class shape childhood experiences, impact on children's life chances and on how they form a sense of self. Children's experience of their childhoods is different within the same geographical spaces and historical times because of the profound structural inequalities that shape the contemporary world, in the advanced (or overdeveloped) capitalist countries of the Global North as well as the incipient and partial capitalist countries of the Global South (Balagopalan 2014). Uneven development is not only global, it is also regional and national. It is the central task of this book to contribute to the conceptualization and description of this multiplicity of childhood, what I call the making of young subjects.

Chapter summaries

In the next chapter I survey the field of Childhood Studies to give the reader a sense of the genealogy of the four key sub-disciplines (anthropology, geography, history and sociology) that have contributed to the discipline. I then develop the core argument of the book over the following seven chapters, in which I show how the classic exclusions of or limitations on liberal rule have played out in the lives of children and in the formation of their subjectivities. In chapter 3, which is loosely structured around the history of childhood, I begin the story by showing how from the beginning of the twentieth century there was a purposeful exclusion of black children from the child labour reform campaign in the USA. This campaign to get children out of work and into school focused its reform energy on white children and indeed claimed the importance of rescuing white children from economic labour because, or so they argued, white children were living in slavery while black children were free. The offence, in other words, was not the labour of children but the unfreedom of whites. Capitalism in the USA, I argue, was a racial capitalism from the outset. My claim is that governing through childhood and governing through racism were strategies for securing the power of the liberal state that emerged at the same time and cannot be unpicked from one another. In chapter 4, drawing mainly on the sociology of childhood, I show how Childhood Studies has understood gender and sexism in relation to children. My empirical material here is drawn from the scholarship on juvenile justice in the USA, and shows how gender is literally policed by the state and how racism and homophobia both enter into the production of children as gendered subjects. Chapter 5 explores geographies of childhood in relation to the formation of class. Here I show how economic exclusion in childhood in the USA is racialized and how it impacts children's sense of respect and recognition.

Chapters 3, 4 and 5, then, explore how governing forces press onto the child from the outside, structuring their experience of the world. In the subsequent chapters, I turn my attention to the child's own activities, practices and responses. Chapter 6 begins with the governing technologies that produce disability, specifically autism, and then explores how autistic communication can be understood culturally and symbolically. Chapter 7 turns to children's bodies to think through how the specific affordances of children's bodies (of which their brains are a part) shape their subject formation. Chapter 8 draws on social and development psychology to interrogate how children think about gender and racial identification, and chapter 9 turns to practices of consumption as sets of cultural resources through which children come to understand the performativity of social identity. Finally, in the concluding chapter, I return to the three core arguments developed in this book, which are that childhood is the ideal target of liberal governmentality; that governing through the child is segmented in highly unequal ways and is structured by racism, sexism and classification; and thirdly that subject formation is not only pressed onto the child from outside but is also taken up by children and shaped by their corporeal and cognitive resources and through their cultural practices. Through the reasons and techniques of government on the one hand, and the affordances of children's bodies and minds on the other, young subjects are made.

2

The Disciplines

Introduction

The purpose of this chapter is to sketch the dominant trends in each of the sub-disciplines that constitute Childhood Studies in order to show the explanatory power of Childhood Studies as an interdisciplinary and multidisciplinary field. Childhood Studies locates children and childhood at the intersection of time, space, society and culture. Each of the field's sub-disciplines (history, geography, sociology, and anthropology) approaches the figure of the child and the site of childhood through the central problematic of their discipline. So for sociology the central problem is structure/agency, for anthropology it is culture or specifically how children are enculturated, and for history and geography it is the difference that time and space make to childhood and to the lives of children and youth. In the following sections I trace the genealogy of these sub-disciplines, their points of origin, the central problems that they engage with and their key concepts.

History

Historians, perhaps more so than geographers and sociologists, tie their claims about childhood to specific places and historical periods. With the exception of Peter Stearn's world history of childhood (2011), most histories of childhood are region or country specific. Indeed, the field of the history of childhood is mostly the history of North American childhood, and, in fact, largely the history of the colonial period and up to the recent past in the USA.

It is a cardinal principle of historical inquiry that explanations for phenomena should be faithful to the period, in other words that contemporary ways of understanding social phenomena should not be projected back into the past. The definition of children in current use by most Childhood Studies scholars is people below the age of 18 years. Somewhat paradoxically, given a prevailing critique of the United Nations Convention on the Rights of the Child (UNCRC), this definition is derived from that Convention. For historians to describe a person as a child who would not be recognized as such by their contemporaries would be anachronistic. Historians are much more likely to take childhood to be the period from birth to a culturally resonant age or a moment in biological development (for example, puberty). The period from puberty up until a historical culturally resonant shift to adulthood occurs is much more likely to be defined by historians as 'youth' than childhood.

The history of childhood, like the history of all marginalized populations, presents specific problems about the trace children did or, for the most part, did not leave in the historical record. The history of institutions and how they refract ideas about childhood has been the focus of many of the histories of childhood, perhaps because institutional records offer a rich archival source for children's histories. These institutional records and other official sources, including records of birth and death, not only give us a record (albeit at times a rather thin one) of children's experiences but also offer evidence of how childhood was structured and governed in the past. Artefacts are another fertile source for reconstructing the history of childhood; for example, gravestones supplement registries of birth and death and also provide evidence of parents' feelings towards their children, or at least how they wanted their feelings to be viewed in public. Other material objects, including artefacts recovered in archaeological digs, can provide a trace of how valued children were and what they did with their time, long after the lives of individual children have disappeared from the historical record (Baxter 2005, 2008, Sofaer Derevenski 2000).

The nineteenth-century emergence of child-saving reforms coincided with the invention of photography, a coincidence that institutions and charities were quick to respond to, widely using photography to document children's entry into institutions and to campaign for the rescue of children whose innocence was so easily and poignantly caught on camera. As a consequence, film and photography archives offer quite extensive contemporary sources for understanding children's lives and childhood in the past. The Lewis Hine archive, for example, which I analyse in the next chapter, is a collection of photographs most of which were commissioned by the National Child Labor Campaign in the early twentieth century. The late nineteenth-century photographs of children before and after their rescue by the children's charity Barnardo's (the pictures were staged) have also been a fertile source for historians of childhood (Koven 1997).

Autobiography and biography, mostly of adults recollecting their childhoods, have been another rich seam for historians of childhood. It is a source fraught with problems, of course, not least the unreliability of personal memory. (The very idea of personal memory is contested by cultural historians who contend that memory always draws on sociocultural narratives.) Nonetheless, looking back is often the best source we have for the construction of subaltern histories that were left out of the record the first time around. Jennifer Ritterhouse (2006) drew on, among other resources, the 'Behind the Veil' archive at Duke University to great effect in *Growing Up Jim Crow*, her haunting account of childhood in the Southern states after the Civil War.

Popular novels have also been drawn on in the writing of children's history. Harriet Beecher Stowe's *Uncle Tom's Cabin* and particularly the portrayal of children in that book have been analysed multiple times by cultural historians of childhood (Bernstein 2011, Duane 2011, Levander 2006, Mitchell 2008).

Key themes

Susan Kidd has suggested that children disrupt the standard periodizations of American (USA) history (Miller 2012). What periodizations could be applied to the history of childhood and to what extent could those periodizations make sense out of national contexts? Unsurprisingly, given the importance of child-saving institutions to the formation of modern childhood (and the archives they have contributed to), the emergence of these institutions in the USA and Europe has provided an effective periodization. Another temporal frame is provided by the periods of industrialization, urbanization and the growth of the bureaucratic nation-state. These have mostly focused on the shift from work to school (from economic to mental labour) and changes in family structure. Of course there will be an overlap here between the emergence of child-saving institutions and of urban-industrial development, since getting children out of work and into school and extending the reach of the state into the family were all benchmarks of the Progressive Era and similar periods in Europe. European imperialism is another time-frame that can be used for exploring changing conceptions of childhood and children's experiences and how the colonial state shaped the ways in which people thought about their children's capacities and vulnerabilities (see, for example Sarada Balagopalan (2014) on India, Saheed Aderinto (2015) on Nigeria, Owen White (1999) on French West Africa and Beverly Grier (2006) on colonial Zimbabwe).

In US history, the colonial period, that is the period from British colonization of North America up to the War of Independence, is a standard periodization, and this has been followed by historians of childhood. Similarly the British Empire is a standard periodization in British history covering the period from the incursion of the East India Company into the Mughal Empire up to the imposition of various forms of colonial rule across roughly one-quarter of the earth, including mandates, indirect rule and settler colonization. How does a periodization based on colonial rule speak to the history of childhood? What space does it leave for a history of colonized peoples? So far, there is scant historical work on the indigenous populations of the Americas, Australia and New Zealand.

Modern world history

I argued in *Childhood in a Global Perspective* (Wells 2015) that as a consequence of globalization it is now possible to think of childhood on a global scale. That is to say that the forces regulating or governing childhood, many of which link together international and national policy, operate on a global scale and have done so since the beginning of European colonialism. The integration of much of the world into the governing orbit of European states, from the conquest of the Americas (*c*.1492) and continuing after decolonization up to the combined forces of international institutions and finance capital, or modernity, thus offers another periodization for the history of childhood. There are three important shifts here, the dynamics of which differ in relation to the position of a national economy or colonial territory vis-à-vis the global political economy, on the one hand, and the class (and racialized class) of people within that, on the other hand. These three shifts are, firstly, from working children to school children; secondly, from large, dispersed families to small, concentrated families; and thirdly, and in many ways most significantly, from children being on the periphery of governing rationales to becoming, arguably, the most highly governed of modern subjects.

Geography

The dissemination of governing practices and ideas about childhood on a global scale accompanied the emergence of modern world history marked by imperialism and postcolonial globalization. This process was highly uneven and differentiated. The governing of childhood in the colonies was not the same as the governing of childhood in the metropoles (Balagopalan 2014), and this spatialization of government continues into the present period. It points to the importance of space, and therefore of geography, in understanding childhood.

Space is a central concept for children's geographies. It prompts questions about what difference geography (place and scale) makes to children's life experiences and to how others perceive children's competencies, capacities and vulnerabilities. Like the other disciplines that contribute to Childhood Studies, children's geographies want to place children at the centre of those questions. This has led to a tendency to focus on the micro spaces of childhood. Although the analysis of micro spaces ignores the significance of other scales, as with the anthropology of childhood, the accumulation of careful description of specific places allows for the development of theories about how childhood is structured spatially and with what effects. Most of this research is concentrated in the age range 9–13 years, or 'middle childhood', and there has been little work done on infant geographies (but see Holt 2013, 2016).

The way the child is conceptualized within geography is somewhat different from that for the sociology of childhood. In the latter a distinct line is drawn between the child and the family; indeed there is an insistence on children being empirically examined, and childhood theoretically framed separately from the family. This is partly, perhaps, because there is a long-standing sociology of the family and sociology of youth that predates the claim in James and Prout (1997) and James, Jenks and Prout (2014) that attending to children and childhood is a new paradigm. In any case, geography has not emphasized the importance of this division. This has allowed geographies of childhood to focus on childhood as relational, not only in the sense that it is always defined in relation to being adult, but also in the sense that children and young people, like adults, are always in relation with others in their occupation of social-spatial worlds. The most recent contribution to the conceptualization of the field is the twelve-volume reference work *Geographies of Children and Young People*, edited by Tracy Skelton (2016–).

The early geography of childhood was interested in how children learned to conceptualize and navigate space in the field of environmental psychology, which is closely related, especially in its claims about cognitive development, to development psychology and pedagogy. The key figure here is James Blaut (see Blaut, McCleary and Blaut 1970, Blaut and Stea 1971, Stea 2005).

A second early theme is in children's urban geographies and the question of how children and young people navigate space, and what kinds of spaces are conducive to the general well-being of children. An important contribution here is Colin Ward's study of children in post-war London (1990). This is significant not only because it made children (actually, boys) visible in the city but also because these images and the accompanying text uncovered how important abandoned spaces such as bomb sites, empty lots and derelict houses were to children's play. The theme of children appropriating abandoned spaces in the city and using them for play or just for hanging around, out of sight of adult supervision, was also an important area of research for the new geography of childhood. Kevin Lynch made a seminal contribution to the geography of urban childhoods with his design of the UNESCO research project *Growing Up in Cities* (Lynch and Banerjee 1977). His research as an urban planner suggested the importance of legibility in increasing children's ability to interpret and traverse urban space comfortably. Louise Chawla took up Lynch's method in the follow-on study in the late 1990s (Chawla 2002).

Geography is a discipline that crosses the science/humanities disciplinary divide, and perhaps for this reason there has not been the same hostility towards the natural world as a determinant of human endeavour as there is in the sociology of childhood. A third theme, then, in children's geographies is environmental geography and children's participation in designing the built environment. Roger Hart (1997, 2002) is the key figure here and his ladder of participation is regularly cited in research design in contemporary studies of childhood. Within this theme, which continues to be highly influential in geographies of childhood, the importance of being in nature for children's well-being is emphasized.

With this as the backstory to contemporary childhood geographies, the beginning of a geography of childhood self-consciously connected with the new social studies of childhood can be dated to a seminal paper by Hugh Matthews and Melanie Limb (1999), in which an agenda for children's geographies is formulated. In 2003 this was followed by the founding of the multidisciplinary *Journal of Children's Geographies*. In 2000 Sarah Holloway and Gill Valentine published an edited collection, *Children's Geographies: Playing, Living, Learning*. The key themes of this second wave of childhood geographies can be conceptualized in various ways but I focus here on place-making (rural, urban, out-of-place), mobilities, and scale (globalization, embodiment). Alternative typologies can be found in Peter Kraftl, John Horton, and Faith Tucker's (2014) contribution on 'geography' to the online *Oxford Bibliographies for Childhood Studies* (http://www.oxfordbibliographies.com/obo/page/childhood-studies) and the volume titles of *Geographies of Children and Young People* (Skelton 2016–).

Place-making

Rural place   Childhood as a trope of the contemporary social world is closely connected to nature and the rural. In contrast to this ideology of childhood and the idea of a rural idyll that supports it, more than one billion children and half the world's population live in urban areas (UNICEF 2012). For this reason at least, and perhaps from a certain degree of iconoclasm, most childhood geographies focus on urban childhood (Matthews, Taylor, Sherwood, Tucker and Limb 2000). An important exception, and a volume that was developed in part to balance this emphasis on the urban especially in the Global South, is Ruth Panelli, Sam Punch and Elspeth Robson's edited collection *Global Perspectives on Rural Childhood and Youth: Young Rural Lives* (2007). Their introduction to this volume offers an excellent overview of rurality and childhood geographies.

Urban place   The association of a good childhood with the rural idyll on the one hand, and moral panics about unruly youth on the other, put children and youth in a contradictory space in relation to the city (Wells 2002, 2005). On the one hand they are a significant part of urban populations globally. On the other hand they are treated as out of place in the city, especially when they are on their own. This has led to curfews on young people in the developed world (Collins and Kearns 2001) and marginalization of homeless children in the developing world (Beazley 2003, Panter-Brick 2004, van Blerk 2012) and the developed world (Ruddick 1996). Related to the paradoxical inclusion/exclusion of young people in urban space is the literature on youth gangs, most of which has been written by sociologists; but important work by geographers that is attentive to the spatial (and not only the sociological or psychosocial dimensions of gang formation) includes Gareth Jones and Dennis Rodgers' (2009) edited collection *Youth Violence in Latin America: Gangs and Juvenile Justice in Perspective*. The inclusion of Kathrin Hörschelmann and Lorraine van Blerk's *Children, Youth and the City* (2011) in the Routledge series on critical introductions to urbanism is indicative of how children's geographies are now influencing the wider discipline. It is also instructive to compare that book to Lynch and Banerjee's 1977 text. Although both take the city-making of children and young people seriously, the latter is also interested in what children are and proposes a relational and intergenerational understanding of both children's lives and childhood.

Out-of-place   All ascribed social identities are spatialized, that is to say the social marks out what spaces people are made to feel un/comfortable in as well as determining, to some degree, how their identities are read. There are various actors from peers to the law who police or regulate who should or should not be in a specific space. Unsurprisingly, who is made to feel out-of-place where and how that is policed are an important theme in children's geographies (Tucker and Matthews 2001, Valentine 1996). Research on street children (Abebe 2008, Young and Barrett 2001, Beazley 2003, van Blerk 2006) has also made a significant contribution to understanding how the social is spatialized. Hugh Matthews and colleagues' (2000) conceptualization of the street as a third space in which teenagers can carve some autonomy from the supervision of school and family, but which also exposes them to hostility from adults who do not want them to use the street for socializing, has some connections with accounts of street children geographies, although for the latter the street has both greater affordances and greater threats.

Mobilities

The movement of children across borders, with and without their parents, is a central theme in childhood geographies. Children crossing borders without their parents speaks to childhood geography's intersection with political geography and how national borders shape and constrain children, reorganize family life and draw political boundaries around which lives should be protected and which lives will be left to die, to use Foucault's evocative phrase. The scale at which children are dying attempting to reach political refuge or economic security in states in Europe and North America is an issue of huge political importance for contemporary children's geographers, and exposes once again that modern protected childhood is a fiction for most of the world's children, including those that are within the governing sphere of the so-called developed world.

While the current (2016) crisis for refugees has not yet made its way into children's geographies, the governance of immigration has been a key concern for children's geographers. In their introduction to a special issue of *Children's Geographies* on borders and revolution, Stuart Aitken and Vicky Plows (2010) discuss the ways that borders impact on children, the violence borders do and the political agency they make necessary. In their research on AIDS in Lesotho and Malawi, Nicola Ansell and Lorraine van Blerk consider children's migration as a strategy to manage the economic and care effects of AIDS on families (Ansell and van Blerk 2004). Peter Hopkins and Malcolm Hill give an account of the experiences that lead children to seek asylum in Scotland (Hopkins and Hill 2008), and in my own work I have considered the social network formation of unaccompanied asylum-seeking children (Wells 2011).

One of the many effects of migration on children and family life is the formation of new networks and the stretching of existing networks across wider scales. This has been explored by Geraldine Pratt in her research on family reunification among Filipino domestic workers in Canada (Pratt 2012), by Brenda Yeoh and colleagues in numerous publications (including Graham, Jordan and Yeoh 2015, Asis, Huang and Yeoh 2004, Hoang, Lam, Yeoh and Graham 2015, Hoang and Yeoh 2015) and in my work on young refugees and privately fostered children in new transnational families (Wells 2011).

Scale

Scale is an important concept in human geography, notwithstanding a lively debate about whether a scalar ontology should be abandoned and replaced with a flat ontology (Jonas 2006, Marston, Jones and Woodward 2005). In children's geographies, as I have mentioned, there has been a predominant focus on the micro scale, partly so that the experience of being a child can be captured through qualitative data. This approach is critiqued in Ansell (2009), who argues children's geographies needs to connect children's everyday experiences empirically and theoretically to the economic flows and institutions that structure that experience. One question for children's geographers is how individuals figure in relation to scale. Julie Cidell (2006) argues that scale is 'the creation of a level of resolution at which phenomena are deemed understandable' (Cidell 2006:197 citing Kelly 2000:10).

Globalization   How globalization is implicated in the structuring of childhood and impacting on children's lives is a central theme in my own work, especially *Childhood in a Global Perspective* (2015). Global restructuring has reshaped family life and youth transitions to adulthood. Cindi Katz, in her widely cited *Growing Up Global* (2004), brings a spatial analysis to the shifting conditions of social reproduction in a developing (Sudan) and developed (USA) context in which the former is experiencing economic growth and the latter depression and disinvestment. Craig Jeffrey reviews academic research on the impacts of global restructuring on children and youth in relation to employment and school (Jeffrey 2010). Globalization and the economic changes that it signifies impact on all aspects of the lives of children and youth and how they are perceived by peers and adults (Ruddick 2003). It makes movement necessary for some, to escape economic and political insecurity, and impossible for others, too poor or too stuck to migrate. The ways in which globalization stretches local networks through migration, social media and 24-hour news cycles also undermine any simple dichotomy of childhood 'here' and childhood 'there'.

Children's bodies/embodiment Embodiment has attracted significant interest among children's geographers, especially in relation to health (Evans, Colls and Hörschelmann 2011). Research on the governing of children's bodies, particularly through discourses of obesity has been an important part of this (Evans 2010). Physical disability and children's geographies is a growing field that, as with health, ties together different scales from the child's individual body to local and national politics and policy. More recently, I have argued for the importance of acknowledging the corporeal vulnerability of children in explicating the impacts of war on children (Wells 2016b).

Sociology

The sociology of childhood originates in the 1990s with the publication of James and Prout's *Constructing and Reconstructing Childhood* in 1997, followed two years later by their collaboration with Chris Jenks on *Theorizing Childhood* (1999). In 1994 Jens Qvortrup, Marjatta Bardy, Giovanni Sgritta and Helmut Wintersberger published the edited collection *Childhood Matters*. Chris Jenks published a contribution on Childhood Studies to Routledge's key ideas in 1996 (second edition 2005). However, Chris Jenks had begun some of the work of developing a new sub-discipline of sociology much earlier, in 1982, with the publication of a reader, *The Sociology of Childhood* (1982). Earlier still there is the widely cited if historically inaccurate book by Phillippe Ariès, *Centuries of Childhood* (1962), and a more activist approach to rethinking childhood in the early 1970s was realized in John Holt's *Escape from Childhood* (first published 1974).

Who or what was the child to sociology before the sociology of childhood? James et al. (1999:9–21) think of this figure as the pre-sociological child, one that was primarily addressed through the intersection of sociology with development psychology, as in Piaget's work (2001); or the figure is a vessel in need of shaping – both empty and half-formed; or, to use another metaphor, the blank slate of John Locke's *An Essay Concerning Human Understanding* (1997, first published 1690). To Rousseau (1991, first published 1762), the child was an innocent and primitive figure. In psychoanalysis, the child's life was understood to foreshadow the adult's. Indeed, in one way or another, or so the sociology of child-hood claimed, the interest of the social sciences in children was entirely in relation to who they would become, what kind of man or woman they would transform into and what efforts were required in childhood to ensure that the developing child would be the parent to the right kind of adult. Children, it seemed, were either Romantic innocents or Puritan sinners, children of Dionysus or Apollo, angels or devils, and entirely at the mercy of social structure (for structural functionalists) or their developing bodies and brains.

In *Theorizing Childhood*, James et al. (1999) suggested that there are several ways to conceptualize childhood, each of which can be connected to where they place the child on the axis of structure and agency. The new sociology of childhood might consider the child as a tribal child with its own distinct culture. The famous collection of English childhood folklore collected by Iona and Peter Opie (2001, first published 1959) might typify an empirical approach to this paradigm. The Opies' col-lection continues to attract attention and is now in the process of being digitized by a research team at the University of Sheffield. Although most contemporary social studies of childhood scholars invoke the socially constructed child, it is arguably in fact the culturally formed 'tribal' child that guides their accounts of childhood practice and social interaction.

A second paradigm suggested by James et al. (1999), the minority child, suggests that the child is a political minority, even when, as in much of sub-Saharan Africa, they are a demographic majority. Children, in this view, are understood as social subjects in similar ways to women, black people in the Americas and Europe, ethnic and tribal minorities in Asia and Africa and indigenous peoples in the Americas and Australia/ New Zealand. This comparison extends to borrowing the theoretical frameworks that have been used to explain the relationship to political economy and the socio-cultural position of subaltern adults. Berry Mayall (2002) and Leena Alanen (1994), for example, both point to the efficacy of standpoint theory, an approach originally developed out of black civil rights and feminist activism and sociology, to theorize child-hood. Standpoint theory developed out of the activists' claim that 'who feels it knows it' (a similar slogan used by disability rights activists is 'nothing about us, without us'). It is premised on the claim, as the slogan suggests, that to understand what it means to inhabit a particular social identity it is necessary to inhabit or live that identity. It is from this perspective that the mantra in Childhood Studies that children are experts in their own lives arises. Although a strong or weak version of standpoint theory continues to be central to how Childhood Studies conceives of its epistemology, this has its critics. David Oswell incisively comments that:

'Neither child nor adult can speak in a manner which draws on their experience as a source of either power or truth' (2013:87).

Standpoint theory presents a problem for adult researchers since they are not the ones experiencing the childhood that they wish to account for, theoretically and empirically. This dissonance between the insistence on some version (weak or strong) of an experiential epistemology has led to a call for children not only to participate in research, but to be co-constructors of knowledge and to be involved in all aspects of research from initial design to final analysis and dissemination. This is now widely considered the 'gold standard' of childhood research although it is rarely done in practice. Allison James in her contribution to the *American Anthropologist*'s special focus on childhood (2007) questions this approach, and suggests that Childhood Studies scholars might find a revisiting of the 'writing culture' debates in anthropology a useful resource for thinking through what it means to represent children, and the pitfalls of claiming to ventriloquize the child's voice.

The fourth way of conceptualizing childhood within the sociology of childhood is the social structural child. If the minority and tribal child leads the researcher towards qualitative methods, analysis of the child in relation to social structures implies the construction and analysis of large-scale data sets. This method has not been central within Childhood Studies (as opposed to research on, say, childhood poverty). This is partly because, perhaps, Childhood Studies have pulled much more in the direction of agency as it relates to childhood in the agency–structure debate. The analysis and construction of large-scale survey sets have been done, for example by economists in the longitudinal study of childhood poverty, *Young Lives* (Porter and Goyal 2016), or in UN reports on children's lives, but quantitative studies reported in the key journals of Childhood Studies (*Childhood*, *Children's Geographies* and *Global Studies of Childhood*) are few and far between.

Structure/agency

A central question for sociological theory has been theorizing what space there is within social structures for the expression of individual agency. Prior to the emergence of the new social studies of childhood, or so the narrative goes, the standard sociological view, derived largely from Talcott Parsons' structuralist functionalist sociology, was that children were empty vessels into which social norms were poured and who, if this was done effectively, would continue these same traditions. If the socialization of children was not done effectively then children would become deviants, and social institutions (for example juvenile justice or reform school) would intervene to correct their development. If there was scope for agency, as the possibility of deviance implied there was, it was limited and ineffectual and would be corrected or contained. The most interesting thing about childhood was not children but who children would become under the influence of the social structures that they were most closely in contact with, especially the school and the family.

In contrast the new sociology of childhood insisted that children are social actors in their own right and exercise agency within the social structures that attempt to mould them. Research should be with them and for them, not on them. It should treat them as subjects who act and not objects who are the passive recipients of the adult gaze. Nevertheless it should also be recognized that their agency, their capacity to act, is structured by age-related constraints, such as risk, surveillance, best interests, that are imposed on them by society or social structures, and seek to regulate and govern children's lives. This insistence on children's agency and the importance of their direct and extensive involvement in research has led to some repetition of studies that seek to demonstrate that children exercise agency, that they construct goals that they act on, and that they shape the actions of others. I have argued elsewhere that this focus on individual agency chimes with contemporary ideas about the self in the liberal democratic capitalist countries (Wells 2016b); in particular, that people are self-actualizing, autonomous, free individuals who make rational choices based on the maximizing of their self-interests and the minimizing of costs. In my view this is not quite the liberation that it is often presented as, precisely because it does fit so well with late capitalist ideology about what it means to be a (good) human, and therefore the importance accorded to children's agency does not hold out quite the promise that perhaps was hoped for at the founding of the new social studies of childhood.

Interpretive reproduction   A widely cited concept for grasping the relative balance of structure and agency in children's lives is 'interpretive reproduction'. William Corsaro developed this concept (2015, first published 1997). It is intended to capture the '[i]nnovative and creative aspects of children's participation in society' (2015:18) through observing and describing how children use language and develop cultural routines. Interpretive reproduction shows how children engage in the collective reproduction of 'their own peer worlds and cultures' (2015:24). It is based on an 'orb-web' model of cultural reproduction. Essentially it captures what Corsaro claims happens when children engage in play and other cultural activities (although play is the one most fully described); this is that they take the concepts offered to them (say, gender) and they then interpret them through their activities, and through this embodied engagement with these concepts they provide a new interpretation. This allows Corsaro to say that, in contrast to classic socialization theory in which the child is presumed to be given a concept and then find out what its norms are and then practise those norms, without reinterpreting or altering, resisting or redefining them, his concept demonstrates that the transmission of social norms from one generation to the next is not smooth or uninterrupted but interpreted. To paraphrase Marx, children make their own culture, but they do not do so in circumstances of their own choosing.

The challenge of poststructuralism

The sociology of childhood took the agential child as the centre of its theory. The child was a modernist subject, self-knowing and self-expressive. The child's selfhood was not problematized. At the moment when most of the social sciences and humanities were taking up the challenge of poststructuralism and rethinking the subject, the sociology of childhood reasserted the modernist agent. To begin to problematize the child as a subject seemed to be to give away the core rationale of Childhood Studies, and what then would be left? Yet the challenge that poststructuralism offers to any concept of agency that is the outward expression of an already constituted interior self cannot really be dodged, precisely because children are at the centre of Childhood Studies. It is obvious that the infant is not the 7-year-old, and the 7-year-old is not the 17-year-old. Most people may live by a narrative of selfhood that is consistent across time, but it often becomes apparent to us, especially in moments of personal change, that at some level this self is a fiction. This sense of a constantly shifting selfhood is surely all the more the case for children, whose changing capacities over time necessarily alter the ways that they relate to the world. There are few people who are as mercurial as small children.

Alan Prout's edited collection *The Body, Childhood and Society* (2000) is one response to this problem. For Prout, the body of the child should be taken as one actor among many in constantly shifting actor-networks. Nick Lee (2005) proposes accepting the instability of childhood and using it as a model for how we think about adulthood so that we understand all humans, not only children, as 'human becomings' that are never completed. Karen Smith (2012, 2014) suggests that the rational, autonomous, individual child is being produced through technologies of governance, a figure she names the Athenian child in reference to the Greek myth that Athena sprang fully formed from the head of Zeus.

David Oswell, in his book *The Agency of Children: From Family to Global Human Rights* (2013), proposes that we think of children's agency as located within assemblages of humans and non-humans, technology, culture and nature; after poststructuralism there can be no view of agency as the individual possession of anybody, child or adult. Indeed agency may refer not to a person but to parts of persons, and this may be particularly the case for children, whose parts are more often drawn into governing assemblages than they are as singular people; for example, he points to medics attending to viral infections or psychologists to cognitive functions (2013:9). He wants to 'locate agency throughout what others might term structure and not to bifurcate the two in terms of a totalizing or individualizing polarity; but to understand the extension of agency along different temporalities and spatialities, not always returned to the individual child, categorically defined, as a point of origin or endpoint' (2013:20). The presumption within Childhood Studies that agency is something ontologically connected to humanness is not warranted, he points out, and needs to be empirically investigated.

Generation

A potentially important concept for Childhood Studies, and one that has been taken up by the Finnish sociologist of childhood Leena Alanen, is that of generation. Karl Mannheim was the first sociologist to frame 'generation' as a sociological concept. It has since entered everyday speech and popular discourse in the attempt to identify the attitudes, dispositions and cultural practices shared by a specific age group, such as Generation X, Gen Y or Millennials. For Alanen the concept allows us to think of children as comparable to a class, that is a collectivity with shared experiences and common objective interests. Mannheim's concept of generation did not map onto children as an age group. Indeed, for the most part his concept of generational identity was formed in the context of political struggles between youth and older generations. Furthermore, as a generation ages it is still a generation formed by specific shared experiences: Generation X remains Generation X, even though that generation is now aged between 40 and 55. Outside of moments of shared political struggle, children do not move through social or political space with common experiences. Their experiences are different because of other ascribed social identities, but also as children their shared experience – of being in school, living in a neighbourhood, belonging to an extended family and sharing its material and symbolic resources – disrupts the possibility of a single identity that rests on the shared opposition child/adult (see also Oswell 2013:101–4 for an extended discussion of these points). I think what Alanen and other theorists using 'generation' to conceptualize the political and social exclusions of childhood are trying to formulate is a term for the practices through which this exclusion is enacted and legitimized (generationing) and an insistence that, even while other differences between children are empirically true (space, time, social identity), their shared differences as an age group are more important in explaining one of the ways in which the distribution of power between social groups (here, adults and children) gets done in the contemporary world. Like all distributions of power it is naturalized and oppositional, and involves the unequal distribution of resources.

Anthropology

In 1973 (republished in *Childhood*, 2001) Charlotte Hardman asked 'Can there be an anthropology of children?' To illustrate the possibilities of a child-centred culture that could be analysed to show meaning and pattern she recounts how children say 'touch wood' and then touch wood (or their own heads) to ward off bad luck. She proposes that this illustrates that children 'reveal a segment of the society's stock of beliefs, values and social interaction, *which is exclusive to them'* (2001:516, emphasis added). In fact, 'touching wood' to ward off bad luck, especially after a run of good luck, is widely done, in England and the USA (where the phrase is 'knock on wood', also the title of a popular song covered by David Bowie in 1974), including knocking one's own head if wood is not easily to hand. The phrase is found in Brewer's *Dictionary of Phrase and Fable*. The point is that what Hardman describes shows neither familiarity with popular culture nor an exclusive practice of childhood culture, undermining if not her implicit claim that there can be an anthropology of childhood then certainly the evidence that she uses to warrant that claim.

Nonetheless, and as Hardman recognizes, there is already an anthropology of childhood. Hardman's concern is that the existing anthropology of childhood was (in 1973) overly focused on the development of children rather than childhood culture and its emic (insider) practices and their patterns and significance. There is certainly truth in that criticism, but nonetheless, as both Heather Montgomery (2009) and David Lancy (2008) show in their respective reviews and analysis of the ethnographies of childhood over the last 150 years, children have had an important place in the ethnographic record. Indeed, in a recent overview, Montgomery makes the case that children 'have been central to the overall development of the discipline' (2012).

Anthropologists of childhood have often aimed to challenge universalist assumptions in the approaches to child and youth culture in their home countries. Margaret Mead (2001, first published 1928), for example, did her study of adolescence in Papua New Guinea to contest the assumption that adolescence was necessarily a traumatic and stressful period. Anthropologists showed through their ethnographies of childhood and youth how practices that were thought to be natural or biological were cultural.

In their introduction to a review of children in anthropology, a focus section of *American Anthropologist*, Myra Bluebond-Langer and Jill Korbin point to the importance of the UNCRC, together with the heightened visibility in a globalizing world of children's suffering, in expanding anthropological interest in children and childhood (2007:241). They contend that 'Studies of children and childhoods are the next logical steps [after the incorporation of women] in a more inclusive view of culture and society.' It is interesting that Bluebond-Langer and Korbin, two of the most significant figures in the anthropology of childhood for their cross-cultural research on childhood illness and death, and child abuse and neglect, respectively, suggest that the anthropology of childhood is only just beginning in 2007.

So which is it? Is the anthropology of childhood only just beginning (Hardman 2001, Bluebond-Langer & Korbin 2007) or has it been there all along (Montgomery 2009, Lancy 2008)?

It depends on what is meant by the anthropology of childhood, on whether it means attending primarily to children, listening to them (rather than their caregivers); but above all, as in the rest of the social studies of childhood, the difference really seems to rest on whether ethnographies of childhood are about translating the other to make the strange familiar, a classic focus of anthropology, or whether ethnographies are intended to contribute to our understanding of child development, of how sets of cultural practices produce particular kinds of adults. For Bluebond-Langer and Korbin this next logical step in anthropology should give a 'more inclusive view, rather than privileging children's voices above all others, it is more productive to integrate children into a more multivocal, multiperspective view of culture and society' (2007:242). They propose a view that assumes children have agency but insists that they are also vulnerable and developing and have 'specific needs for nurturance' (2007:242).

In his contribution to the special focus that Bluebond-Langer and Korbin edited, a review of ethnographies of childhood in domestic and community settings throughout the twentieth century, Robert LeVine points out that 'The ethnography of childhood, then, is based on the premise – constantly reexamined in empirical research – that the conditions and shape of childhood tend to vary in central tendency from one population to another, are sensitive to population-specific contexts, and are not comprehensible without detailed knowledge of the socially and culturally organized contexts that give them meaning' (2007:247). This is incontrovertible in many ways, and yet it does imply that in a specific population there is such a thing as childhood in the singular. Indeed, in many ethnographies of childhood what is offered is a description of a general childhood in a specific culture, with little attention given to how childhood is articulated with economic position, with gender or with ethnicity. Many ethnographers may not have had to contend with ethnicity as a marker of difference within childhood, because they were writing about people that shared language, cultural practices, origin myths and religious belief. However, many anthropologists now conduct research in urban centres (that are ethnically diverse) and in any case, all societies are gendered and generational.

LeVine begins with Margaret Mead's seminal account of children growing up in Samoa and Malinowski's study of family life among the Trobianders in Melanesia (2005, first published 1929). The latter was written partly in response to Freud's claims that the Oedipal complex was universal. Trobianders were a matrilineal society. LeVine comments that 'Malinowski's crystalline descriptions and vivid anecdotes were carefully selected to make this point: Trobriand father and mother are of equal status; fathers participate in infant care and take great pride in their infants; children are free and independent; and, although parents sometimes beat their children, Malinowski also observed "quite as often" (1929:45) children beating their parents' (LeVine 2007:249). Other contributions to the ethnography of childhood also borrowed from the theoretical frameworks of psychology. This was especially true of the culture and personality school that Margaret Mead and Ruth Benedict developed from Frank Boas' conceptual work, even if their aim was to undermine the claims of psychology to universality. A key concept for Boas was plasticity, LeVine says, and that meant that given the gradual development of the child's nervous system, environment and geography must affect this. Therefore there could be no universal child. This role of anthropology to contest the universalizing claims of psychology remains significant. LeVine also points out that most research in development psychology is done in Western countries, although a majority of the world's children live in the developing world. So he proposes that not only the conceptual but also the empirical basis of development psychology is flawed, and that '[t]he resulting knowledge deficit has not been recognized by the child development research field, even in the agenda-setting report by a National Academy of Sciences panel on "The Science of Early Childhood Development"' (LeVine 2007:250).

A generation of British anthropologists, Malinowski's students, produced ethnographic studies of childhood that laid the groundwork for a non-psychological study of children, often focused on kinship and ritual, sometimes on education and socialization. Audrey Richards' *Chisungu* (1995, first published 1956) described girls' initiation among the Bemba of Zambia. Evans-Pritchard's *The Nuer* (2001, first published 1940) and his *Kinship and Marriage Among the Nuer* (1990, first published 1953) included observations about Nuer childhood. Margaret Read published a book-length study of childhood among the Ngoni of Nyasaland/ Malawi, *Children of Their Fathers* (1987, first published 1960). Meyer Fortes published his *The Web of Kinship Among the Tallensi* (1949) (Levine 2007:250–1).

One of the most significant contributions to the anthropology of childhood was Beatrice and John Whiting's (1975) six cultures study. Their intention was to develop a systematic comparison of children's enculturation and the causes (for example in socio-economic organization) and consequences (in psychocultural effects) of being raised in different societies. If its original goals were not realized, it did establish the basis for an ethnography of childhood and the studies themselves contain rich ethnographic detail. Beatrice Whiting with Caroline Edwards extended and used some of the original data for a 1988 comparison of fourteen communities (Whiting and Edwards 1994) (see LeVine 2007:252–4).

Despite the evidence from LeVine's review of a century of anthropology of childhood, he concludes that 'ethnographic documentation by itself, however excellent, cannot create an anthropology of childhood of more than marginal significance to anthropologists ... , or for that matter to other social scientists, without further theory building and cross-cultural comparison' (Levine 2007:256).

One of the founders of the new social studies of childhood, Allison James, was trained as an anthropologist. This had an important influence on the conceptualization of how the new social studies of childhood would attend to children's 'voice'. Methods borrowed from anthropology, specifically participant observation and key informant interviews, and translated into sociology as the qualitative interview are the key methods, not only of the anthropology of childhood but of the sociology and geography of childhood. LeVine is concerned that the proliferation of ethnographies is not enough and proposes that a new fieldwork guide, like the one used in the six cultures study, might be useful to ensure development of the sub-discipline. Allison James, in the same special issue, suggests that the anthropological debates on 'writing culture' should be revisited to give theoretical purchase to the question of what is being represented when we write children's cultures (James 2007).

The classic ethnographic texts focused on the place of children in the learning of culture. Their central interest was in how children come to be competent cultural participants. Central themes in that work have been the start and end of childhood and, especially, the place of ritual and rites of passage in the enculturation of children.

Rites of passage

The rite of passage through which children become women and men, or, in the case of infant circumcision, in which incomplete beings become human, has attracted the attention of anthropologists. On boys' circumcision, the classic texts are T. O. Beidelman's *The Cool Knife* (1997), Maurice Bloch's *From Blessing to Violence* (1986) on boys' circumcision in Morocco, and Victor Turner's accounts of Ndembu ritual (1970, first published 1967). It is, though, girls' genital cutting that has been the focus of most recent research on these rites of passage. For a comprehensive review of the literature and arguments see Silverman (2004). Few areas of anthropology, as Silverman comments, have attracted as much public interest as circumcision rites. I review the literature in Kenya and Sudan and make an argument for understanding the cultural logic of cutting in the making of gender and generation (Wells 2012). Silverman makes the important point that if there can be a cross-cultural comparative study of circumcision then it might be one that contrasts a Euro-Christian sensibility, in which personhood resides in the complete body and salvation in an unembodied self, with cultures in which body modification is precisely what enables personhood. She points out that '[a]lthough an anathema to most Western sensibilities, the body is not everywhere complete upon birth' (Silverman 2004:426).

Most of the anthropological literature on female circumcision engages very directly with the global campaign for its eradication and the local response to these campaigns (e.g. Moore 2009). Nancy Lutkehaus and Paul Roscoe's' edited collection, first published in 1985, was the first volume that gave empirical accounts of girls' initiation in Melanesia (Lutkehaus and Roscoe 1995). In their preface they note that Audrey Richards' account of Chisungu initiation, published in 1956 and written in 1935, remains 'the most complete and detailed description of a girl's initiation ceremony' (Lutkehaus and Roscoe 1995:xiii citing Brown 1963:837). In fact most address female genital cutting (FGC) in the context of women's (rather than girls') health, and specifically reproductive health. I am aware of only one ethnography of girls' (rather than retrospective or explanatory accounts of women's) experiences; Leonard's research on girls adopting the practice in Southern Chad in a community that traditionally did not cut (2000). Janice Boddy's (2007) *Civilizing Women: British Crusades in Colonial Sudan* is a compelling historical anthropology of the beginning of the anti-circumcision campaign during the colonial period in Sudan. Claudie Gosselin's (2000) thesis is on the campaign against FGC in Mali. Henrietta Moore's (2009) paper 'Epistemology and Ethics: Perspectives from Africa' discusses the introduction of alternative rites of passage in Kenya. Most of these studies are done by European and North American anthropologists; for a rare anthropological account from an emic perspective, see Fuambai Ahmadu, a Sierra Leonean anthropologist living in the USA who returned to Sierra Leone to be initiated into the women's society (2000). Hoda Salad (2015), herself a British-Somali Muslim, provides a fascinating account of interviews with Somali women living in the UK who had undergone either Sunni or Pharaonic circumcision as girls. She found a surprising willingness on the part of women who had undergone the Pharaonic form to abandon the practice if they found that, as the researcher contended, there was no religious basis for it. She also found that those women who had undergone a weak version of Sunni cutting (essentially a prick of the clitoral hood) were reluctant to abandon the practice since they had positive memories of their circumcision and the pride they felt in becoming a woman.

Out of place

As in the wider discipline, and as the debate on FGC illustrates, the anthropology of childhood wants to establish that cultural concepts are often incommensurable but that this does not mean that one culture's ideas about what a good childhood is are necessarily better or worse than another culture's. This is particularly emphasized in relation to the cultural body, the family and what makes children culturally out of place (see earlier discussion for the same theme in geography). At the same time, a debate within anthropology about what the ethical responsibilities of anthropologists are to the people they study is intensified in the anthropology of childhood by our responsibilities as adults towards children.

An interest in those children who are out of place and who offer perhaps relatively clear examples of separate cultures of childhood has led to an interest in child soldiers, street children and working children (especially, but not only, street vendors). These children are often very visible in public space and are often living at a distance or perhaps entirely independently of parents and other adult gatekeepers. Research with them therefore poses specific ethical issues about the responsibilities of researchers towards their subjects both during the research and after they 'leave the field'. The description of these young people as 'children' is also not an emic description and borrows from the language of international social policy. Most of the young people whose lives are described in these ethnographies would not be considered children, either by themselves or by others, in their own societies or indeed in the Global North. This is not to say they are not vulnerable or marginalized nor to suggest that they are adults, but rather to point out that the adoption of the terms of international policy loses the emic perspective of the young that the anthropology of childhood is in other respects committed to uncovering, and has provided. Ethnographies of young soldiers, homeless youth and young street vendors have produced some of the most vivid writing about the lives of teenagers. These include, on homeless youth, Tobias Hecht's ground-breaking *At Home in the Street* (1998); Christopher Kovats-Bernat's *Sleeping Rough in Port-au-Prince* (2006), on young soldiers; Matt Utas' (2003) doctoral dissertation *Sweet Battlefields: Youth and the Liberian Civil War*; and Danny Hoffman's research on young soldiers in Sierra Leone (Hoffman 2011). Chris Coulter offers a rare account of girls' experience of war (2009). On street vendors, Thomas Offit's *Conquistadores de la Calle: Child Street Labor in Guatemala City* (2008) makes a compelling argument for the differences in the everyday lives and cultures of homeless youth and street vendors.

What is a child for anthropology?

How does anthropology answer the question of what is a child? One approach is to divide it into development-related periods in the life course. This is how the physical anthropologist and evolutionary life history theorist Barry Bogin (2006) approaches childhood. His interest, as with other life history theorists, is to explain why humans have an extended period of immaturity after infancy that is not shared with other primates, including chimpanzees. He divides the human life course into eight periods after birth, based on changes in dental growth, skeletal growth, sex hormones and biological reproductive capacity. For him, childhood is the period from weaning to around the age of 7 years. The end of childhood is the end of a period of intense dependency on others for food preparation and is accompanied by changes in cognitive ability. For most Childhood Studies scholars, 18 years is taken as the end of childhood because this is the definition given in the UNCRC. There are other periods of immaturity that Bogin defines (juvenile – until the onset of puberty – and adolescence) that most Childhood Studies scholars would also want to include in their field. It is interesting that Bogin gives a universal definition that is based not on a global legal structure but on the conditions of typically developing children's everyday lives.

However, of more significance is how Bogin's periodization of the life course enters into his explanation of why humans have this extended period of immaturity. Humans developed a more cooperative approach to child-rearing than other primates, which involved juveniles and adolescents, fathers, grandparents, and non-kin in the care of children, including finding and preparing food for them. This allowed women to wean their children early and reproduce more quickly than other primates. Bogin concludes, 'In sum, childhood and cooperative breeding helped evolve human life history' (2006:230). In other words, it is our collective responsibility for the care of children that makes us human.

Conclusion

Childhood Studies is necessarily an interdisciplinary field. It is only by locating childhood and children's lives at the point where time, space, society and culture meet that we can give an adequate account of childhood. In the following pages I show how this interdisciplinary approach illuminates how childhood subjects are produced. I explore the ways that governing forces press onto children and shape the conditions for the formation of their subjectivities. In the second part of the book I then engage with children's bodily and cognitive capacities to show how children themselves work with the conditions that shape their lives. Childhood is as unequal a space as adulthood is, as this book will show, but it does make a difference to how that inequality is played out and how it is taken up by individuals that the subjects we are discussing are young subjects, biologically immature, and with vulnerabilities and capacities that are not shared by adults.

3

Governing Through Race, Governing Through Childhood

Introduction

In the next three chapters I take three sub-disciplines of Childhood Studies, specifically history, sociology and geography, and explore how they have conceptualized and represented children and childhood in relation to formations of race, gender and class, respectively. I am not intending to suggest through this division that these disciplines cannot speak across their disciplinary borders to understand how race, class and gender play out in the lives of children and in the formation of childhood subjectivities. Indeed, in this chapter, which is primarily focused on history, I draw on the sociology of race to provide some of the theoretical tools to explain racism and racialization in childhood.

The reason I begin with racism and history is because I want to make an argument that the history of childhood and the history of racism are intimately tied to one another. In this chapter I argue that the modern idea of childhood and the modern idea of race were brought into existence during the same period and continue to shape how contemporary states govern. I show that the fact that these two concepts emerged at the same time was not simply a coincidence but is critical to understanding how government produces subjects and legitimates its claims to rule. It shows both that the child came to be a central figure in whose name the liberal state governs and that racism enabled the 'white republic' (Blum 2005) of the USA to justify both the extent of and the limits to its jurisdiction.

This is a very different story from the one that is usually told about the history of race and racism within Childhood Studies. The dominant narrative is that once poor children became the target of social reformers there were gradual but steady improvements for all children. Childhood in this narrative was 'discovered' by enlightened governments in Europe and North America and was gradually disseminated to the rest of the world, a project that continues in the current period through international development.

That narrative of the progressive history of childhood occludes the fact that racism structured the lives of children throughout the colonial and postcolonial world; that at exactly the same moment that the importance of protecting white children in Western Europe and North America was shaping law and social policy and changing intergenerational relationships, African/descent and Asian/descent children were being systematically excluded from these same protections. These systematic exclusions have not been widely researched but have been addressed in Grier's (2006) important work on child labour in Colonial Zimbabwe, and in research on racist population policy in French West Africa (White 1999), British Hong Kong (Pomfret 2009) and British and French Empires in East Asia (Pomfret 2016). There is also a still relatively small but nonetheless important literature on the exclusion of black Americans from the expansion of child-saving (Ward 2012) and from the emergence of the ideology of the modern child (King 1998, 2005).

It is important to recognize that these exclusions were systematic, not accidental. It is not that black and Asian children were somehow overlooked but that the inculcation in children of race and racism was and continues to be at the heart of modern childhood as it is at the heart of the modern state. This chapter takes forward Levander's (2006) comments in her study of the relationship between racism and liberty: 'The emergence of the modern nation-state and of the modern child in the late eighteenth century and nineteenth century have been subjects of intensive critical inquiry in the last two decades, yet missing from these two rich bodies of work [on liberalism and childhood] has been an assessment of how these two ideas work in tandem' (2006:6) and how they are articulated through racism.

If Childhood Studies has generally not been alert to how the governing of race and the governing of childhood have informed and shaped one another, and continue to do so, it has also not been attentive to the ways that children themselves are inducted into racist orders, into understanding themselves as people with a race and into enacting or resisting racism. Children's racial identifications and their investment in or enactment of racist exclusions have unfortunately been left, with notable exceptions among a group of cultural historians (Bernstein 2011, Duane 2011,

Mitchell 2008), to the discipline of social psychology. Social psychologists, by and large, insist on the universal proclivity of humans to identify 'ingroups' and 'outgroups' and to exclude others on the basis of physiological differences that are presumed to be a sign of other, putatively deeper underlying differences. The current fascination with neuroscience has only reinforced these tendencies, with popular science and social psychology disseminating ideas about how structures within the brain, the so-called mirror neurons, make us more empathetic to the experiences and feelings of 'people like us' and indifferent to those of people who are 'not like us'. The social question of how we come to think of some people as similar to ourselves, and others as radically dissimilar from ourselves, is left unanswered and, indeed, largely unasked. I explore these issues further in chapter 8 on the integration of development psychology with social identity theory.

This chapter aims to fill these lacunae in two ways: firstly through a discussion of the theoretical tools of the sociology of race and how these might inform our understanding of childhood, and secondly through an analysis of the exclusion of African-American children from education after emancipation and from child labour reform campaigns in the early twentieth century.

Sociology of race

One of the key questions for Childhood Studies when trying to integrate an analysis of racism and race into the discipline has to be: what is race and what is its relationship to racism and, indeed, to anti-racism? In Childhood Studies the silence about race and (anti-)racism may emanate from a certain discomfort about whether speaking with children about race will produce the object (race-identification) that it purports to describe and in doing so may further racism instead of undermining it. Secondly, there may be some concern that speaking about racism might expose or even generate racist discourse or racist aggression in children. Thirdly, there is an idea that talking with children about racism will make them aware of a social-political fact of which they are presumed to be innocent. Children may not be thought to see racial difference or at least not to ascribe significance to or attribute qualities to racial difference, or to understand white privilege and black exclusion. White children using racist language, for example, might be excused with the comment that 'they don't understand what they're saying' or, more obliquely, 'he's just a kid'. Related to this is an ambivalent attitude towards what it means to hold white children to account for racism. This is not only in relation to when they may make racist statements or enact racist exclusions (van

Ausdale and Feagin 2001, Connolly 1998), but also thinking at a more structural level of the benefits that accrue to white children as white people in a racist order. It is perhaps thought to be unreasonable, hurtful or even sullying the innocence of childhood to suggest that white children might benefit in some way from racism.

Too often this ambivalence about talking with children about race and racism or trying to understand children's investments in racial identification, racism, anti-racism and resistance to racism leads to a kind of substitution of sociological analysis by apparent facts; for example, counting the ethnicity of the children in a study without explaining the significance of ethnicity as a variable. If it is left without analysis or explanation this can make it appear that race or ethnicity (rather than, say, racism or discrimination) is the underlying cause of the phenomenon under investigation. This has the effect of attributing action to race rather than analysing the underlying experience, knowledge and understanding that might explain how differences in attitudes or experience apparently map onto differences in skin colour. This slippage reifies race and makes it appear as an actor. This is what Karen Fields and Barbara Fields (2014) call, in their book of the same name, *Racecraft*. They use this term as analogous to 'witchcraft' to suggest the way that a specific ideological field that has no reality (magic or race) is taken as the cause of events. They argue for a naming of the effect of racism and naming the agents of racism, rather than of race.

What precisely it means to understand the place of children within the terrain of racism and racialization is a complicated question. Racism is an exercise of power and children as an age category are a powerless group – what kinds of power do children borrow from the identities that they are ascribed with? We know that children do engage, by themselves and with adults, in racist acts and that white children benefit in often quite concrete ways from racism (for example, in the USA consistently more public resources are spent on white children than on black children in education, health and housing). The symbolic inclusions and exclusions of racism are also important. I am thinking here of who gets represented doing what in film and television or in story books (a point that I take up in chapter 9) or more generally of who gets respect and recognition (Fraser 2003, Honneth 1995). The extent to which racism saturates public institutions, including policing, immigration and housing (as we shall see in chapter 5), means that class privilege often offers limited protection to middle-class black adults and their children against racist exclusions.

Childhood Studies insists on the social construction of childhood; similarly historians and sociologists of race insist on the social construction of race. But to say that an ascribed social identity and its associated practices (age, gender, ethnicity, class) are socially constructed says little about how the work of social construction gets done: what makes institutions or individuals feel confident in their ascription of an identity to a person? Of course, race is socially constructed, and to insist on this point is an important corrective to those who would argue that race is a biological fact, but it is also important to keep in sight that race is socially constructed by racism. Barbara and Karen Fields are withering in their criticism of the substitution of race for racism. They say: ' "Race" appears in the titles of an ever-growing number of scholarly books and articles as a euphemism for slavery, disfranchisement, segregation, lynching, mass murder, and related historical atrocities; or as unintentionally belittling shorthand for "persons of African descent and anything pertaining to them" ' (Fields and Fields 2014:100). What they are arguing here is that all of these forms of violence and exclusion are caused not by race but by racism. Yes, they say, race is socially constructed; it is also a fiction; but not all social constructions are fictive. Racism is also socially constructed but unlike race, racism 'is not a fiction, an illusion, a superstition, or a hoax. It is a crime against humanity' (2014:101) and it has very real, concrete effects on the lives of black people and other people of colour.

I think what the Fields are arguing is that race is not primarily about identification. They quote the great African-American sociologist W. E. B. du Bois: 'The black man is not someone of a specified ancestry or culture, he decided ... A black man "is a person who must ride 'Jim Crow' in Georgia" ' (2014:158 citing Du Bois 1992:153). Barbara Fields argues that in a racist order only those subjected to racism can be said to have a race and that 'the equation of Afro-Americans' peoplehood with race is a corollary of racism' (Fields 2001:50). In the article in which she makes this statement she is arguing against the empirical or conceptual usefulness of 'Whiteness Studies', which she thinks gives white people a racial identity that historically they do not hold (whites were more likely to think of themselves if immigrants as German, Italian, Jewish, or if Anglos as simply 'American') and displaces the actual agency of whites' racist actions (for example, segregated schools are caused by the racism of specific actors who are white, and should not be attributed to an amorphous or abstract 'whiteness'). Furthermore this identity generates a kind of parallel structure that implies both whites and black people are hurt by racism. This is an important argument for Childhood Studies because it means that questions about whether children have the cognitive ability to understand racial identification or to be racist is somewhat beside the point. Racial identification is ascribed to black children (and not to white children) and has real effects on their life chances regardless of whether black children, white children or other children of colour understand what these ascriptions signify.

She is also arguing against another key concept in the sociology of race: racialization. Racialization refers to the practices through which a person is ascribed with a race. Racialization, like the device of writing race in quotation marks as "race" to signify its fictional quality, makes visible and opens up questions about the work that goes into the construction of race. Most social theorists writing about race (at least from a progressive political position), myself included, understand race to be made through racializing practices and therefore to be inseparable from racism. Racism is understood to be ground zero in the production of race, rather than, as everyday discourse might have it, that racism is a response to a pre-existing racial difference.

Barbara Fields' objection is that using the concept of racialization, rather than racism, to describe how race is conjured into existence distances racism from the actions of specific actors and the structures and institutions they activate and inhabit. This is a valid point for sure, but in relation to children it may be that the term 'racialization' helps to think through how children learn to think of themselves and/or others as people with a race. It would seem odd, at best, to say that black children are practising racism when they learn to think of themselves as having a race, although it is analytically powerful to theorize that when black children learn to think of themselves as having a race it is wider racist discourses and structures that provide the tools that make this work meaningful. This theory contrasts with those theories that claim that the tools to address racism in children's lives are to be found in multicultural education.

But at the level of the mundane practices that operationalize racism, that, as it were, make a bridge between an ideological commitment and the daily lives of people, racialization may be a useful concept. Take the practice, for example, widespread in London state schools, of encouraging children to identify their parents' or grandparents' country of origin as their home country. Now, by definition all of these children attending London schools are in some sense or another English; they live in England, they attend an English-speaking school, they are being immersed in an English curriculum. The effect of asking them to identify with another country, which is usually done visually in classroom displays of flags and maps, is that all of the black and Asian children in the classroom, regardless of how many or how few generations their families have lived in England, are represented as being from 'somewhere else'. Some of the white children, those who are recent arrivals and whose first language is not English, will also be attached in these displays to somewhere else. But most white children will be simply tied to England (almost literally, since these displays usually involve a picture of a child with a piece of string or wool linking their picture to another place). These are practices of racialization; they produce racial identities. Yet it is invariably done as an attempt to acknowledge and perhaps celebrate in the classroom the diversity of children's family origins, languages spoken at home, and other forms of cultural capital; in other words, with an underlying anti-racist intent (see Wells 2007a).

When schools specifically attempt to address racism and black self-organization against racism in the UK, the signs of racism and resistance are always taken from somewhere else (usually the USA or South Africa) (Wells 2007a, 2007b). In Black History Month as it is taught in UK schools, three subjects predominate: the role of white people in the abolition of slavery, Nelson Mandela's peaceful statesmanship, and Mary Seacole's nursing career in the Crimean War. The contemporary landscape of racism, the origin of racism in a specific historical moment, black people's resistance to racism from slavery, through the anti-colonial nationalist struggles, into the post-war settlement in the UK, and onto black resistance and anti-racist struggles today – none of that is even hinted at.

So in these mundane, everyday practices of racialization, black and Asian children are encouraged to think of themselves as being from somewhere else, and to forge an identity based on their parents', or grandparents', or great-grandparents' country of origin. Furthermore, the identity that they are encouraged to embrace is simply that of another country, devoid of the history of struggle against racism, and even without the history of colonial occupation that generated ties between one place and another that led their families at some point to claim their right to live in the UK.

The modernity of race

Most scholars agree that race is a modern concept. This is contrary to a common-sense view that racism is a trans-historical practice that has always been present in human culture because people are 'hardwired' to organize other humans into sub-categories that we then discriminate against. In addition to the common-sense discourse of this view, it is also prevalent in psychology, and social psychology. These disciplines have generated a large literature that purportedly demonstrates that young children are predisposed to prejudice because of neurological structures (see chapter 8). The fallacious idea that humans are made up of distinct groups of people whose shared visible physiological differences (e.g. in hair texture, skin colour) are exterior signs of a more meaningful difference (e.g. in intelligence, morals, strength or indeed culture) is a fundamentally racist idea, despite which it continues to animate much social policy and social relations.

Against this view of the timelessness of race and racism, I argue that race is a modern idea. It arose out of the contradiction between the importance of slavery, a quintessentially unfree economic practice, for emergent capitalist nations and their professed commitment to political and economic freedom. The claim that capitalism is democratic and free, in contrast to the various forms of unfreedom that preceded it, was vividly in contradiction with the dependence of capitalism on the labour of enslaved people.

The transatlantic slave trade was neither the first slave trade in history, nor the first in which slave-owners were visibly different (e.g.in skin colour) from enslaved peoples. There were visible physiological differences between North Africans, who organized the transcontinental slave trade, and enslaved sub-Saharan Africans, for example. The transatlantic slave trade was the first in which skin colour gradually became read by white slavers as a sign of a pre-existing condition of unfreedom. (It should be obvious that black slavers or black slaves would not see in blackness a sign of unfreedom.) Indeed the early slave trade did not have a general organizing concept that justified in terms of any essential difference the reasons why some humans were shackled and others were free. The attachment of unfreedom to black skin colour gradually emerged in the discourse on slavery in the United States. If this claim seems surprising it should be recalled that although the importance of liberty (or freedom) in European political philosophy goes back at least to Aristotle, this co-existed with the unfreedom of a majority of the population. Serfdom, essentially bonded, unfree labour, ended in Britain in the fourteenth century but did not end in France until after the 1789 revolution and in Eastern Europe until the mid-nineteenth century. Serfdom was justified on the basis that there were essential, literally God-given, differences between serfs and lords, but this difference was not racialized (Hall 2004:12). Slavery itself, then, does not depend on a racialized distinction between the free person and the enslaved person. Racism is not necessary for slavery to flourish.

What racism did make possible, and in some sense still does, is to reconcile two opposing ideologies – liberty (or freedom) and slavery (or unfreedom) – within the same governing formation. English colonialists fought the American War of Independence (the Revolutionary War) for independence from Britain. The war was framed by an ideology of liberty that legitimated the demand for separation from England and for self-governance. When the war (1775–83) ended, the Constitution (1788) proclaimed that 'All men are created equal.' Yet this claim of the equality of all 'men' excluded slaves. Just as the English colonialists demanded independence as a sign of their inherent equality with Englishmen in England, they could have recognized the necessity of freeing Africans and African-Americans from slavery to recognize the fundamental equality of African men with European men. That they did not was not yet a sign of their racist belief in the inherently unfree nature of Africans. Indeed, many African-Americans secured their freedom after the Revolutionary War in a process of political struggle. African-Americans fought in the Revolutionary War, both as patriots and as loyalists (to the British Crown) and in either case to press their demands for freedom.

It took another seventy-five years (1865) until the adoption of the Thirteenth Amendment following the Civil War (1861–5) finally to end slavery in the USA. It is worth reflecting on this date. It is less than four generations ago. This means that in the living memory of many Southerners someone in their family was either a slave or a slave-owner. Someone who is now around 80 years old, born in about 1935, could have had a grandparent and would have had a great-grandparent who lived through slavery. The material and symbolic effects of slavery continue to reverberate through US political economy, society and culture. Slavery did not end racism; the resistance of African-Americans to racism and their involvement in the Revolutionary War as patriots and the Civil War as Unionists did not end the constitution of the USA as a 'racial democracy' in which to be Anglo-American was/is to be assured of a personal and political sovereignty, twinned with a 'racial despotism' (Omi and Winant 2015) in which to be African-American was/is to have sovereignty attenuated at best.

It is widely claimed that white enslavers (slave-owners and traders) thought that Africans were less than human or perhaps not human at all, that it was this belief through which they justified their enslavement of Africans, and that the transatlantic slave trade and the visible physiological differences (skin colour, hair texture) between Europeans and Africans around which it was organized were the origin of modern racism. This belief is contradicted by the historiography of slavery in the USA. Whites were as aware of the humanness of Africans as of their own humanness, and of course Africans countered any sense of their less-than-humanness through the exercise of their own agency. The belief that slave-owners thought of slaves as like horses or cattle is mostly warranted by reference to two practices: one, the listing of slaves as a capital asset, alongside livestock and crops in slave-owners' accounts; and two, the standing of a slave as three-fifths of a citizen for the purpose of representation and taxation. Yet at this point women for the purpose of representation counted not at all – but it would be not only counter-intuitive but counter-empirical to suggest that men did not think of women as human.

None of this is to deny the deep inequality that was American slavery or the violence and threat of violence that slaves were constantly subjected to. Indeed, for African-Americans the period following slavery was arguably more structured around racial governance than the period of slavery. Commentators note that white abolitionists often reassured their white constituents and white Southern states that abolition would not change the racial order since African-Americans were naturally inferior to whites. This theory of essential racial difference was forged in the crucible of the Revolutionary War and reinforced during the Civil War, rather than being self-evident to whites when there was no need to provide an ideological basis for the enslavement of Africans and African-Americans.

Children and racist governance

The figure of the child took centre stage in this intensification of racist governance. Levander (2004, 2006), for example, shows that the abolitionist texts that featured child characters, both black and white, inscribed within them a racist ideology that insists that whiteness is the essential colour of liberty, and that although slavery is a 'stain' on the nation, racial equality was not the goal of the abolitionists. The figure of the child deployed by abolitionists is therefore taken as a collapsing together of the child and the nation and of white supremacy and the 'infantile citizen'. Ward concurs (2012:43) that many white abolitionists were also racist. Lincoln himself was against race integration and sought to win support for the colonization of (and deportation to) Liberia by African-Americans.

This 'free' nation needed 'unfree' labour to settle and cultivate land for the profit of the Anglo-American colonialists. The intensification of racist ideology occurred after the Revolutionary War, when changes in Southern agriculture expanded the demand for unfree labour. This expanded demand from the Revolutionary War to the Civil War had an enormous impact on Southern black families.

Within a generation of the end of the Civil War and the end of slavery, the US government in concert with various civil society actors began to address the deep inequalities generated by industrial capitalism and to reform the institutions of the welfare state. However, this so-called Gilded Age or Progressive Era in US politics, from 1890 to 1920, was for African-Americans 'the darkest age since the Civil War and a period of retrogression in black–white relations' (Levander 2006:159). Indeed,

Ward sees the Progressive Era state as a 'white supremacist parental state [that] predated American independence, but its ideological and institutional scaffolding grew rapidly with the establishment of the Republic, the waning decades of racial slavery, and the so-called enlightenment of the juvenile justice system' (2012:45).

What I have argued in this section is that racism underpinned the development of the US state, and that capitalism in the USA cannot be separated from what is sometimes called 'racial capitalism'. Racist exclusions were not anomalous in the architecture of liberal capitalism, they were its foundation stones. This is not a new argument, and many others have made it (Mills 2011, Omi and Winant 2015); what is less well-developed in the extant scholarship is that the foundations of racial capitalism are connected to the ideology of modern childhood. Others have begun to make these connections (for example, Bernstein 2011, Levander 2006). In the next section I develop more fully this argument about the connection between governing through racism and governing through childhood.

Education after slavery

Child labour reform focused on taking children out of work and enrolling them in school. Many of the photographs of working children taken by the US reform photographer Lewis Hine, and analysed in the next section, are of schools. Although some of the photos are of schools for black children (all schools were segregated in the South), the majority are of schools for white children. More photographs are of schools than of cotton (either mills or fields). Frequently Hine comments on enrolment and absenteeism, due to 'the cotton' or 'the beet work'. The implication is that white children are absent from school because their parents wanted them to work in the fields or the mills and that black children are in school while white children are working.

Former slaves and yeoman farmers shared a strong dislike of being supervised by white landowners but they had very different views on children's education. White yeoman farmers did not want government officials telling them to send their children to school. In contrast, after the Civil War African-American families did want their children educated but white planters, and the governing bodies that represented them, used first violence and later withholding of resources to prevent this. African-American parents and children were the pioneers of public education in the immediate post-Civil War South, and their considerable gains immediately after the end of the Civil War were wrested from them by the combined actions of the national and federal state legislators and the terrorism of white Southerners, especially poor whites.

The dominant historical narrative of black education in this period is that it was achieved through the benevolence of white Northerners who came south to ensure that Reconstruction would benefit African-Americans. The dominant historiography claims that the teachers were mostly young white women and that they were motivated by abolitionist sentiment or politics. Indeed, some historians claim that white Southerners' opposition to African-American education was in response to these Northerners and their disdain for the South. In *Schooling the Freed People* (2010) Ronald Butchart overturns this dominant historical narrative. Drawing on a much wider archive than other historians, he shows that teachers were in fact mostly Southerners, both white and African-American, and that many of the white Southerners applied to be teachers out of economic compulsion, following financial losses in the Civil War (Butchart 2010:54–7, 67–71), and many had no commitment to the abolitionist cause and were in fact often racist. African-Americans were only 12 per cent of the US population (North and South) but between 1861 and 1876 African-American teachers 'outnumbered northern white teachers four to three' (Butchart 2010:19), and many of them were Northern black veterans. Regardless of their political position or their racial identities, these teachers and their students and schools were subjected to racist violence including shooting, arson, assault, kidnapping and murder. White supremacists engaged in 'open terrorism aimed at destroying the black dream of intellectual emancipation through education' (Butchart 2010:156; see also chapter 6).

Education and literacy, denied under slavery, made up one of the most concrete demands of African-Americans after emancipation. They 'acted on the possibilities of freedom with an overwhelming surge toward the schoolhouse door' (Butchart 2010:2). If many of the economic possibilities after the end of slavery did not feel so different to slavery itself, education held out the promise of political and economic power. For this reason African-Americans organized schools, demanded that they be taxed to pay for schools, and hired teachers. Far from being a gift of the state, or of white Northerners, '[t]he education of the freed people was, first and foremost, an education by African Americans, the work of the freed people themselves and of black Americans from the northern states' (Butchart 2010:3). Within ten years of the end of the Civil War they had established over one hundred secondary and postsecondary schools (Butchart 2010:4).

The demand for schools from freed people and other black Southerners (that is, those who were free before emancipation) was not matched by a demand from poor whites for schools for their children. This was not, as the child labour reform archive seems to imply, because black children were not in work and white children were. Black parents also needed the labour of their children. As Butchart recounts, '[o]lder students whose labor was needed in the fields worked early and showed up at the schoolhouse door after midday despite many hours of work' (Butchart 2010:7). If poor whites in the antebellum South were illiterate because of 'custom and a general [white] southern indifference to public, universal education' (Butchart 2010:15), poor blacks were illiterate because during slavery it was illegal for slaves to be educated and 'in many states, even for free blacks' (2010:15).

African-Americans' push for schooling did not survive the onslaught against them from whites of all classes. By the so-called Gilded Age, black children were less likely to be in school than their white peers and government expenditure on black children's schooling was significantly less than on white children's schooling. In 1910, according to Moehling (2004:31, table 1) black boys aged 10 to 16 were more likely than white boys to be working (nearly two-thirds of black boys and less than one-half of white boys) and black girls were nearly three times more likely than white girls to be working. She concludes that state disinvestment in black education was more important than family structure in accounting for this difference.

Child labour reform

Many of the gains made in the immediate aftermath of the Civil War were lost in the period of reconstruction. White landowners and white yeoman farmers, albeit with different economic interests, sought to lock African-American workers out of industrial labour. In the early twentieth century, as the structure of the Southern economy changed, white yeoman farmers were increasingly dividing their household labour between agriculture and industry. White child labour in industry became the target of social reformers. Lewis Hine, a white social reform photographer, was commissioned by the National Child Labor Committee (NCLC) to take documentary photographs to publicize the conditions of working children for a middle-class audience. The photographs he took are available at the NCLC Collection (http://www.loc.gov/pictures/collection/nclc). In this archive there are over 5,000 images of working children, only thirty-five of which are of black children. The images are accompanied by captions that give sparse, factual information about the subjects: their ages, when they started working, their roles and whether or not they also attended school.

Although race is hardly mentioned in these captions, and racism is never mentioned, I will show that the framing of the problem of child labour as a problem of white child labour was critical to how the reform campaign sought to secure the support of middle-class reformers and white workers.

In her book *The Whiteness of Child Labor Reform in the New South* (2004) Sallee shows that white trades unionists abandoned a socialist, non-racist agenda of labour reform for a campaign that insisted on the inappropriateness of white child labour, not of child labour in general. Others have commented on the affront to racist ideas that the image of white children, specifically Anglo-American children, working held (e.g. Dimock 1993). Dimock argues that 'Hine's child labor photographs must be read carefully and cautiously "against the grain" given their complicity in the construction of the working-class "other"' (1993:43). That may be one critique to make, and clearly these images are packaged for the gaze of the middle-class reformer who sees in child labour not the inequality of capitalism but the fecklessness and neglect of working-class parents. However, what also needs commenting on is why this working-class 'other' was always a white child. The reason was that the cross-class alliance that the NCLC wanted to build had to be forged on another terrain than a pro-labour, anti-capitalist critique and so the connection that was made across the class line was to white, perhaps specifically Anglo-American racism.

White mill labour

The focus of the NCLC's work was on the Carolina Piedmont, which was the heart of the cotton industry in the South at the end of the nineteenth century. Cotton mills almost only hired white labour. In the mid-nineteenth century, when the cotton industry was being established in the Piedmont, free white workers and black slaves worked in small factories, including many children (Lander 1953), but by the end of the nineteenth century the mill workforce was almost entirely white.

The cotton mills were the centre of industrial child labour: 20 per cent of workers in the cotton mills were under the age of 16 years, compared to 5 per cent in Northern cotton mills. I have already mentioned the focus of the Hine archive on white workers. In his biography of Hine, Freedman comments that 'Throughout the segregated South, mill work was reserved for whites. Blacks were seldom hired. Most mill hands were impoverished white share-croppers and tenant farmers who had abandoned worn-out farms for the promise of steady employment in the mills'

(2008:32). Freedman's short text *Kids at Work: Lewis Hine and the Crusade Against Child Labor* (2008) includes fifty-eight photographs; not one of them is of a black child working, despite the fact that many of them are of cotton field workers – as which black children worked – and not only of mill workers. In a review of Davidson's 1939 *Child Labor Legislation in the Southern Textile States*, Mabry comments that 'outside of the textile industry child labor constituted a problem of no great magnitude' (1940:74). In her 1937 paper 'Early Development of Public Opinion Against Southern Child Labor', Davidson comments that, '[t]he reformers struck one note of popular appeal when they declared that while the poor white child was forced to work the black child was going to school, and the future domination of the whites was thus jeopardized' (1937:244). In *Like a Family* (Hall et al. 1987), the authors also comment that the mills workforce was almost entirely white, and they remark that of the more than 200 oral testimonies that they collected in their oral history of Piedmont industrialization, all but six of the respondents were white.

Making segregation look natural

The cause of the mill workforce being almost entirely white is not commented on, as if the whiteness of labour in the mills was a fact of life rather than the outcome of racist exclusions. Hall et al. claim that white workers were not racist and they were more concerned about the hardships of daily life than racist exclusions of black workers from the mills. Yet this is surely disingenuous. White workers refused to work alongside black workers in the mills and white mill owners had no economic or political interest in forcing white workers to accept black workers into the mills. Although some union organizers saw the necessity of organizing black and white workers, the racism not only of white workers but of white planters and the governing class in the South brought any attempt at integrated labour organizing into violent confrontation with the police. So the racism of white workers was not the only reason for the exclusion of black workers from the mills, but it certainly contributed to making the mills a 'closed shop' for white workers.

In *Racecraft*, Barbara and Karen Fields (Fields and Fields 2014) make the powerful point that analysis of race makes race itself (usually in fact skin colour) appear as an agent. They insist on the importance of naming racism as the action that produces race. Their point resonates powerfully here with the history of child labour reform in the USA that has tended to say that 'the mills were white', rather than that racist action on the part of whites – workers, industrialists and planters – kept the mills white. They also argue that whites in the South did not have a shared culture, a shared ideology or shared economic interests. This is not to say that white yeoman farmers were not racists. Their racism, they argue, sprang from their association of African-Americans with slavery. If this is correct then the racism of white workers in the mills followed on from their clinging to an ideology of agricultural independence that was compromised by their family labour in the mills and would be compromised further by working alongside African-Americans, whose bodies signified to whites the condition of slavery. This is racism, of course, as surely as the racism of white planters led them to insist on their rights to African-American labour even after emancipation. Their point is that the fact that planters and yeoman farmers had white skin and were racist did not mean that their racist ideology was of the same type or arose from the same conditions as the racism of the planter class. Nonetheless, the shared racism of white yeoman farmers and white planters was what kept the mills white. The planter class needed agricultural labour as much after abolition as before it, and segregation in the mills meant that the foundation of Southern industrial capitalism was largely barred to black workers.

For the yeoman farmer, waged labour was a form of slavery (and for child labour reformers too, child labour was a form of slavery) and yeoman farmers were struggling to hold onto their identities as independent farmers and the land itself, even while their families were at the vanguard of changing the family economy from independent subsistence farmers to industrial workers. In calling child labour a form of slavery, reformers were talking in racist code to both Anglo-American reformers and white yeoman farmers turned mill workers.

Women and child workers were a significant part of the Southern textile mill workforce. Men frequently tried to hold onto land; combining mill work with farming and leaving the mills at harvest time to do the more lucrative work of cotton harvesting. Children often preferred mill work to farm work; for young boys (who worked as doffers and sweepers), the pattern of work in the mills gave them more free time than they had in the fields, at least during the harvest. White children did not have any great interest in staying in school, preferring to work and contribute to the family wage and their own pocket money once they were, or could claim to be, 12 years old. The parents of child mill workers were used to being able to dispose of their children's time and felt they had the right to do so; they resented the interference of Northern reformers in their family economy.

As a consequence of the racist exclusion of black workers from the mills, and the decision of child labour reformers to focus on the mills as the worst form of child labour, the history of child labour in the USA is largely represented as a history of white children. It excludes black children's labour almost entirely; indeed it would be possible to suggest, on the basis of the archive and the historiography of Southern labour, that after emancipation black children were either in school or, if not in school, then at least not working.

The exclusion of black children from this archive was not a visual artifice of the already segregated mills. Although child labour reform focused on the textile industry, it did not only focus on the mills. Nearly 700 of Hine's photographs are of cotton workers, in the fields and in the mills; not a single one of these is a black worker. Here, surely, there is a more deliberate exclusion of black children from labour reform and child welfare more generally. For while it can be argued that black children do not appear in the documentary photographic archive of the mills because of a pre-existing exclusion of black workers, the same cannot be said for workers in the cotton fields. If the textile mills are taken as the most important site of child labour, in relation to both the numbers of children working and the harshness of their working conditions, such an argument can only be made if agricultural labour is bracketed out of the term 'labour'. What would warrant such an exclusion? One possible explanation is that agricultural labour was the main employer of black children's labour and that the rationale for the exclusion is, if not intentionally racist (from subsequent scholars: it was intentionally racist on the part of contemporary whites), then implicitly so. It naturalizes black agricultural labour and does not see in it the harshness of labour – agricultural or industrial – because it is labour done by black people.

In those industries that were not segregated, black child labour is excluded from representation in the Hine archive, either literally through the cropping and framing of the image to focus only on white subjects or in the accompanying texts that refer only to the white children in the images. When black workers are mentioned it is frequently to cast them as potential corruptors of white youth; for example, the caption to an image of lumber workers in Baltimore reads 'Many girls and boys, old and young, working here with the negroes who are often not good associates'. In a set of photographs of glass workers at a glass factory in Alexandria, black child labourers are cropped or out of focus. In one photo, for example, a black boy is framed at the edge of a group of white boys and in another the photo has been cropped to exclude this black boy almost entirely, only the edge of his face remaining visible. That said, there are two other photographs of glass workers in glass factories in New Jersey, one a group of four young black workers and another a cropped version of the same group, and one of adult workers in a glass factory; a 'holding-mold boy' is the object of the photograph, though dimly seen.

The only images in the entire collection of black farmers are two photographs of Charlie Howard and his two sons, aged 6 and 11 years old. The caption reads, 'Father says children will go to Rocky Ridge School when it opens'. In this image, the figures of the farmer and his sons are barely legible and the lack of clarity in the image contrasts with the rest of the archive, which in general has high production values.

It is relevant that Hine calls Charlie Howard and three other photos of boys and girls in the 4-H Club 'colored', a respectful form of address in the early twentieth century but not one that Hine consistently uses. Here, linked with the 4-H Clubs (agricultural extension service clubs for rural boys and girls; the 4-Hs are Head, Heart, Hands, Health), it signifies the 'uplift' of African-Americans and implicitly contrasts this with the working and living conditions of white children.

It has not only been child labour reform in the South that has been, so to speak, coded white; the historiography of child labour since emancipation has also been so coded. An analysis of Hine's photographs that is attentive to the history of racism makes visible the erasure of black children's labour in the South in the historical record. It brings back into focus, as it were, those photographs where Hine does show traces of black children's labour; for example, black workers in the glass, wood, tobacco and oyster industries did include children, even while his captions often then deny their presence. We have to turn to other sources to try uncover the extent of children's labour in the margins of the history of adult labour.

In *White Land, Black Labor,* Flynn (1983) discusses the post-Civil War struggle of African-Americans to control their own labour and how this shaped the decisions of black Southerners about the family economy. He comments that, freed people 'used their right to withdraw their labour perhaps most dramatically as women and children adopted new economic roles. After emancipation, single black women and widows often worked as wage hands in cotton, but *wives and children usually refused employment* in the fields' (Flynn 1983:61, emphasis added). Yet further on he says that

> *Like their children*, they [married women] returned to the field to chop and pick cotton for the superior wages available during ... growing or harvesting season. And they sometimes even cultivated on shares a few acres of cotton and corn separate from the landowner's 'general crops' and out from under his supervision. Farther up the agricultural ladder, the wives of sharecroppers and renters regularly joined their husbands *and children in the field* after housework was finished for the day. (Flynn 1983:61, emphasis added)

In other words, it was not agricultural work itself that married women and children withdrew from but the 'close supervision' of white landowners. Freed people refused to endure white landowners attempting to control their children's labour after emancipation. In 1872 in Schley County 'a freed man named Allen Stallings burned the house of his employer at the insistence of his wife, who was infuriated that the landowner had whipped her "little son". She said that "the boy was not his" and that he "would be sorry for" what he had done' (Flynn 1983: 63).

Conclusion

This chapter has explicated and applied key concepts from the sociology of race, including racialization, to show how governing technologies provide the means through which children are encouraged to think of themselves and others as people with a race. I have shown that racist ideas about differences between humans are not trans-historical; rather they were forged in a specific historical context. That same historical context gave rise to the idea of the modern child – a figure set apart from public life and immersed in childish occupations of school and play and who is conceptualized as a developing potential whose development must be carefully nurtured. In the Progressive Era or the Gilded Age, labour reformers were demanding the extension of child-saving to Southern industry. This same period when governing technologies – that is to say national legislation but also philanthropists, charities and trades unionists – were demanding an end to child labour under the sign of the rights of the child, racism was intensifying in the South against black children and their families.

Through an analysis of the Hine archive I have suggested that the choice of the mills as the target for child labour reform was not because this was where most children were working but because it was where most white children were working. In other words, the reformers used racist codes to suggest that the affront of mill workers was that they were not in school when black children were, that they were suffering like slaves when black children were free. I have argued that reformers deployed racist tropes to curtail child labour in the South for two reasons. One is that the alliance that campaigned against child labour was not an alliance of workers' organizations; it wanted to retain the substance of capitalist labour relations whilst removing its worse excesses. The second is that it needed the support of white planters and white yeoman families, especially fathers, to secure an end to some forms of child labour. Just as white abolitionists had appealed for support from white voters by claiming both that slavery was unjust and that

African-Americans were not the equals of Euro-Americans and that abolition would not therefore fundamentally change the governing order, Progressive Era reformers now claimed that African-American 'uplift' threatened white supremacy and would continue to do so as long as white children were 'slaves'.

What I hope this analysis highlights is the necessity of interrogating what work governing through the figure of the child accomplishes, and of interrupting the progressive narrative in the history of childhood, to make visible the ways that children's lives have been and continue to be structured by racism.

4

Policing Gender

Introduction

This chapter is in two parts. The first part offers a theoretical framework for thinking about gender in Childhood Studies. It does this through setting out how gender has been treated within Childhood Studies and the related fields of Girlhood and Boyhood Studies. It then develops an account of Judith Butler's analysis of gendered performativity and its relevance to Childhood Studies. In the second part of the chapter I use the example of juvenile justice in the USA to interrogate how these theoretical tools may give us the means to understand how gender governs the lives of children and young people.

Childhood Studies and Gender Studies

In her review of the literature and debates at the intersection between Childhood and Gender Studies Emily Kane (2013) notes that the two disciplines share key theoretical principles. They both understand their core concepts to be socially constructed and increasingly recognize the intersection of gendered inequalities with other inequalities (especially race and class). Gender Studies and Childhood Studies both insist on the relationality of social identities (that is to say, that binary identities, whether adult/child or male/female, are constructed in opposition to one another) and increasingly emphasize how gender is structured in relation to sexuality. Kane notes that within Childhood Studies 'The literature documents the many ways in which children's daily lives are shaped by gender in a wide variety of cultural contexts' (2013:16).

However, although it is certainly the case that childhood scholars attend to gender, they often take it as a variable that explains patterns of social interaction and the acquisition by children of conventional ideas of how boys and girls should behave. Notwithstanding the desire to show that gender is socially constructed, the reifying effects are very similar to those produced through an understanding of gender as grounded in biology. Certainly, there is attention to children's agency in constructing and maintaining gendered boundaries but the outcome remains the same, in terms of the perceived stability of gendered practices. Indeed, children's play and discourse are often shown to exhibit a more conservative interpretation of gender roles than may exist in their social worlds.

In any case, although we may reasonably claim anything written about girls or boys or transgender/gender-non-conforming children as being about children and therefore within the frame of Childhood Studies, many scholars whose research focuses on children and youth would not necessarily recognize themselves as contributing to Childhood Studies, rather than, say, to the sociology of gender or to Cultural Studies. Thus the extent to which gender has entered Childhood Studies is difficult to determine because the scope of the field (Childhood Studies) is potentially so broad. Furthermore, a separate field of Girl Studies that has emerged since the end of the last (twentieth) century has positioned itself as somewhat tangential to Childhood Studies. Although it speaks to the core issues of Childhood Studies, particularly agency, there seems to be little cross-contact between Girl Studies and Childhood Studies. Claudia Mitchell and Jacqueline Reid-Walsh, both Canadian scholars, have been important figures in this literature. Mitchell is a professor in the Faculty of Education at McGill University and an honorary professor at KwaZulu Natal University, South Africa, and her commitment to Africanist scholarship in Girl Studies has influenced the scope of the journal she co-edits, *Girlhood*, giving a welcome extension of the sociology of gender and Cultural Studies to non-Western contexts. Mitchell also has a co-edited volume with Carrie Rentschler: *Girlhood and the Politics of Place* (2016). Included in that collection are papers by key scholars in a feminist-oriented Girlhood Studies, including Jessica Ringrose, Marnina Gonick, Catherine Driscoll and Geraldine Bloustien. Bloustien may also be considered a pioneer in this field, as she published *Girl Making* in 2003. It is a seminal contribution, not least in its methodology, its focus on the lives of working-class girls and its close analytical attention to the intersections of gender, class and race in the subjectivities of her respondents. Yet none of these authors are routinely cited within Childhood Studies or themselves cite more than the foundational texts (for example, James et al.'s *Theorizing Childhood*) in their work.

Nonetheless, it is within Girl Studies rather than Childhood Studies that much of the work of theorizing what gender means in children's lives has been done. It therefore offers Childhood Studies important theoretical tools for understanding the formation of gendered subjectivities. One strand of theorizing within that work has been connecting ideals of young femininity to liberal models of the self. Anita Harris in *Future Girl*, for example, says that young women have 'become a focus for the construction of an ideal late modern subject who is self-making, resilient and flexible' (Harris 2004b:6). Like Valerie Walkerdine and colleagues in their widely cited *Growing Up Girl* (Walkerdine, Lucey and Melody 2001), Harris sees girls as being positioned as both 'can-do' and 'at-risk', and 'as ideal citizens, closely regulated in schools, work, leisure and new welfare and justice' (Harris 2004b:11).

Harris locates the emergence of Girl Studies in criticism of Youth Studies as focusing on boys or 'boyology'. In contrast, then, to the origins of Childhood Studies in a critique on the one hand of how disciplines simply ignored children's perspectives and experiences, relying entirely on adult interlocutors, and on the other hand of socialization and pedagogy's focus on children's developmental potential, rather than their lived experience as children, Girl Studies positions itself within the Cultural Studies tradition and its interest in youth (sub)cultures.

Another contrast to Childhood Studies is in the clear feminist commitment of Girl Studies. A feminist epistemology is often claimed for Childhood Studies (see, for example, Mayall 2002) but it is not consistently maintained. Girl Studies, as Harris notes, was part of feminist interventions into Youth Studies in the late 1970s and early 1980s. This was also a period in which teenage girls and young women were themselves organizing and reshaping cultural fields, for example in the emergence of Riot Grrrl, young feminist zines and other feminist interventions. This leads Harris, in *Future Girl* (2004b) and *All About the Girl* (2004a), to declare that the end of the last century was a period of girl power. If it was, that is looking increasingly hollow in the twenty-first century. Certainly, the weakening of prohibitions on girls playing with 'boys' toys' and wearing trousers in school was partly a response to young feminists' self-organization, but these styles have subsequently been co-opted by commodity capitalism; sexual violence and harassment against girls and their exclusion from public space, and the ways that their inclusion in public space is policed around discourses of 'good' girls and 'sluts', suggest that 'girl power' overstates the gains for girls of late twentieth-century feminism.

Interest in girls and the specific dynamics of girls' transitions in ado-lescence motivated by feminist analysis also led to Caroline Gilligan's (1993) widely cited research in psychology. Gilligan and colleagues, writing in the early 1990s, were concerned that girls became less vocal as they entered their teens, losing their 'resistance and authentic voices when they engage with cultural requirements to shape their identities in line with dominant femininities' (Harris 2004a:xviii). Other work took up that theme, including the American Association of University Women research published in 1992 and based on survey data from 3,000 boys and girls in US public schools. Their research was concerned with girls' low academic achievement relative to boys in schools. The research identified school practices that undermined girls' confidence. Then in 1994 Mary Pipher, a clinical psychologist, published a bestselling book, *Reviving Ophelia*, based on her clinical cases. It sold one and a half million copies and stayed in the *New York Times* bestseller list for three years (Ward and Benjamin 2004:16). It lent a strong narrative support to the claim that girls lost confidence as they entered their teens and that institutions needed to do more to support stronger identities for girls. Subsequent research suggested that African-American girls manage to retain a strong sense of self and self-expression through adolescence and 'often appear more willing to advocate for their needs and to resist injuri-ous definitions of womanhood and femininity' (Ward and Benjamin 2004:20).

In the UK Angela McRobbie's (1991) 'Settling Accounts with Sub-culture: A Feminist Critique' argued that subcultural Youth Studies, in particular Dick Hebdige's *Subculture: The Meaning of Style* (1991, first published 1979) in its focus on public space, ignored girls' cultures. This led to a focus on bedroom cultures in Girl Studies that arguably reinforces rather than critiques a gendered public/private male/female binary. This literature established the fundamental issues for Girl Studies as popular cultures, school and media, and emphasized the impor-tance of young women's voices and spaces (Harris 2004a), but Harris also argues that this wave was challenged by the complexities of girls' lives.

The programmes for change that emerged out of concern in the late 1990s with the falling self-esteem of adolescent girls were focused on changing institutions. By the end of the twentieth century, under the pervasive influence of neo-liberalism, the emphasis had shifted from institutions failing girls to, simply, girls failing. The problem in this new paradigm was individual behaviour, not structural or institutional sexism. At the same time, according to Ward and Benjamin, Girl Studies dissi-pated into several sub-disciplines that rarely connect, including educa-tion, reproductive health and psychology (2004:19). In an effort to avoid overgeneralizing the experiences of girls, they argue, Girl Studies has moved from a claim that girls share the same experience to a claim that they all have entirely different experiences. As these authors comment, 'what's lost in this argument is the recognition that all American girls are influenced by, and must negotiate, persistent gender bias in institutions (e.g. schools, health care systems, organized religion) and the ubiquity of American popular culture' (2004:21). Chesney-Lind and Irwin (2008) in *Beyond Bad Girls* identify a similar genealogy of Girlhood Studies, and in particular home in on the media concern with 'bad girls' and 'relational aggression' and the negative effects this has had on how institutions respond to girls, a point that I pick up in the second part of this chapter.

Boyhood Studies

In 2007 the journal *Boyhood Studies* was founded, published by Berghahn, who also publish *Girlhood Studies*. If feminism provides the ideological underpinnings for Girl Studies, Boyhood Studies seems decidedly anti-feminist in its framing; for example, an early issue on the 'war on boys' and 'misandry' includes an article by the anti-feminist writer Christina Hoff Sommers, author of *Who Stole Feminism?*

One of the problems with the emerging research on boys and masculinity is that it misreads constraints in social expectations as a form of oppression of boys and men. Kane remarks that 'Though gender inequalities advantage boys and men in many ways, scholars increasingly recognize that social expectations for masculinity also narrow the range of options considered acceptable for boys and men in troubling ways' (Kane 2013:19). This kind of sentiment has now become a commonplace, that is, the idea that the attachment of emotion and relationships to femininity stigmatizes these practices and prevents boys from the full range of human behaviour. There is, however, little research evidence that boys find these constraints 'troubling'. In the research for *Young Masculinities* (Frosh, Phoenix and Pattman 2004) the researcher comments on the differences in how boys talk about girls and emotion when they are on their own and when they are in focus groups. In the latter they display stereotypical views about girls and sexuality, freely expressing both sexism and homophobia. This does illustrate that how boys do masculinity is shaped by contexts of social interaction and social institutions, but this is the case for all genders, not only for boys. As Lynne Segal comments, 'The "masculinity in crisis" literature is problematic insofar as it ignores the central issue: the pay-offs men receive (or hope to receive) from their claims to manhood' (2001:239).

Indeed, the reason that girls have managed to broaden their range of available behaviours is partly through feminist struggles, but also because boys' activities are valued and therefore for a girl to attach herself to "boys" activities is, with the important exception of desiring other girls, not to engage in stigmatized practices. Stigma is attached, however, to same-sex desire, so that girls who continue with their 'tomboy' dispositions past puberty are likely to be stigmatized as 'lesbians' and must display appropriate hetero-feminine behaviours to avoid this stigma. Judith (now Jack) Halberstam has commented that tomboyism is 'punished when it … threatens to extend beyond childhood and into adolescence' (Halberstam 1998:6; see also Nayak and Kehily 2013:157–81). Instead of acknowledgement of the misogyny and homophobia that underlie parents' and children's concerns about boys playing with dolls, a concern that is not paralleled in relation to girls playing with cars, we find that researchers focus on the restriction that this imposes on boys' play (Kane 2013, Thorne 1993). Given the range of boys' spatial freedoms and the extent of their bodily freedoms in comparison to girls', turning to the limits of boys' emotional range as a sign of their gender inequality (rather than of an anti-feminine gendered order) seems to reconstruct gender as equal but different, rather than making visible the harms that girls suffer in a gendered regime.

Doing gender

Judith Butler's theory of performativity may help develop our understanding of the child's experience of gender and the relationship between gender and sexuality for children. Butler's arguments in *Gender Trouble* (1990), *Bodies That Matter* (2011) and other texts are widely cited in Gender Studies but have been much less influential in Childhood Studies. Indeed, Emily Kane's review of the intersection between these two literatures, *Rethinking Gender and Sexuality in Childhood* (2013), does not cite Butler's work at all. The absence of Butler's work on gender in Childhood Studies is unfortunate (for an exception see Nayak and Kehily 2013) because Butler's central claims have great potential for understanding how children come to think of themselves as people with a gender and how they 'do gender'.

In brief, Butler's core argument is that the gendered positions available to people depend on the fiction of a gender binary that is oppositional and hierarchical and which is only intelligible through a heterosexual matrix. In other words the fiction offered to us is that there are two genders, male and female (this is the binary), that are oppositional to one another, so that the attributes of one are the opposite of the attributes of the other (think strong/weak, stoical/emotional, culture/nature), and that these oppositions are hierarchical – so that the male characteristics of this binary are valued and empowered over the female side. The heterosexual matrix is a concept intended to suggest that these gendered positions are always articulated through sexuality, so that to be a properly gendered subject is also to be a heterosexual subject.

Gender Trouble was first published in 1990, and has since had several editions and reprints, most recently in 2010. It is subtitled *Feminism and the Subversion of Identity*. The subtitle is important partly because, as Butler makes clear in her preface to the 1999 edition, this text was an intervention within feminism. It is a 'self-criticism that promises a more democratic and inclusive life for the [feminist] movement' (1999:vii). In it Butler is exploring how people come to think of themselves as having a gender and with what consequences for an 'intelligible' life gender is constructed as a binary and underwritten by, or through, a compulsory heterosexuality.

The idea that gender is constructed is at the heart of feminist politics and is now more or less accepted throughout the social sciences (though see chapter 8 on psychology for the re-instantiation of biology as the basis of gender through contemporary discourses about the gendered brain). For anyone familiar with Childhood Studies, the parallels with the claim that childhood is a social construction may seem, at first glance, obvious. However, there are important divergences between different understandings of the term 'social construction', and in particular between a humanist concept of social construction and the one deployed by poststructuralists, including Judith Butler. In particular, in Childhood Studies the importance of 'uncovering' children's agency has been at the heart of the discipline. The way that agency is conceptualized in Childhood Studies is as the expression of the will of an individual. The child is understood as having an interiority that she or he (their gender being already predetermined by their genitals) seeks to give expression to in the world through language and other acts. The question of where this interiority came from, how it is formed and how its formation might relate to such categories as gender and race is bracketed. The concept of children's agency within Childhood Studies relies on a modernist concept of the individual as complete, coherent and stable.

The concept of the individual child that predominates in Childhood Studies is remarkable, not only for its refusal of the challenge to this modernist concept of the self that poststructuralism has delivered, but also because childhood, more than any other point on the life course, seems to be a time when the instability, incoherence and fragmentation of the self are most visible. Indeed, the effort that goes into refuting the challenge that children pose to the modernist fiction of the coherent self may well be a source of much of the violence that children are exposed to from others (adults and children) as well as institutions (Wells 2016b, Wells, Burman, Montgomery and Watson 2014).

The social construction paradigm that Childhood Studies draws on is one that is in keeping with structuralist versions of gender that claim that gender is the culture that is written on the biology of sex. This echoes James and Prout's claim that 'the immaturity of children is a biological fact of life but the ways in which it is understood and made meaningful is [*sic*] a fact of culture' (1997:7). For both Childhood Studies and Gender Studies, the hope is that by showing that the way childhood and gender are practised is mutable across time and space (that is, they are socially constructed, whether in a humanist or a poststructuralist paradigm), the inequalities that gender and generational regimes prescribe can be challenged and undone. The unaddressed issue here is whether the differences between adults and children are more foundational than this allows, in which case the inequalities between children and adults will not be undone, and in some respects should not be undone, simply through recourse to 'social construction'. This is a point that I develop further in chapter 7.

In fact, it is not at all clear that appeals to biology as structuring social identity prevent, and appeals to the social as structuring identity facilitate, a move towards a more egalitarian or less repressive regime of either childhood or gender. Indeed, the search for a biological underpinning for difference (as for example in the search for the 'gay gene') has been motivated in part by the desire to argue that if we 'cannot help' being gay (because we are biologically or neurologically different to heterosexuals) then it is unfair to discriminate against us. This confidence in the ability of biology to shield individuals as categories of persons from discrimination is puzzling or just naive given a long history of incarceration, discrimination and violence against people who are presumed to be biologically different to the dominant norm.

For poststructuralism, in any case, this biology (nature)/gender (culture) distinction is unviable because it is through gender as a discourse that bodies are established as belonging to a particular gender. There cannot be a prediscursive sex any more than there can be a prediscursive gender, because the attribution of gender to this person with a clitoris and a vagina or that person with a penis and scrotum is itself an act of gendered discourse. Gender 'is not to culture as sex is to nature; gender is also the discursive/cultural means by which "sexed nature" or "a natural sex" is produced and established as "prediscursive", prior to culture, a politically neutral surface on which culture acts' (Butler 1990:10). Sociology, Butler insists, has 'sought to understand the notion of the person in terms of an agency that claims ontological priority to the various roles and functions through which it assumes visibility and meaning' (1990:22). In other words, for conventional sociology, the person has agency before it has a gender. A person, as it were, puts on their gender. The problem with this formulation for poststructuralists is that doing gender is what gives a subject visibility and meaning; so there can be no prior agency, no non-gendered person who chooses to take up their gender in one way or another. As Butler puts it, ' "persons" only become intelligible through becoming gendered in conformity with recognizable standards of gendered intelligibility' (1990:22).

If Butler is right then perhaps there cannot be a field called 'Childhood Studies' because there cannot be an ungendered child to occupy it. There is not a child (non-gendered) who then puts on a gender or who learns first how to be a child and then how to be a gendered child. Rather, it is through the gendering of the child that one of the fictions of a coherence of the self across time and space, an apparently external coherence that expresses an already internal coherence, is expressed. Butler cites Haar: 'The subject, the self, the individual, are just so many false concepts, since they transform into substances fictitious unities having at the start only a linguistic reality' (Butler 1990:29, citing Haar 1977:17–18). This linguistic reality, the gendered subject, is established through an oppositional and hierarchical relationship to the other gender (the 'opposite' gender) that 'thereby requires both a stable and oppositional heterosexuality' (1990:31). So for poststructuralists, there is no gendered identity that is then expressed through actions or claims; rather 'that identity is performatively constituted by the very "expressions" that are said to be its results' (1990:34).

Gender Trouble has little to say about how the performativity of gender changes over time, how the cultural intelligibility of the gendered child is achieved (if achievement is the right word), how girls and boys repeat their performances (and also how they refuse them). Butler talks only of women and men, but nonetheless the girl and boy are visible in her text through her discussion of the 'repeated stylization of the body, a set of repeated acts within a highly rigid regulatory frame that congeal over time to produce the appearance of substance, of a natural sort of being' (1990:45). She argues that the appearance of gender can be analysed by breaking it down into its constitutive acts. For children this might mean such acts as asking a pregnant woman if she is expecting a boy or a girl, or buying clothes for babies that are culturally read as gender appropriate. It might mean the toys that children of different genders are encouraged to play with, or the different ways their parents hold them. These 'constitutive acts' only make sense within what Butler calls 'compulsory frames' and the 'various forces', including the family, school and the law, that police the conformity between constitutive acts and compulsory frames (1990:45).

In the next section I examine how gender and sexual identification are literally policed within the juvenile justice system. I show that girls are punished for gender-inappropriate behaviour and that these punishments are also enacted within a classed and racist regime, so that black and working-class girls are more likely to be incarcerated, and white and middle-class girls are more likely to be subject to softer forms of coercion and regulation.

Governing structures in gender and sexual identification

The insistence that the body is not the origin or site on which race and gender identities are then inscribed, but rather the body itself is constituted through the gender and raced (or racist and sexist) regimes that govern subjects, is an important and compelling rhetorical point. However, poststructuralist accounts of gender have not been sufficiently attentive to the material conditions by which bodies are interpellated as gendered subjects. In this section I aim to explore the 'compulsory frames set by various forces that police the social appearance of gender' (1990:45) quite literally, by investigating how the US law produces gendered subjects.

The law is a core structure in the interpellation of subjects. The actors that animate the law, from social workers to police officers to judges and magistrates, have literally policed girls' sexualities through the juvenile justice system. My account, drawing on secondary sources, brings empirical weight to Butler's claim that compulsory heterosexuality underlies legible gender identities but also, as she claims, that same-sex desire has to be foreclosed if a rehabilitated, properly feminine gendered identity is to be instantiated. This foreclosure (it cannot be called repression since it may continue to be enacted but have no public or legitimate visibility) of same-sex desire and the regulation of appropriate heterosexual desire runs through the juvenile justice system for girls from its inception in the Progressive Era to the present day (Agyepong 2013). Women in the criminal justice system also have their sexuality policed, to be sure, but it is important to emphasize that, precisely because they are minors, girls are more vulnerable to state control than are women. In other words, the state's claim to be engaged in saving or protecting children allows for the suspension or simply non-existence of the constitutional norms of the liberal state. A final point that this account of the USA's twentieth- and early twenty-first-century juvenile justice system shows is the impossibility in a racist system of understanding the experience of girls as a unified class of people. Certainly, all girls have their sexuality policed to secure conformity with, and punish deviance from, a particular heterosexual feminine norm, but in a racist order, as we shall see, all of these elements – what forms of policing and punishment are deployed and what counts as a heterosexual feminine norm – are racialized and classed.

In 2013 just over 1 million children were arrested in the USA. In the context of a population of nearly 320 million and a child population (under 18) of about 73.5 million these figures, representing, as they do, about 1.5 per cent of the child population, may seem relatively insignificant (notwithstanding the fact that in global public policy the 1 million figure seems to be the tipping point at which an issue comes to be of significance). Even if we divide the population into African-American and white to explore whether the administration of juvenile justice is racialized (it is), the figures are still relatively small as a part of the overall population. There are about 11.3 million black children in the USA (roughly 15 per cent of all children) and 49 million white children (roughly two-thirds of all children). About 3.3 per cent of black children and 1.3 per cent of white children were arrested in 2013. Therefore black children were two and half times as likely as white children to be subjected to legal process in 2013. Boys are about twice as likely to be arrested as girls are. While these figures are low as a share of the total US population, in absolute numbers they are far from negligible. Furthermore, juvenile justice is a significant part of the government apparatus and apprehends boys and girls for different kinds of offences, as we shall see. It therefore brings to light how the construction of gender is not simply a matter of individual lifestyle or cultural choice but is shaped by wider governing structures.

Control of sexuality

The first juvenile court opened in Chicago, Illinois in 1899. This heralded the beginning of the institutionalization of the child-saving movement. It was, as that label suggests, a movement persuaded of the mutability of the child's character, and therefore the possibility of redemption if the child were given the right conditions in which to reform his or her character. The juvenile justice system was saturated with racist presumptions and black children were not seen as redeemable in the ways that white children were. Black and white girls were treated in the same institutions, but they were seen as different kinds of girls. In her paper on the policing of gender in a correctional facility in Illinois in the first half of the twentieth century (1893–1945), Tera Agyepong shows that 'notions of childhood innocence and rehabilitation were not universal but circumscribed by race' (2013:271) through which 'images of African American girls connoted inherently deviant, unfixable and dangerous delinquents' (2013:272). Most of the prisoners were white girls, but although African-American girls were only 10–15 per cent of the prison population between 1896 and 1920, this had risen to 35 per cent by 1928 even though African-Americans were only 2 per cent of the Illinois population (2013:274).

Reinforcing Butler's point about the importance of the regulation of sexuality in gender norms, the main reason why girls in the early twentieth century were referred to the courts was for 'sex delinquency'. Yet, although most of the girls at the Geneva School were there because the state wanted them to reform what it viewed as their sexual deviance, black girls were both more likely to be incarcerated and less likely to be seen as reformable. African-American girls, Agyepong argues, were thought by reformers to be sexually irredeemable, and the sexual exploitation of black girls was ignored in public policy. She cites as an example the passing of the Mann Act in 1910 to protect girls from sexual exploitation by men through controlling their movement across internal borders in an effort to suppress the 'white slave traffic': '[t]he modification of the word "slavery" with "white" was meant to distinguish the trade from black slavery, and thus rendered the sexual abuse and trafficking of black girls and women both normal and invisible' (2013:274).

Scholars concur that the central role of juvenile justice in the early twentieth-century USA was to police girls' sexuality. The 'girl problem' in the late nineteenth and early twentieth centuries was at the centre of US reformers' attitudes to the place of girls in juvenile justice and welfare. It was concerned with the control and regulation of girls' sexualities and was framed through a discourse of protection – from themselves and others. Agyepong situates her study within this wider context. Meda Chesney-Lind and Katherine Irwin agree that control of girls' and women's sexuality was 'at the center rather than the periphery of the early history of the juvenile justice system' (Chesney-Lind and Irwin 2008:157). The child-savers and juvenile courts of the Progressive Era focused on 'monitoring the behavior of young girls, particularly [white] immigrant girls and girls of color, to prevent their straying from the path of sexual purity' (Pasko 2010:1101).

Black girls were assumed by white social workers, police and courts to be both more promiscuous and more violent than white girls and, as in the wider dominant discourses about black femininity in the USA, were characterized as masculine, strong and sexually predatory. When black and white girls in the Geneva reformatory that Agyepong studied were in sexual relationships with each other, adults (contemporary researchers in the emerging social sciences, and reformatory staff) assumed that black girls imposed their sexual attention on white girls (2013:279). In 1935 a Master's student at Illinois published her thesis on girls on parole from Geneva and claimed that 'The violent attachment of one girl for another takes on a heterosexual character, the aggressor adopting the masculine role and the other girl playing the feminine part ... when the attachment occurs between a colored and a white girl, the former invariably assumes the masculine role' (2013:280). Staff members sought explanations for white girls' involvement with black girls in terms of the temporary nature of the associations and understood them as a parody of heterosexual relationships. Since black girls were already thought to be sexually deviant, the reformatory staff felt that there was no need to explain their sexual relationships with white girls (2013:282).

A generation later, in the early twenty-first century, girls engaged in same-sex relationships while detained in the juvenile justice system were still thought to be expressing a pathological desire. Thus, in her research on contemporary juvenile justice and gendered decision-making, one of Pasko's (2010) interviewees, the director of a residential facility, explains:

> No, not every girl in here has told us that they were sexually abused. But we know all of them have been. That's just the truth. Whenever a girl exhibits these behaviours [sexual activity with other girls], it is always because of PTSD, impulse control disorders, sometime intermittent explosive disorder ... There is a history of sexual abuse, whether they tell us or not. (Pasko 2010:1121)

Pasko points out that girls who, on release from prison, enter into relationships with men that are coercive or transactional are still seen as affirming a heterosexual identity whereas girls who have sex with girls while in detention can never affirm a lesbian or bisexual identity. The discourse of 'gay for the stay' informs the staff's understanding of girls' sexuality. Their inability to see same-sex activity, let alone a lesbian or bisexual identity, as valid surely plays some part in the responses in girls' detention centres to the passing of the Prison Rape Elimination Act (PREA). This act is a 'zero-tolerance' policy for prison rape which 'seeks to identify, prevent, and sanction sexual violence in all custodial settings' (Pasko 2010:1125). It was intended to protect men in prison from rape by other men. Pasko found in her research that staff interpreted the PREA Act to require a 'no-touching' rule between girls in detention, including no sitting next to one another on the bus, and only using one arm for hugging in therapy sessions (and otherwise no touching at all). Although staff expressed their discomfort with the implementation of PREA through close regulation and surveillance of girls, they nonetheless did so in terms that assumed that sex involves an instigator and a (dominated) subject. For girls this means an increased likelihood that detention may lead to them being listed on the sex offenders' register, further decreasing their opportunities when they are released.

Courts ignore lesbian and bisexual identities, and girls in juvenile detention are 'encouraged to develop a heterosexual understanding of themselves and their sexuality and to engage in hetero-feminine forms of gender conformity. Pressure to conform takes the form of pressure to wear makeup and "feminine" clothing, prohibitions on shaved heads, "reparative therapy" [i.e. conversion to heterosexuality] to address sexual identity confusion, and heterosexual life skills and safe sex education' (Pasko 2010:1113).

The persistence of a discourse that girls are being incarcerated for their own good and to protect them from their own sexuality has also obscured the extent to which girls are actually being detained for resisting sexual violence and oppressive gender norms. Schaffner (2006) shows that many of the reasons that girls are detained for violence and for status offences can be traced to avoiding sexual assault at home (running away from abusive homes, especially from mother's boyfriends), attaching to an older man (often, a friend of their mothers) who then pimps them out. These are gendered experiences; of course boys are also subjected to sexual violence and abuse but girls are more likely to know their abuser (90 per cent do, and therefore have nowhere to escape to) and in any case are more likely to experience sexual assault (86 per cent of sexual assaults are of girls) (Schaffner 2006). Similarly, in their study of the 'school to prison pipeline for girls', Simkins, Hirsch, Horvat and Moss (2004), using semi-structured interviews with thirty-five girls incarcerated in the juvenile justice system and twenty-six women with criminal histories, found that childhood physical and sexual abuse led to their incarceration. Entry into the juvenile justice system as a way to escape sexual abuse has a long history: Anne Knupfer, in her analysis of the juvenile court in Chicago (1904–27), found that nearly 70 per cent of the girls who were institutionalized were victims of incest, 'although this "discovery" was noted mostly as fact and not as a mitigating circumstance' (Knupfer 2001 cited in Pasko 2010:1102).

African-American social reformers' opposition to segregation at Geneva eventually succeeded in getting it desegregated (as the reformers did across the USA; see Ward 2012). Despite the formal shifts in the juvenile justice system towards integrated institutions, racism and sexism structured girls' engagement with governing structures (school, family, justice) and this did not fundamentally change throughout the twentieth century and into the current period. The 1974 Juvenile Justice and Delinquency Prevention Act focused on the treatment of 'status offenders' (status offences only apply to minors, for example leaving home) and the problem of involving the 'judicial system in the moral behaviour of youth' (Chesney-Lind and Irwin 2008:157). The Act was re-authorized in 1992 and called for more equitable treatment of girls in the system. The 1974 Act did lead initially to a fall in rates of incarceration of girls (Chesney-Lind and Irwin 2008:158). This progress was subsequently halted when, recognizing that girls were often returning to the streets if they were not incarcerated: 'The public, led by juvenile court judges, pointed to this pattern and clamored for a return to the time-honored means of protecting female status offenders: incarceration' (Chesney-Lind and Irwin 2008:159). Following the 1992 re-authorization of the 1974 Act, funds were made available by the Clinton administration and then cancelled by the Bush administration, after the September 11, 2001 attacks on New York.

Arrest and incarceration rates for all girls have increased in the USA and girls continue to be arrested and incarcerated for what one could call 'crimes against gender'; that is, behaving in ways that do not conform to gendered normative ideals. Ironically, it is because they are minors that they are more available to government regulation than adults are. The punitive regulation of their demeanour, sexuality and interactional styles is made possible through their availability to institutions that are nominally charged with their protection (schools and juvenile justice). African-American and Latina girls are disproportionately captured by these systems of regulation; a pattern that continues into adulthood, with African-American women accounting for almost half (48 per cent) of all incarcerated women in the USA although the African-American population is under 13 per cent (Chesney-Lind and Irwin 2008:188). The phenomenal increase in the incarceration of black women is 'largely a product of the war on drugs' (Chesney-Lind and Irwin 2008:186) whereas for girls of colour the relabelling of status offences as 'person' offences 'is moving the juvenile justice system into the same racialized patterns of incarceration that we see in the adult system' (Chesney-Lind and Irwin 2008:186).

Minor infractions and girls' incarceration

A discourse of increasing gender equality, and indeed the emergence of a new discourse that boys are being left behind, want to suggest that the sexist regulation and control of girls is a problem for 'developing' countries, a problem of pre-modern, non-capitalist or anti-liberal societies' antiquated ideas about gender norms. However, these discourses are belied by the levels of sexual violence that girls in the 'developed' world face at school, in the neighbourhood and at home, and by the punitive response to girls who do not (or indeed, given the ways that ideal femininity is raced and classed, cannot) conform to gender norms. Chesney-Lind and Irwin comment that families and schools 'are intensely monitoring girls, [mis]recognizing their misbehaviours (which are usually minor), and then sending them into the juvenile justice system in increasing numbers' (Chesney-Lind and Irwin 2008:5).

A concern about apparent increases in school violence by girls (a response to the 1999 Columbine High School shootings, which is ironic since mass school shootings have all been carried out by white boys) has finally brought attention to white girls' aggression (rather than assuming that female violence is only done by black girls), but emphasizes gender programming as a solution, rather than (as has been done for black girls) incarceration (Chesney-Lind and Irwin 2008:24). Although arrests for violence by girls increased relative to boys between 1986 and 2004, this increase was significantly out of step with self-reported data on violence, victim reports, hospital admissions and health department data (Chesney-Lind and Irwin 2008:27), which implies that 'the surge in girls' violence arrests reflects an intensified policing of youthful misbehaviors, rather than a dramatic change in girls' behaviors' (Chesney-Lind and Irwin 2008:28). These authors account for this rise in arrests by the increasing arrest of girls at home and in peer groups at school, and suggest that these are the contexts where girls are more likely than boys to offend, albeit the offences will be minor ones. Chesney-Lind and Irwin show that the causes of increased arrests from home are parents using arrest as a form of 'time out', parents calling the police when their daughters do not come home (a strategy they are less likely to use with boys), parents calling the police when their daughters hit them (often in retaliation for being hit, and the child gets charged for assault but the parent does not). For example, Leslie Acoca (1999) (cited in Chesney-Lind and Irwin 2008:86) reports, in a review of 1,000 girls' files from four California counties, a typical instance in which 'father lunged at her while she was calling the police about a domestic dispute. She (girl) hit him.' Other trivial offences, including 'throwing cookies at her mother', led to girls being arrested. Buzawa and Hotaling (2006:29 cited in Chesney-Lind and Irwin 2008:96) reported two cases involving daughters who retaliated after their mothers hit them, in which the parents were treated as the 'injured parties' and the girls were arrested.

Partly as a consequence of the media attention to 'relational' bullying being relabelled as violence, and together with the emergence of 'zero-tolerance' schools, girls' misdemeanours are treated more seriously than they warrant: an 11-year-old arrested at school for possession of a weapon, a butter knife, for which she was handcuffed and jailed; a girl expelled under anti-drug rules for giving a classmate Midol, an over-the-counter pain relief drug for menstrual cramps; another girl expelled for bringing ibuprofen to school; and another 11-year-old student arrested and removed from school in handcuffs 'after a shoving incident' (Chesney-Lind and Irwin 2008:152).

Girls are being arrested in increasing numbers (one-third of juvenile arrests in 2004) for violent offences. Girls have 'more person offense referrals than boys: 26 per cent compared to 23 per cent' (Chesney-Lind and Irwin 2008:164); '[t]his pattern suggests that the social control of girls is once again on the criminal justice agenda with a crucial change. In this century, the control is being justified by girls' "violence", whereas in the last century [the twentieth] it was their "sexuality"' (Chesney-Lind and Irwin 2008:164). Despite the large increases, one-third of all arrests of girls are for running away or petty theft (generally, for girls, shoplifting) and nearly three-quarters of girls who enter juvenile justice are not detained again on a new referral. Detentions increased for girls for minor offences, with one-third detained for a 'technical violation' (for example of probation conditions).

Nearly half of girls in detention are African-American, even though white girls are two-thirds (65 per cent) of the at-risk population. This is important to highlight given that there is a general awareness that black children are disproportionately incarcerated but that this recognition is framed by a presumption that it is accounted for by underlying variables, such as high rates of poverty or family dysfunction, rather than being an effect of racism in the criminal and juvenile justice and welfare systems. White girls are more likely to be referred for treatment and to have their offences attributed to low self-esteem or abandonment, whereas the offences of "non-white" girls are more likely to be attributed to lifestyle choices. Another study found that despite similar histories of sexual victimization, white girls tended to be charged with status offences and black girls with criminal charges. African-American girls make up only 18 per cent of New York's youth population but 54 per cent of girls sent to New York's juvenile facilities (Chesney-Lind and Irwin 2008:172). A study by the American Bar Association and National Bar Association (2001) found that African-American girls are far less likely than white girls to have their cases dismissed and make up nearly half of those in secure detention.

Several studies show that one of the reasons for girls' violence is attempting to defend themselves against sexual harassment. In a study in Ohio (Holsinger, Belknap and Sutherland 1999 cited in Chesney-Lind and Irwin 2008:171), although girls were just as likely as boys to have been incarcerated for violent offences, closer examination showed that the girls' infractions were relatively minor and included self-defence.

'After being taunted and threatened by a boy at school and receiving no protection from school authorities, [one girl] hid a knife in her sock. While school authorities did not intervene in the boy's harassment, they did enforce the zero-tolerance for weapons policy against the girl' (Chesney-Lind and Irwin 2008:171). Schaffner (2006:66) gives the example of a girl detained for violence who said 'I was suspended from school because this boy put his hands on me and I tried to hit him back. Now I'm sittin' up in here! Shit!' A 1997 Department of Justice and Education study (cited in Schaffner 2006:66) reported 4,200 rapes and sexual assaults each year on school grounds. Brown, Chesney-Lind and Stein (2007:1259) argue that sexual harassment in school is now being reframed as degendered 'bullying', removing the possibility for redress in the courts under civil rights legislation. These authors note that in the globalization of a discourse of bullying, largely borrowing from European research, actionable offences in US law are being reframed as interactional problems. They say, '[t]o engage 6th through 10th graders [UK years 7–11] in this discourse of bullying without acknowledging the realities of sexual or racial harassment is to infantilize and mislead them because some of the behaviours described as bullying are, in fact, criminal conduct, or could be covered by sexual harassment or other civil rights in education laws' (2007:1259). They also note that to incorporate school shootings as a response to bullying and then to extend that to other more mundane forms of harm and violence 'is to deny a central and operating feature in boy culture, namely the maniacally driven, tireless efforts to define oneself as "not gay"' (Brown et al. 2007:1261).

Chesney-Lind and Irwin are arguing that 'Law enforcement, parents, social workers, and teachers were once more concerned with controlling girls' sexuality than they were with their violence, but recent research suggests that is changing' (2008:175). Yet underlying the reasons why girls are runaways and involved in violence is largely misogyny – with results including sexual abuse, sexual harassment and sexual violence, rape and the threat of rape. In Washington State, for example, following the passing of a state truancy act after the murder of a teenage girl which allows parents to obtain court orders requiring their children to attend school and obey their parents, or risk contempt proceedings and detention, girls are being taken into detention for their own protection; but this protection is itself a protection from men and boys and the threat they pose to women and girls. Once in detention centres, girls continue to experience sexual abuse, harassment and violence from staff. In *Girls in Trouble with the Law* (2006) Laurie Schaffner notes the circulation of a discourse of violent boys and 'sexy' (that is, sex-work-involved) girls that is belied by the statistics: in 2004, 14,500 girls were arrested for aggravated assault (83,000 for assault), and fewer than 1,500 for prostitution. Of 662,000 arrests, two-thirds were not for violence or prostitution but for status offences and other minor offences (37 per cent) and theft (21 per cent). In 2013, although black people are 13.2 per cent of the US population, black children were 35.3 per cent of all juvenile arrests. Nearly one-third of all arrests were of girls and one-third of these were black girls. The largest group arrested were in the age range 13–15 years and about half of all arrests were dealt with informally (Sickmund, Sladky and Kang 2015). Most children were not detained in a residential facility. In 2013, 46,421 boys and 7,727 girls were detained in a residential juvenile facility. Despite being only 15 per cent of the total child population, whereas whites are 66 per cent, more black boys (18,977 in 2013) are held in detention than white boys (14,579 in that year). Black girls are also disproportionately detained (2,984 white girls and 1,568 black girls in 2013; http://www.ojjdp.gov/ojstatbb/ezacjrp/asp/Age_Sex_Race.asp). Some 5 per cent of these detentions were for status offences including running away, truancy, under-age drinking and incorrigibility.

Conclusion

In this chapter I have drawn on sociological theory to explore what it means for children that they are gendered subjects. Attending to the complexity of children's subject formation I have shown that girls' behaviour is regulated and intensely governed and they are more likely to be punished for minor infractions and status offences than boys are. However, it is also clear that black children, boys and girls, are treated as less redeemable than white children and that this has serious consequences for how governing forces police gender differently for black children and white children in the USA. The racism that shapes how childhood is governed is refracted through sexism, for sure, but nonetheless it is clear that the gendered privilege of boys is also refracted through racism. In short, despite the protection and privilege that boys are inducted into, being a boy does not protect black boys in the ways that it protects white boys. To give a full account of childhood subjectivity, then, we need to understand the complex ways in which racism and sexism amplify and refract one another to give subjects access to spaces of privilege or to spaces of loss and disadvantage. This would include understanding other forms of racism, against, for example, Latina/o and Native American children, and how these amplify and refract sexism.

5

Class Discrimination in Childhood

Introduction: class and childhood

In this book I am exploring how children come to think of themselves as kinds of people, as social subjects. In the previous chapters I discussed this in relation to race and gender. In this chapter I explore subject-making and class in children's lives. There are important differences in how these three social positions or identities might shape children's sense of self. One of these is that gender and, in different ways, race are legible in ways that class is not. Gender is not a hidden concept in children's lives. We know that children relate easily to the idea that they have a gender and that it shapes how they think of themselves and others. Likewise, many children who live in countries where race has been a central technology of governance, as we explored in chapter 3, will be familiar with the idea that they and others have a race and/or an ethnicity. It is unlikely that most children will use these terms to describe people; they are more likely to identify that someone is a boy or a girl, and perhaps the colour of their skin. They might point to a national identity, particularly one that is not the dominant identity, or to the language they speak. But although they are unlikely to use the terms that social scientists use they will, nonetheless, be familiar with the idea that they are not only a child but, in some socially meaningful way, also have a gender and perhaps a race or ethnicity. Class is another social position, another way of interpellating subjects that shapes our life chances and, perhaps, our dispositions. However, it is not so clear that children (or indeed adults) think of themselves as classed subjects.

This chapter explores what class might mean in the lives of children and whether it shapes not only their life chances but also their dispositions. It starts with sketching what class is, how it relates to childhood and how we might locate children in relation to class. It then turns to one of the dominant explanations for how class shapes disposition and how in turn this impacts on education: the idea of a culture of poverty. This is followed by an examination of forms of capital and the idea of a working-class habitus. In the final two sections I explore how neighbourhoods impact on children's well-being and how class intersects with racism in the USA to contain black children in poor neighbourhoods. In the conclusion I argue that class has a decisive impact on children's lives but that it is not widely experienced as a primary subject position or social identity.

A recent study (Savage et al. 2013), conducted by Mike Savage at the London School of Economics and Fiona Devine at the University of Manchester, carried out through BBC Lab UK, surveyed 160,000 British people and concluded that the working class was gradually disappearing and the structure of class, understood as a concept related to levels of economic, social and cultural capital, should best be understood as seven categories from precariat to elite. In fact, the precariat sound remarkably like Marx's definition of the petty bourgeoisie; that class who own their own means of production but have little economic capital. The survey produced a lively debate, with key British scholars of working-class lives/ sociology contesting these new categorizations and, in particular, the weakening of connections between material conditions and class categories. Savage deployed Bourdieu's forms of capital (cultural, social and economic) as the markers of class position; raising again the possibility that class is culture. For our purposes, a further problem is that none of the people surveyed were aged under 18; again, the presumption being that children do not have a class because they are not economic actors (and presumably also do not have social or cultural capital).

Many years ago, I was in a sociology of childhood academic seminar at which, to general assent, one of the participants blithely said something like 'of course children don't have a class'. This was at the beginning of my academic career, and it struck me as one of the many effects on their distorted understanding of the world that most academics come from established (that is to say, for two or more generations) bourgeois families and have little understanding of how economics impinges on the lives of working-class children. The person speaking may have meant that if class is defined in Marxist terms as a relationship to the means of production then children, at least if they are not working children (as many children globally are, including in the advanced capitalist countries), do not have a direct relationship to the means of production and therefore do not have a class. Most sociology and social policy does not define class in relation to the means of production; it defines it in relation to household earnings. So the contributor may also have meant that since children do not contribute to household earnings they cannot really be said to have a class position. Yet scholars of Childhood Studies would surely not accept that children should be bracketed out of socio-economic life simply because they do not do paid work or pay for the labour of others.

In her study of white, African-American and Mexican-American girls and their attitudes to learning and post-school transitions in a Californian school, *Women without Class*, Julie Bettie (2014) argues that people (in general, adults and children) do not experience themselves through class. Rather, she claims, ethnicity and gender are the social identities that appear meaningful to people as explanations for success or failure, for patterns of social interaction, and for the likelihood of future success. In Lareau's (2011) study, *Unequal Childhoods: Class, Race and Family Life*, she maintains that ethnicity is not the determinant of school success; in fact class is. She shows that Euro-American and African-American parents within the same economic class share attitudes to parenting that shape children's school experiences and will eventually impact on their post-school transitions. Despite her analysis showing that class is the underlying variable that impacts school experiences and post-school opportunities, Lareau also recognizes that her respondents do not themselves perceive class to be the shaper of their experiences or their sense of selfhood.

Research with children on class has deployed a range of concepts and facts as proxies for class. In education research, for example, free school meals, in the UK, and household income, in the USA, are taken as proxies for children's working-class status. In psychology, parent's educational attainment is used as a proxy for children's class. In Childhood Studies, indices of neighbourhood deprivation are frequently used as proxies for household, and therefore children's, class position.

Class and education

The main way in which class has been considered in Childhood Studies is in relation to education. This has principally been in research on middle-class families and how they make school choices (mostly UK focused), and research on working-class children and their experience of school. The latter, which is also mostly from the UK, is mainly interested in how working-class children negotiate (or not) the gap between home life and school life. This gap is understood as a cultural dissonance between the social relations and cultural goods that are valued at home and in working-class neighbourhoods and the social relations and cultural goods that are valued at school. The underlying research question for most of these studies is, implicitly or explicitly: why do working-class children fail at school? Echoing the 'culture of poverty' argument that has been used in the USA to blame working-class and especially African-American families for failing to lift themselves out of poverty, this research assumes that the dissonance between home life and school life leads to working-class students either excluding themselves from school (through truanting or non-participation) or being excluded by teachers who presume that children cannot or will not benefit from education.

The classic study in this tradition is Paul Willis' (2006) *Learning to Labour: How Working Class Kids Get Working Class Jobs*. First published in 1977, this ethnography of a group of boys at school in an English town is still widely cited. The thesis of the book is neatly summed up in the title: working-class children (or at least white working-class boys) learn at school that their role as adults is to do low-skilled manual work. The boys Willis studied were the 'rebel' boys in the school. Willis' main point is that their culture of resistance makes it impossible for them to transform their class position. Although widely cited as a book that respects working-class culture and is sympathetic to the school refusal of working-class students, in the final analysis it can feel a bit as though Willis is blaming working-class children for their inability to succeed at school.

Willis' work is often cited along with Oscar Lewis' ethnographic studies from which he developed the concept of a 'culture of poverty' and with John Ogbu's research that suggested that black students underachieved for fear of being taken to be 'acting white'. In a review article of these three studies, Watras (2014) notes that they have all been critiqued by sociologists and psychologists for developing strong theories on the basis of limited ethnographic data. For psychologists, culture cannot explain individual behaviour, and for sociologists, the core claims made by all three studies are not substantiated by wider sociological data, including data cited within the studies. What is perhaps more puzzling is that all three studies appear to blame the group attitudes of subaltern groups (white working-class, Puerto Ricans, African-Americans, respectively) for the underachievement of individual members in school. This work, particularly Ogbu's, has impacted on educational policy in the USA, yet it seems to ignore material issues in school such as inadequate levels of funding for schools in working-class neighbourhoods.

In a similar vein, Annette Lareau, in her research on the social reproduction of class inequality and especially in her book *Unequal*

Childhoods (2011), claims that working-class and middle-class parents deploy different styles of parenting that impact on their own and their children's attitudes to education. In her analysis of the data from her ethnographic study of twelve families she identifies two parenting styles, which she labels 'concerted cultivation' and 'natural learning'. She says that these typified the attitudes of middle-class and working-class parents, respectively, to education. Lareau clearly values the working-class parents' strategies and can see some benefits for children in being left largely to their own devices outside of school, rather than having to endure an endless round of extra-curricular activities. However, she also argues that schools fail working-class children because their parents have not equipped them with the dispositions to secure the attention and engagement of teachers.

In the UK, statistics on educational achievement (number and grade of qualifications at exit) are collected by ethnicity, gender and socio-economic status (SES). These statistics show that white working-class students attain the fewest qualifications in comparison to any other ethnic group, and that within this group boys achieve fewer qualifications than girls. The publication of these statistics led to the discovery of the white working-class student; that is to say, not the working class but specifically the *white* working class. Frequently the qualifier 'working-class' was left out of these claims, and scholars and journalists alike talked about schools failing white boys. For example in 2007, research commissioned by the Joseph Rowntree Trust from the London School of Economics reported that 'White British boys [are the] most persistent low educational achievers' (https://www.jrf.org.uk/press/white-british-boys-most-persistent-low-educational-achievers-practical-measures-could-improve). In 2006, Gillian Evans published her ethnography of a working-class neighbourhood in south London with the title *Educational Failure and Working Class White Children in Britain*. Like Oscar Lewis' 'culture of poverty', Willis' 'learning to labour' and Ogbu's 'oppositional culture', Evans' ethnography claimed that working-class children failed at school because of the dissonance between what was needed and valued to succeed at school and what was needed and valued to succeed at home and in the neighbourhood. It seemed that Evans was arguing that white children have a specific dissonance between home/neighbourhood and school cultures that black or other ethnic minority children of the same class did not share.

In 2005, I and Roger Hewitt (at the Centre for Urban and Community Research, Goldsmiths, University of London) were commissioned by the London Borough of Camden to undertake research with white working-class students at a successful London comprehensive school who were failing at school and who were unlikely to choose to stay on for further study after the then end of compulsory schooling at age 16 years. The commissioning authority clearly felt that there was a need to understand the attitudes of white working-class students to education and transitions to adulthood, given the statistics circulating about the school failure of white working-class students. The underlying assumption, as in Evans' research, was that there was something peculiar or specific about *white* working-class attitudes, behaviours, dispositions and that the *white* working class has a particular culture (a way of life) that does not value education.

With hindsight I wonder if we should have resisted this particular framing. Our respondents did share particular experiences of education and beliefs about the future and what a successful transition to adulthood might look like that appeared to be rooted in working-class experience. Students described experiences of school that involved low-quality teaching, poorly disciplined classrooms and chronic boredom. They looked forward to leaving school and becoming adult. For both boys and girls the mechanisms through which these transitions were to be accomplished drew on traditional ideas about learning a trade (typically, hairdressing or make-up for girls, car mechanic for boys) and, for the girls, becoming mothers. The girls talked about the importance of mothering to children and their desire to stay at home to care for their children when they themselves became parents. Their narratives echo those of other studies. Linda McDowell's research, for example, on white working-class boys has shown that in their reflections on their transitions to adulthood when they were in the last year of school they hoped to enter the same kinds of jobs as their fathers had in the car and steel industries. Subsequently she wrote about their experiences after leaving school (McDowell 2002, 2003), and about both the difficulty they had in securing permanent jobs and also their continued desire 'to settle down with a good job, a nice house, and a family' (2002:55; see also Nayak 2006). McDowell notes that her sample is all white boys but that 'lack of access to employment is a key part of the growing social exclusion of young British Asians' (McDowell 2002:56). It seems likely, given that the Joseph Rowntree Trust commissioned McDowell's research, that the inclusion of white boys only in the study was part of the presumption that there is something specific in the experience of white working-class boys *qua whites* that was shaping their experience.

The belief that, since white boys were now the most likely to have persistent low achievement, racism in schools and in education was no longer an issue was criticized by the anti-racist education scholars David Gillborn and Alison Kirton in a paper called 'White Heat' (2000). They argued that this belief 'misrepresents the true situation of race equality (where students in many minority groups continue to experience significant and consistent inequalities of opportunity) and it is dangerous because it threatens to reinforce processes whereby the class bias shared by white [working-class] youth is reconceptualised as a race bias' (2000:271). Gillborn and Kirton's paper also points to the poor resource base of schools in working-class neighbourhoods in an epoch of quasi-markets in compulsory education. Importantly though, and precisely under the influence of these discourses that encourage white working-class people to perceive themselves as being ignored by a liberal establishment that (for reasons never disclosed) prefers to direct resources towards black and Asian citizens, the white respondents in their research believe that the school's limited budget is a consequence of resources being diverted to predominantly Asian schools.

Forms of capital

Although the racist discourse that Gillborn and Kirton identify is an almost inevitable outcome of locating educational failure in whiteness (rather than in class), what these claims perhaps really have in their sights is the construction of a white-working-class culture that makes working-class students responsible for their own school failure because of their investment in what is, essentially, *mutatis mutandis*, a 'culture of poverty'. Ironically, this 'culture of poverty' thesis is common ground between those who denigrate working-class lives (as chavs and the like) and those who celebrate working-class lives (as the salt of the earth). For the latter, there is a small body of research that examines the consequences for children (mainly girls) of academic success that then provides them with pathways out of working-class life, leading to a kind of crisis of identity (e.g. Walkerdine et al. 2001, Reay 2001): what Ingram (2009:421) calls 'wounding the working-class identity' and Sennett and Cobb (1973) call *The Hidden Injuries of Class*. Ingram's study is centred on the question of whether or not it is 'really necessary to resist having a working-class identity in order to achieve [academic] success' (2009:421).

   Another way of framing the dissonance between working-class dispositions and school expectations is with the concepts of cultural capital and habitus. Originally developed by Pierre Bourdieu (1986), these concepts have been very influential in educational research on class. They have been used to explain both why working-class children might fail at school and how the class privilege of middle-class children is reproduced at school. Annette Lareau used these concepts in her study of working-class and middle-class families' dispositions towards education. Cultural capital is a resource, and like all resources some people have access to it and others do not. Habitus is the dispositions that people inhabit; it includes what people say and what they do. In some readings of habitus it is embodied, in others it is more about ingrained attitudes. But in whichever way habitus is understood, the critical point is that it is not freely chosen. Habitus is therefore a useful concept for thinking about how children develop habits, ways of being that come to feel natural and instinctual.

Despite the wide deployment in educational research of Bourdieu's core concepts (cultural capital and habitus) it is difficult to specify precisely what they are, let alone to trace how they affect interactions in the classroom and educational outcomes (qualifications, and post-school careers) for children of different classes.

Lareau's research, and Bourdieu and Passeron (1990), assume a more or less stable or predictable school environment into which students enter. In this relatively homogeneous landscape it is assumed to hold true that working-class children will have (as a class) little academic success, given that teachers, curricula and the moral universe of the school expect and reward middle-class cultural capital. However, other researchers have noted that different schools in the same neighbourhoods have different expectations of their students even when those students are more or less from the same class. So, for example, grammar schools in the UK assume that all their students, regardless of their family's class position, will persist in the academic accomplishment that brought them into a selective public/state (that is, government-funded) school.

Some scholars have developed the concept of 'institutional habitus' to conceptualize differences between different schools that may educate some of the same kinds of students (in terms of class origin and neighbourhood locality). This concept was developed first by McDonough (1997) in the USA and then by Diane Reay in the UK, more recently further developed by Ingram in her study of a secondary modern and a grammar school in Belfast, and robustly critiqued by Atkinson (2011). One of the problems with the concept of 'institutional habitus', as Atkinson points out, is that institutions do not act, have dispositions or attitudes; only humans have these capacities. But an additional problem is that the criticism levelled at schools is that they require of their working-class students an adherence to what has been called 'middle-class' culture. Ingram explicitly appends 'whiteness' (although, oddly in the context of Northern Ireland, not 'Catholicism') to her cultural frame in order to suggest that, as Mac an Ghaill (1988) found for the cultural dissonance between black students and (white) schools, cultural dissonance between students and schools opens up space for two broad reactions: acculturation or refusal. So, in effect, the argument, echoing perhaps those working-class students who are not doing so well at school, is that working-class children who do enjoy and thrive in academic study are 'acting posh'.

Treating class as culture in this way presumes that knowledge of the world not derived from immediate or everyday experience – scientific knowledge, knowledge of philosophy or of grammatical concepts, analytical appreciation of literary structures, and so on – is simply bourgeois ideology and bourgeois culture masquerading as some deeper insight into the physical and social world.

Now clearly, for most working-class children, certainly in the UK, their school education does not deliver them anywhere close to the intellectual tools they will need to comprehend and analyse either their own experiences as people located in relation to a specific economic, political and social formation, or the underlying structures of the physical world. But it is important to hold onto the fact that this failure is a failure on the part of schools. So when Ingram says 'There is a sense that although (dis)engaged in the process of schooling, learning for these boys is otherworldly, outside their lived experience, their habitus' (2009:429), she takes this to be because their habitus (ways of being, doing, speaking and thinking) is opposed to education. Yet in other parts of the same paper she describes how the secondary modern these students attended had essentially given up on any pretence of educating its students. At the same time she (approvingly, it seems) suggests that the secondary modern (rather than the academic-path grammar school) shared the habitus of the students. Notwithstanding Atkinson's criticism that an institution cannot have a habitus, it seems from the logic of the rest of Ingram's paper that a shared habitus between the student and the school, a lack of dissonance, should have made the secondary school students more 'at home', as it were, than the working-class students at the grammar school. Yet being 'at home' did not make them less likely to fail at academic study.

Working-class neighbourhoods and outcomes for children

Neither schools nor homes are free-floating spaces; they do not exist only in relation to the broader political economy but are also situated in specific places. This is the third space in which class shapes children's experiences (the first two being family and school). Working-class neighbourhoods in urban areas, which might be identified by census data on indices of deprivation, share certain characteristics, especially densely populated spaces with small housing units with little indoor space (either purpose-built apartments or houses more or less formally divided into households), few social amenities, few shops and so on. The social relationships shaped by these material conditions are not generated by a cultural predisposition (for example based on a shared ethnicity) towards particular ways of behaving. Nonetheless, these spatial-social conditions have particular affordances for social relationships that produce certain cultural practices and even cultural goods. Researchers frequently comment on the close-knit social relationships in densely populated working-class areas, the sense of belonging – what Les Back described in *New Ethnicities and Urban Culture* (1996) as 'neighbourhood nationalism' – that young people often express to a specific locale. In the research cited in the previous section, Ingram talks of the attachment her young respondents expressed to their neighbourhood. One of the central tropes of these discourses is that 'everyone knows you'.

At the same time as they valorized their neighbourhood as close-knit, Ingram's respondents also denigrated it as unsafe and dirty. In research that I conducted in Tottenham, incidentally the neighbourhood where I was raised, I found that my respondents, all aged 10 and 11 years, also felt that their neighbourhood was stigmatized. Respondents were preoccupied by fears of crime that, notwithstanding Critical Legal Studies critiques of the construction of crime, were to some extent rooted in their daily experiences and local news stories. It was interesting that their main preoccupation, though, was paedophiles, that is to say a fear of kidnapping and sexual abuse at the hands of strangers; a threat which we know is statistically very rare (Wells 2005). Similarly, in her research in Detroit, Erin Winkler (2012) found that her young African-American respondents were aware that their own neighbourhoods were seen as undesirable. In our research in a north London borough (with Sophie Watson) we found a sense shared by children and their parents that their working-class neighbourhood was unsafe, and a subsequent vacating of public space as children played either at home or at school.

Social geographers emphasize the relationship between a sense of place and a sense of self; that who you are is in some sense bound up with where you are. This raises important questions for thinking about how working-class children in stigmatized neighbourhoods form a sense of self. What does it mean to feel that where you live, where in some sense you 'are from' or 'belong', is 'shit'? Neighbourhood stigma has been shown by social epidemiology studies to impact adversely on children: for example, children living in areas of concentrated social housing are vulnerable to a range of poor outcomes for health and well-being (Flouri, Midouhas and Tzatzaki 2015, Osypuk 2015). Martens et al. (2014), in a study of the effects of the socio-economic status of neighbourhood on the outcomes on a range of indictors for children living in social housing in Winnipeg, Canada, found that children living in social housing had poorer outcomes than their peers.

The impact on development of living in poor neighbourhoods is not only due to the subjective effect of feeling disrespected. In a study in

Rhode Island, USA, Vivier and colleagues found that children living in pre-1950s housing and in the highest quintile for poverty were exposed to significant levels of lead poisoning. They report that even 'low levels of lead poisoning are associated with irreversible, deleterious effects on a child's development leading to learning and behavioural disorders, hearing impairment, decreased intelligence quotient (IQ), and diminished attention span. At high levels, lead poisoning can cause convulsions, coma, and even death' (Vivier et al. 2011:1196), while Yousey-Hindes and Hadler (2011) found that census tracts with low socio-economic status and high crowding were correlated with levels of hospital admission for paediatric influenza 'at least 3 times greater than that in low-poverty and low-crowding tracts'. Living in poor neighbourhoods, then, is literally bad for your health, and it impacts on children more than adults because of their greater biological vulnerability to environmental hazards.

There are now a large number of quantitative studies that show a correlation between neighbourhood poverty and poor outcomes for children and youth. Studies are trying to identify the causal mechanisms of this neighbourhood effect. In a mixed-methods study in Denver, Colorado, and Canada, Galster and Santiago (2006) asked parents if there was a neighbourhood effect on their children and what kinds of neighbourhood characteristics affected children's outcomes. Interestingly, about one-third of their respondents disagreed that there was a neighbourhood effect, either because their children were too young or because they (the parents) could counter any negative effects. The rest of their sample cited lack of social norms and 'collective efficacy', the influence of children's peers, exposure to crime and violence, and the lack of institutional resources. This ties in nicely with a series of studies and reviews conducted by Tama Leventhal and Jeanne Brooks-Gunn, who, in a summary of their work in 2003, sketch a series of theoretical models that may underlie neighbourhood effect: institutional resources, relationships and ties, norms and collective efficacy. Pettit (2004), exploring the impact on children's social ties of the Gautreaux experiment, found that families in low-income housing projects appreciated the range of affordable after-school activities for their children but were also very concerned about high levels of crime and violence, including murder. (The Gautreaux experiment refers to a Chicago housing policy of giving housing vouchers to African-American families so that they could rent in predominantly white areas, thereby desegrating public housing, as instructed by the Supreme Court ruling in 1976 following a 1966 American Civil Liberties Union class action lawsuit, *Dorothy Gautreaux v. Chicago Housing Authority (CHA)*. The experiment was the basis for the subsequent Moving to Opportunity programmes, described in the next subsection.)

Martens et al. (2014) also show that older children in social housing had better outcomes when they lived in wealthier areas. For adolescents this might suggest that place and peers mitigate the impacts of poverty. These authors note, for example that other studies have shown that the socio-economic status of the school is a better predictor of student outcomes than is the socio-economic status of students, including for poorer students in wealthier neighbourhood schools. Further support for this claim is found in several other studies, including Caughy, Leonard, Beron and Murdoch (2013), who found that the influence of what they call 'proximal peers' – that is, not only a child's chosen peer group but simply the children that are around in their neighbourhood – and the influence of poor conditions in the neighbourhood (such as broken fences, peeling paint on houses, and rubbish not emptied) were positively correlated with behavioural problems in children. A large study of 342 neighbourhoods, with over 8,700 residents, conducted in 1995 by Sampson and colleagues found that neighbourhood collective efficacy for children was correlated with affluence and residential stability; in other words, that wealthier neighbourhoods took more shared responsibility for other people's children than did poor neighbourhoods (Sampson, Morenoff and Felton 1999).

How racism mediates class and space

On the other hand a study by Rebecca Fauth Tama Leventhal and Jeanne Brooks-Gunn (2007), analysing the impacts of a court-ordered housing desegregation scheme to move lottery-selected families from black and Latina/o working-class and poor neighbourhoods to white middle-class neighbourhoods in Yonkers, New York, found that children's schooling outcomes did not improve and on standard testing both movers and stayers had the same scores. Further, children who moved were more likely as adolescents to experience anxiety and depression than those who stayed. They propose that the negative effects of moving might follow from discrimination against them in their new neighbourhood.

Robert Sampson and colleagues have conducted a series of studies in Chicago on 'durable inequality' and neighbourhood poverty. In a study with Perkins, Sampson found that transitions to adulthood for a large random sample of Chicago residents compounded individual and neighbourhood deprivation for black people but not for whites or Latinas/os (Perkins and Sampson 2015). These writers do not explore in their paper on compound deprivation what the underlying causes are of these differences. In an earlier paper on residential choice, Robert Sampson and Patrick Sharkey note that black people often choose African-American neighbourhoods over more affluent white neighbourhoods, even when they could exercise such a choice. These authors comment that 'African American families trade off more affluent (white) neighborhoods for ones perceived to be more hospitable and racially diverse, a not unreasonable calculus given the grim history of race relations in Chicago' (Sampson and Sharkey 2008:26).

In the USA, being African-American continues to overlap with living in poor neighbourhoods, even when individual households are not all poor. Class discrimination overlaps with racism to the extent that, as Bettie (2014) suggests, class disappears as an explanation for why people work in low-wage jobs, attend poorly resourced schools or live in areas of high crime, violence and police brutality. Research notes that 'being black' is a predictor of poor educational outcomes and that the effects of the Moving to Opportunity (MTO) experiments, in which randomly selected low-income families with children living in public housing were moved to better housing in wealthier neighbourhoods, flattened out within about ten years, so that the outcomes for black youth who moved with MTO and those who stayed were similar even if school outcomes were initially better. This overlap means that it is more likely that people experience poor outcomes for African-American children and youth and ascribe these to blackness rather than to class or, indeed, racism. Few of the studies of children's lives in either school or neighbourhood theorize the causes of neighbourhood 'social disorganization' or the low levels of educational attainment of African-American children.

If robust research shows that educational attainment, neighbourhood collective efficacy and effective relations and ties are correlated with being an African-American child, then it is of great political importance to explain these correlations. It is important, for example, to make visible the significance of a lack of intergenerational wealth transfer and a paucity of varied social networks to the persistence of racialized poverty. These are effects of a long history of racist exclusion of black people, including children, in the USA, as was historicized in the previous chapters. The effect of racism over the longue durée is that most black households do not have assets to protect their families from economic shocks such as unemployment, increased rent prices and inflation. Social networks may be strong but if there are few resources to travel across them then they are not necessarily protective or enabling.

It is also important to recognize the impacts of contemporary racism on black neighbourhoods in the USA. Contemporary racism at social levels prevents black households from moving into middle-class, white areas that are better served by resources such as open spaces, schools and even grocery stores. At the institutional level, racism leads to underinvestment in schools in black neighbourhoods and in infrastructure, and to a complete failure to protect neighbourhoods from violence. Indeed, the police may themselves be the instigators of violence against black children and teens, as we have recently witnessed in a series of shootings of black children by US police and the subsequent emergence of resistance to police brutality against black people, especially black children and youth, in the Black Lives Matter movement. The scale of police murder of citizens in the USA is astounding. In 2015 alone the police killed nearly 1,200 people in the USA, and black people were more than twice as likely as white people to be the victim of police shootings. In the age group 15–24, black boys and young black men were nine times as likely as white men of the same age to be killed by the police. The police killed nineteen black children in 2015 and twelve white children; black children under the age of 18 years are only 14 per cent of the US population; white children are 52 per cent (http://www.theguardian.com/us-news/ng-interactive/2015/jun/01/the-counted-police-killings-us-database).

Conclusion

Economic deprivation and class discrimination have significant impacts on children's lives. The consequences of living in environments that are, literally, poisonous impact children's health and development. The failure of the state to protect children in their neighbourhoods and, in fact, the violent policing of poor and black communities in the USA attest to the importance of economic inequality in shaping children's life chances and sense of self. Far from experiencing government as biopolitical, as increasing health and welfare, black and poor children and their families in the USA witness and experience government violence. In the UK, working-class children's school failure is mystified and attributed to their (working-class) whiteness. The state presses down on children and their families in the name of improving their lives, and yet continues to make their lives more and more difficult to live. What these three chapters have shown is that childhood is never innocent; in the modern world, what kinds of childhood are available to which children is always part of governing strategies. The scope for agency is extremely constrained by economic conditions, by racism and class discrimination and by the blunt power of the state over their lives, for most children.

6

Disability in Childhood Studies

Introduction

The central question that this book addresses is: how are childhood subjectivities produced in the iterative relationship, the constant back and forth, between the materiality of the child or the child as a corporeal being, and the modes of governing that aim to shape children and childhood and the socio-cultural fields that children participate in? In the previous chapters I showed how governing forces press onto children, structuring their lives through racism, sexism and class discrimination. The focus of this chapter is on the governance of childhood disability, in which the relationship is highly visible between the materiality of the child's body (and mind), the political economy that structures and stratifies children's life chances and the socio-cultural fields through which political economy is taken up into the practices of everyday life and a felt sense of selfhood.

I take as my focus in this chapter the governance of neurological disability, specifically in relation to autism. I take autism as my focus for three reasons. Firstly, neurological or cognitive disability is now the most prevalent form of childhood disability in developed countries. Secondly, neurological disability challenges a fundamental idea about the child: that she or he is a development potential and that the purpose of governing childhood is to ensure that a child emerges into a healthy and *productive* adulthood. Thirdly, the governance of childhood neurological disability is a particularly intense site for governing childhood, but it is different only in the degree of intensity and not in the quality of governing. Many of the technologies aimed at autistic children, for example observation, measurement, surveillance and modification, are also aimed at non-autistic children, but at a different level of intensity. In the management of childhood disability the boundaries between private and public are eroded, as families are required to 'invite the psychiatrists and the state into the middle class family' (Eyal, Hart, Onculer, Oren and Rossi 2010:89) so that they can demonstrate their compliance with early intervention strategies (de Wolfe 2014). Disability is accomplishing for the contemporary state what poverty accomplished for it in the early twentieth century (Donzelot 1980, Chen 2005), that is the opening up of family life to the scrutiny of government and the internalization into the family, even the white middle-class family who are more able to resist government intrusion, of the norms of governance. In return, government offers families support and recruits their children into disability research; for example, in the USA the Children's Health Act 2000 'called for the coordination of autism research efforts ... and authorized unprecedented federal support for investigations' (Silverman 2012:30), and in 2006 the Combating Autism Act further increased support.

Disabled children in Childhood Studies

In contrast to government policy and health research on childhood disability, research on disability has been largely absent in Childhood Studies. There has been little published on disability in the main Childhood Studies journals. The journal *Childhood* has the most citations, at seventy-one since its launch in 1993. However, a review of their abstracts shows that the majority of the papers that mentioned disability are not directly related to research on or with disabled children but simply mention disabled children in passing.

What are we to make of this inattention to the lives of significant numbers of children? Following the work of key scholars who work at the intersection of Disability Studies and Childhood Studies, particularly Katherine Runswick-Cole (Curran and Runswick-Cole, 2013, 2014), I want to suggest that thinking about disability in relation to personhood and subjectivity provokes problems for Childhood Studies if it continues to insist on the bounded, free, independent and rational character of the contemporary child's agency. This framing of childhood agency is uncomfortable with the constraints on freedom and independence that characterize the subjectivity of many disabled children. This explanation is supported by the focus of the only paper in the journal *Childhood* that is directly on the experiences of autistic children being about self-identity (Winstone, Huntington, Goldsack, Kyrou and Millward 2014). Winstone and colleagues show in their paper that, when they were conducting research with autistic youth using qualitative interviews, young people were unable or unwilling to elaborate on concepts of the self. In interviews that involved activities the same children were more discursive and, according to the researchers, constructed a narrative of self that was continuous through time, that is to say one in which they had a discourse about what kind of person they are, and what kind of future they want. It is interesting to ask: what would the conclusion be if their respondents had not eventually displayed this sense of a continuous self through time, as many autistic people do not? Is the ability to project the self forwards in time necessary for the enactment of agency? Is there a sense, then, in which the kinds of disabilities that Childhood Studies can accommodate, within a paradigm that somehow locates the validity of the field in a particular version of agency, are those of children whose disability is assumed not to shape their sense of self in the world fundamentally?

This chapter contrasts a psychological model of autism that is grounded in neuroscience research, and has become the preferred mode of governing autism, with cultural and psychoanalytically informed models that insist that children with autism are also participants in socio-cultural life.

The invention of autism

The invention of autism as a diagnostic label can be dated to the mid-twentieth century. Several processes converged to make the invention of autism possible at that point in time: the concentration and visibility of children in various institutions, including the clinic and the school in large urban areas; the growth of ideas about children as developing potentials whose development could be misdirected; and, above all, the focus on children as a central problem of government. Were it not for the congruence of these factors, parents would not have been bringing their children to psychiatrists to challenge their diagnoses of being 'feeble-minded' and, even if they had done so, the psychiatrists they consulted would not have had the institutional sway to make their diagnosis stick.

The invention of autism is conventionally dated to 1943, when Leo Kanner a psychiatrist who has been referred to as 'the father of child psychiatry', published a paper in the second issue of the journal *Nervous Child* in which, on the basis of eleven case studies, he described a collection of behaviours that he called autism. Kanner had been the director of the Behavior Clinic for Children at Johns Hopkins University since 1931. He had seen the children he described in 'Autistic Disturbances of Affective Contact' at the clinic. He borrowed the term 'autistic' from the

Swiss psychologist Eugen Bleuler, who had coined it in 1910 from the Greek *auto* meaning self and the English suffix *-ism* to describe symptoms of schizophrenia (Silverman 2012:33). Autism was initially understood as a childhood form of schizophrenia in which fantasy predominates over reality. The year after Kanner published his paper, the Viennese psychiatrist Hans Asperger published a paper (1991, first published 1944) on a group of children that he had observed and whom he also labelled autistic, again borrowing the term from Bleuler (Silverman 2012:37). Lorna Wing, a psychiatrist whose daughter Susie was autistic, returned to Asperger's case studies several decades later, and it is from her rediscovery of Asperger's research, her conviction that autistic behaviours were part of a spectrum of human communication, and, most importantly, her involvement in compiling the entry for autism in the Diagnostic Statistical Manual of Mental Disorders that the term was brought into the lexicon of autism (Wing 1981).

Kanner's paper focuses on the social relationships and emotional dispositions of the children he observed. After a narrative sketch of each child, the discussion section of Kanner's seminal paper notes that

> The outstanding, 'pathognomonic', fundamental disorder is the children's inability to relate themselves in the ordinary way to people and situations from the beginning of life. Their parents referred to them as having always been 'self-sufficient'; 'like in a shell'; 'happiest when left alone'; 'acting as if people weren't there'; 'perfectly oblivious to everything about him'; 'giving the impression of a silent wisdom'; 'failing to develop the usual amount of social awareness'; 'acting almost as if hypnotized'. This is not, as in schizophrenic children or adults, a departure from an initially present relationship ... There is from the start an *extreme aloneness* that, whenever possible, disregards, ignores, shuts out anything that comes to the child from outside ... or, if this is no longer sufficient, [is] resented painfully as distressing interference. (Kanner 1943:242)

The eleven children in Kanner's sketches shared characteristics that are now used to diagnose autism. These include: confusing pronouns in speech as a result of the literal repetition of statements ('You spilt your milk' to mean 'I spilt my milk'); an inability to use language to communicate meaningfully, although with different levels of fluency in language ranging from an extensive vocabulary to having command of a few or no words; problems with eating in the first few months of life; relating to objects easily and to people as if they are also objects.

In the final section of his paper, Kanner comments that although the characteristics described in the paper of 'extreme autism [aloneness], obsessiveness, stereotypy, and echolalia [repeating phrases, especially questions]' are similar to 'basic schizophrenic phenomena' (1943:248) there were important differences that he noted. Firstly, childhood schizophrenia is characterized by gradual change but the children in his paper 'have all shown their extreme aloneness from the very beginning of life, not responding to anything from the outside world' (1943:248). Secondly, they all 'are able to establish and maintain an excellent, purposeful, and "intelligent" relation to [those] objects that do not threaten to interfere with their aloneness' and '[a]ll of the children's activities and utterances are governed rigidly and consistently by the powerful desire for aloneness and sameness' (1943:249). He considers briefly, and dismisses, the significance of the parent's preoccupation with 'abstractions of a scientific, literary, or artistic nature' and their limited 'genuine interest in people' before concluding, abruptly, in the last sentence that 'here we seem to have pure-culture examples of *inborn disturbances of affective contact*' (1943:250, emphasis in the original).

Parents came to see Kanner because they wanted to dispute the labelling of their children as 'feeble-minded'. Children who were labelled as cognitively impaired ('mental retardation', in the language of the day) or as childhood schizophrenics were likely to be incarcerated in an institution. The parents that came to Kanner believed that their children were not 'feeble-minded', and Kanner concurred. He believed that a diagnosis of autism would apply to very few children, and he wanted it to be carefully distinguished from schizophrenia or cognitive impairment, with which it was likely to often be confused.

In this early period of the 'discovery' of autism the emphasis, following Kanner's clinical observations, was on a rare condition characterized by the extreme aloneness of these children. Gradually, the emphasis on aloneness became less significant in the diagnosis of autism, which led to dramatic increases in diagnosis. In *The Autism Matrix* Gil Eyal and colleagues (2010) claim that this rapid increase in diagnoses of autism can be explained by deinstitutionalization in the context of a matrix of networks (of parents, occupational therapists, behavioural psychologists and others) that supported an expansion of the concept from a relatively rare and quite specific condition (Kanner's 'extreme aloneness') to a spectrum of behaviours.

Biopolitics: deinstitutionalization and increases in diagnosis

Young children were not incarcerated or diagnosed in the first half of the twentieth century. Prior to 1945 there was a legal prohibition on institutionalizing children under the age of 5 years. Young children were not viewed as having the same social interactional styles and competencies as older children and adults, and given the intensity of development in the early years, a firm diagnosis of developmental delay in a young child could be quickly superseded by later development.

Post-war, increased surveillance of middle-class childhood enabled a shift in how the government's responsibilities towards young children were conceptualized, and 'having healthy and normal children became an ethical goal, and adult life fulfilment became a matter of successful parenting' (Eyal et al. 2010:85). Parents were encouraged to grieve for their lost child but to leave him or her to the care of the institution so that they could devote their energies to their 'normal' children. During the Second World War in the USA parents' groups formed to push for the expansion of funds for the institutionalization of children 'in the name of protecting the family from the burden, especially the emotional burden, posed by the retarded child' (2010:90). They invited the psychiatrists and the state into the middle-class family (2010:89).

In 1970 the White House Conference on Children recommended early development screening and preventative measures to 'reduce the incidence of mental retardation' and recommended the care of 'the mentally retarded in the community' (Eyal et al. 2010:97). From the 1980s onwards, institutionalization of children was discouraged and a programme of fairly rapid deinstitutionalization began. Eyal and colleagues correlate the rate of increase in autism spectrum disorder (ASD) to the pace of deinstitutionalization of children in psychiatric wards and care homes. In 1989, the prevalence rate was 1 in 2,500. In 2013, the prevalence rate in a report by the Centers for Disease Control and Prevention (CDC) on a parent survey was about 1 in 50. Three years earlier, in 2010, the CDC had claimed that 1 in 68 children had ASD. This means that the diagnosis of ASD has doubled (1 in 68) or tripled (1 in 50) since 2000, when CDC was reporting prevalence rates of 1 in 150 (http://www.cdc.gov/ncbddd/autism/data.html) (Eyal et al. 2010:2). This rapid increase can be correlated with patterns of deinstitutionalization. The diagnosis of ASD per 10,000 of the population increased from 0.7 to 55–7 in the USA; from 4.1 to 38.9 in the UK; and from 10.1 to 28.4–35.2 in Canada. In contrast, in France, which continues to institutionalize children, the ASD prevalence rate barely increased from 1989 to 1997 (from 4.5 to 5.35) (Eyal et al. 2010:61). In 2007, more than 108,000 French children with disabilities, a majority with intellectual disability including autism, were in residential institutions whereas in the UK, only 2,245 children were, and this is despite the existence of an active parent group, Vaincre l'Autisme, that has taken the French government to court for institutionalizing children (Eyal et al. 2010:62).

Factors that made deinstitutionalization possible

Deinstitutionalization did not happen by itself. It was made possible through a combination of factors including intensified surveillance of children, democratization of expertise, and the emergence of a new domain of 'atypical' children, new therapies and new commitments to the rights of the disabled (Eyal et al. 2010:64). The democratization of expertise allowed parents to challenge psychiatrists' judgements about their children's capacities, new therapies meant that containment was no longer the only response to developmental delay or childhood mental illness, and the emergence of a disability rights movement made the incarceration of disabled children a political issue.

When the response to a diagnosis of delayed or abnormal development was simply to incarcerate the child it did not really matter to professionals if children in institutions had cognitive disabilities, schizophrenia or autism, since the only medical response was separation and containment. What institutions did do was discriminate between middle-class families and working-class families and between black children and white children. Middle-class white families were expected to manage their children within the child guidance clinics, and working-class and black families frequently had their children removed from them against their will.

After deinstitutionalization, children who would have been labelled as 'mentally retarded' got relabelled as on the autistic spectrum because the latter, but not the former, allows for the possibility of intervention, treatment and normalization. The spectrum, but not Kanner's original diagnosis, includes, Eyal and colleagues are arguing, a very broad range of development disabilities (Eyal et al. 2010:18). Once the diagnosis was relaxed, and perhaps less stigmatized (Farrugia 2009), parents, teachers and experts 'begin to see it where they did not do so before' (Eyal et al. 2010:19). From 1991 in the USA, autism was included in the Individuals with Disabilities in Education Act (IDEA), which further extended the push towards diagnosis and, 'once there are concrete benefits to getting the diagnosis, parents demand it and clinicians are happy to make it' (Eyal et al. 2010:19).

Theory of mind and the social brain

The theories that have come to predominate in the diagnosis of autism are increasingly centred on neurological theories about the social brain and on the importance that development psychology places on a theory of mind. Theory of mind is the ability to theorize that others have internal states that motivate their actions. Although we cannot know what people think when they act, we generally induce from their action that they have an internal motivation that is consistent with or explains their action. The development of a theory of other people's minds is considered by psychologists to be one of the major achievements of childhood development. They understand it as a kind of mental structure that makes it possible for us to believe that other people's actions are rational, predictable and meaningful. Autistic children are thought to lack this theory of other (people's) mind(s).

In the 1990s, the US government funded 'the decade of the brain', which led to a proliferation of studies designed to unlock the complexity of the brain and to answer the question of the relationship of the brain to the self, to the location of the mind and even to the soul. On the basis of these studies it is claimed that what we conceptualize as the mind is an artefact of the brain's activity. We imagine a unified, internal self, a thinking 'I' that has beliefs, intention and morality (as theory of mind predicts), but this imagination is an effect orchestrated by the brain's modular structure. There is no singular self but rather multiple selves given an appearance of depth and continuity by the various modal sites of the brain that, as it were, orchestrates a sense of self by synaptic communication across brain cells. The unified 'I' is an effect of synaptic connections.

That people are fundamentally social is one of the central premises of the social sciences and philosophy and increasingly of the physical sciences. Neuroscience suggests that this capacity for sociality is an effect of the structure of the human brain. Specific parts of the brain are associated with social tasks such as empathy and theory of mind. Research on brain injury suggests that the brain is not 'an indivisible whole but a confederation of relatively independent modules, each of which [is] relatively discrete and [has] specific functions' (Rose and Abi-Rached 2013:143). Particular regions of the brain – the amygdala, orbital frontal cortex and temporal cortex – are considered to be the dominant regions involved in 'social cognition' (Rose and Abi-Rached 2013:144). However, because of the plasticity of the brain and its 'redundancy' (non-active parts) it is not a straightforward matter to predict how people will behave from imaging of their brains (Rose and Abi-Rached 2013:145). In 1999, the mapping of a 'mirror' system in the brain suggested that when others do something, the neural pathways involved in that action are activated in primates, including humans, who are simply watching the action and that the observer feels an appropriate response (pain, pleasure and so on). If this is true then it is 'not through *theorizing* about others, but through [literally] *feeling what they feel*, that we understand the mental state of others' (Rose and Abi-Rached 2013:147).

It is these parts of the brain and its associated tasks that much of recent research on autism is most interested in. The primary hypothesis from neuropsychiatry is that in autism 'empathizing abilities are impaired and systemizing abilities are augmented' (Rose and Abi-Rached 2013:149 citing Baron-Cohen and Belmonte 2005:119) and that some, as yet unknown, neurological processes underlie these abilities (or deficits, depending on your point of view). It is still assumed that whatever these neurological processes are, they have a genetic origin.

Cause and treatment

For the last thirty to forty years, research on autism and ASD has concentrated on identifying neurobiological and genetic markers. The assumption is that some combination of genetic and environmental influences changes the structure of the brain in the early months of a child's development, possibly in the womb.

One of the bases for the claim that ASD has some kind of genetic cause is twin studies. The CDC says that 'Studies have shown that among identical twins, if one child has ASD, then the other will be affected about 36–95% of the time. In non-identical twins, if one child has ASD, then the other is affected about 0–31% of the time' (http://www.cdc.gov/ncbddd/autism/data.html). A range of 36–95 per cent seems extraordinarily wide and surely suggests that if there is an underlying genetic cause to autism, it is only activated in specific environmental conditions that could be different for identical twins even when they are raised in the same family. This wide range has done nothing to undermine the claim that autism has a genetic basis. Michael Rutter, who was one of the original board members of the *Journal of Autism*, notes the over 90 per cent heritability of autism in identical twin studies as evidence for the genetic basis of autism. He is convinced that although there has been little progress in the last ten years in identifying the genes, there is a genetic basis to autism, although there is probably not only one gene implicated (Rutter 2011). The change in emphasis from Kanner's forward-looking treatments to the search for a genetic origin 'reflects an increasing focus on psychiatric genetics in general and a deepening conviction that autism treatment is necessary, that it will involve the use of pharmaceuticals, and that developing these techniques depends on locating autism genes' (Silverman 2012:144).

Kanner wanted to unify the emerging field of child psychiatry. He wanted children who were institutionalized for developmental delays or deficits and middle-class children who were the clients of child guidance clinics to be treated as part of the same domain; that is, amenable to the same kinds of diagnosis and treatment. His aim was to develop the 'practical communal, educational, and clinical possibilities for human engineering' (Eyal et al. 2010:87). The unification of the field was helped along by developments in psycho-pharmaceuticals from the mid-1960s. Silverman argues that the availability of these drugs encouraged many psychiatrists 'to see most behavioural anomalies as neurological or neurochemical in origin, *even in advance of any concrete evidence that this was the case*' (Silverman 2012:41, emphasis added). In 1971 Kanner founded the *Journal of Autism and Childhood Schizophrenia*. This provided an institutional base for the continued unification of child psychiatry and included on the editorial board members of all psy-professions. In 1979 its name was changed to the *Journal of Autism and Developmental Disorders*, separating mental illness from developmental disorders and finally breaking the link with schizophrenia and autism, as Kanner had hoped to do since his original article (Silverman 2012:40). Gradually parents become the experts in the lives of their children and various low-tech treatments, especially applied behaviour analysis (ABA) become the mainstay of 'treatment' for autistic children.

In the USA, and other countries where the neurobiological and epi/genetic thesis of autism prevails treatment is now primarily through ABA, supported by various other therapies including speech therapy. ABA is based on Skinnerian behaviourism and claims that learning takes place through antecedent–behaviour–consequence chains, often called the ABC of ABA. Although ABA is an evidence-based practice that has been proven to increase language development in randomized control trials, it is also widely recognized that the accomplishments learned through ABA are often not generalizable by the child to other settings, are often resisted by children, and do not impact on social communication more broadly. In a systematic review of research published in peer-reviewed journals since 1998, Rogers and Vismara (2008) show that the claims made for early intervention leading to recovery from autism (Lovaas 1987, McEachin, Smith and Lovaas 1993) have not been repeated in subsequent studies.

The review of the academic literature carried out by Rogers and Vismara (2008) shows the importance of context to the ability of children to learn and to continue to self-direct their learning. This is the principle behind pivotal response training (PRT) or the identification of the pivot or key moments that push learning forward through the child's own interests and engagement. Practitioners describe PRT as 'naturally occurring' (although it involves constant intervention and close scrutiny of the child's every action). It has been tested in trials and found to be more effective than other forms of ABA (Mohammadzaheri, Koegel, Rezaee and Rafiee 2014). Some practitioners maintain that ABA (not necessarily PRT) can lead to recovery from autism. In a paper published in 2009 Doreen Granpeesheh and colleagues review the cases of thirty-eight patients who were diagnosed with autism and who, following intensive ABA, developed in ways that were indistinguishable from their typically developing peers. Since autism is diagnosed entirely on the basis of behaviour this suggests that these individuals were no longer autistic. The thirty-eight clinical notes reviewed were all of children who began treatment relatively early (on average at 3 years and 4 months), and the key point that the paper makes is that early diagnosis and treatment (early intensive behavioural intervention, EIBI) is more likely to lead to development changes and 'recovery' from autism. Interestingly, given the push towards specialist schools for autistic children, Rogers and Vismara (2008:25) report that some research has found that 'children with autism demonstrate more typical play and social behavior, and less atypical behavior, when in the presence of typical peers as compared to peers with autism, both in dyadic play (Smith et al., 2002) and in a preschool class-room (McGee et al., 1993)'.

The economics of autism

One of the claims often made about the move away from institutionaliza-tion and towards community care is that the neo-liberal state sought to leverage the advocacy of parents and disability organizations and public outrage about the treatment of people with disabilities in institutions in order to move the economy of care away from the state and back into the family. However, this claim is undermined by the fact that the costs of current treatment regimes for children with ASD are considerable (and deinstitutionalization only affected mental health care; rates of prison incarceration and its associated costs have soared over the same period). Parents of children with ASD have higher health care and non-health costs, including additional school costs (Lavelle et al. 2014). Medical costs for children with ASD are 4.1–6.2 times higher than for those without ASD. In 2005 the average annual medical costs for Medicaid-enrolled children with ASD were $10,709 per child, which was about six times higher than costs for children without ASD ($1,812) (Peacock, Amendah, Ouyang and Grosse 2012). In addition to medical costs, intensive behavioural interventions for children with ASD in the USA cost $40,000 to $60,000 per child per year (Amendah, Grosse, Peacock and Mandell 2011). Although ABA is also prescribed for children with intellectual disabilities, 'in the *actual* practice of special education, given limited budgets, only autistic children and their parents are able to make a legitimate claim to the considerable resources and investments that

ABA requires' (Eyal et al. 2010:33). This is because a diagnosis of autism holds out the prospect of a 'cure' within a specific window of intervention, whilst intellectual disability does not.

Alternative views: psychoanalysis, ethnography and neurodiversity

ABA is based on the assumption that the behaviour and language of autistic children are, so to say, misfiring. That is, autistic traits such as repeating phrases, reversing pronouns, refusing to speak, head-banging and other repetitive behaviours are not meaningful and have no symbolic or communicative significance. For neurobiologists, autistic behaviours are signs of an underlying difference in the structure of the brain, and the behaviours that are generated by this underlying difference are, essentially, and other than as signs of the disorder itself, meaningless. Psychologists and neuroscientists claim that 'most autistic children are basically acultural' (Tomasello, Kruger and Ratner 1993:504).

There have been few, if any, challenges within psychiatry and psychology to the view that autistic children are intensely alone and non-communicative and that their behaviour and language lack symbolic significance. It has been left to other disciplines, particularly anthropology and psychoanalysis, and to the neurodiversity movement to insist that autistic children are socially and culturally engaged and that their behaviour is symbolic.

Ethnographic studies at the start of this century are challenging the view that autistic people are radically different in their communicative practice to other humans. Solomon and Bagatell (2010) remind us 'there is less and less attention in autism research to phenomena that cannot be studied at the neurobiological or molecular level, such as human experience, social interaction, and cross-cultural variation' (Solomon and Bagatell 2010:2). In her ethnography of the parents of children with autism, Juliette de Wolfe (2014) shows that autistic children are located within a web of relations of social kin. In contrast to the view that children with autism are acultural, ethnographic accounts situate autistic children within the finely grained fabric of everyday life. Ochs and Solomon (2010) in their ongoing research with ASD children propose that all people develop sociality within domains of 'social co-ordination'. So, for example, although they agree that autistic children have 'impairments' in theory of mind, these researchers draw on their data of appropriate conversational turn-taking between high-functioning ASD and Asperger's children and others to argue that theory of mind should be considered in relation to two discrete domains: interpersonal and socio-cultural. While the former may be impaired the latter (what they call 'doing together') may be fully accessible within a zone of 'proximal relevance' (2010:77, 78). Ochs and Solomon say, 'Like ships that pass each other in the dark, sometimes these proximally relevant remarks pass by interlocutors unnoticed. Sometimes they are generously accepted. But in the social world outside family members and teachers, the proximally relevant, somewhat odd comments of autistic children sometimes confuse and annoy interlocutors' (2010:79). What of the social interaction of autistic children who 'have little or no speech, social eye gaze, facial expressions, or gestures; and little ability to initiate or sustain joint attention – all required for face-to-face social interaction' (2010:81)? Here, Ochs and Solomon suggest that when the specific competencies of autistic children are taken into account in domains of social communication then it is possible to produce an ordered domain between the autistic child(ren) and their interlocutors. Following the work of the Indian educator Soma Mukhopadhyay (2008), Ochs and Solomon show that talk that is side by side rather than face to face, and steady to rapid rather than slow, and affect-neutral rather than affect-laden (meaning 'baby talk' or talking loudly to show appreciation) facilitates the production of what they call an ordered social domain. In this social domain, they propose, autistic children both understand and participate in symbolic communication.

Another way of thinking about the diagnosis of autism and its cultural significance is as status offences. Status offences are actions that are only considered wrong when specific categories of persons do them. So, for example, breaking juvenile curfews is a status offence because it is illegal during curfew for a youth but not an adult to be out in public. Pretend play or a refusal to participate in pretend play, and a presumed inability to 'get' imaginative play, are indicators of autism. Adults are not, generally, required to participate in pretend play, so we might say that children are penalized for not doing childhood in the ways that our culture imagines it should be done. The underlying hypothesis that links a failure to play with autism is that children who fail to pretend play are not able to develop a theory of (other people's) mind(s).

Psychoanalysis and autism

Many critics of psychoanalysis for the treatment of autism wonder how the talking cure can be effective with children who often do not talk. Like anthropology, psychoanalysis presumes that autistic behaviours are meaningful and require interpretation by the psychoanalyst that will be accepted by the child and internalized as accurate or meaningful representations of their own feelings. In particular, psychoanalysts believe that autistic behaviours signify the inability of the young child to manage the separation between themselves and their mother (see Tustin 1992). Given these views it is unsurprising that parents feel that psychoanalysis blames them, particularly mothers, for their children's autism.

The Wall Susan Robert's documentary *The Wall* represents the case against the efficacy of psychoanalysis in the treatment of autistic children (http://www.dailymotion.com/video/x16d4fv_le-mur-ou-la-psychanalyse-a-l-epreuve-de-l-autisme_school). The documentary follows two families who both have sons with a diagnosis for autism. One of the boys, Guillaume, was diagnosed at the age of 4 years by a child psychiatrist. The parents refused permission for their child to attend group psychotherapy but did not specify that they were also opposed to individual psychotherapy, and so the clinic then entered him into psychoanalysis. After the individual psychoanalysis his parents were given a report that said he had 'sexual phobia, that he was liquefying, hallucinating words'. It was, the mother said, 'roughly like she had put Guillaume in a text of Lacan. It's so scary.' The parents refused to give permission for Guillaume to continue with psychotherapy and they began to use the Picture Exchange Communication System (PECS). This is a system of using pictures to communicate that is widely used in the USA with autistic children. He attended a specialist school for a while and then returned to regular school, where he is now in grade 7 (UK year 8) and doing well, especially in maths. He plays 'games that teenagers no longer play', say his parents, but the school have given the other students an explanation for his behaviour, and he is fine in school.

In contrast to this child is the other autistic boy in the film, whom Guillaume introduces us to at the start of the film. His name is Julien and he is about 14 years of age. When Guillaume introduces Julien the camera pans to a tall, skinny boy sitting on the sofa; he kicks the coffee table in front of him as he rocks back and forth looking at the camera. He does not speak and he needs assistance with most everyday activities. At the end of the film we are told that Julien attends a child psychiatry clinic and goes to a day centre where they take good care of him. Earlier in the film his mother had explained how he likes to go outside and that at the school he cycles and roller-skates indoors, but that he cannot do that outside because he forgets to brake. In the closing scenes of the film he is sitting on a rock in front of a wall, looking towards the sea, shaking his head from side to side. He reaches down and picks up mud in his hands and runs it through his fingers. He looks up, directly at the camera, and then slightly smiles. The voiceover explains that if he had specific educational inputs, such as Treatment and Education of Autistic and

Related Communication Handicapped Children (TEEACH), PECS and ABA he would become continent, less dependent and maybe even able to speak.

In contrast to the confident claims of amelioration offered by ABA programmes, psychoanalysts have no such convictions. Professor Pierre Delion, a psychoanalyst and head of child psychiatry at Centre Hospitalier Régional Universitaire (CHRU) de Lille, when asked in the documentary 'What can an autistic child reasonably expect in terms of result?' says, 'But I can't answer this, this is not a matter for a psychoanalyst!' (44:54). The same question to Laurent Danon Boileau, a linguist and psychoanalyst, gets this response after a lengthy pause: 'The pleasure of taking interest in a soap bubble' and, after another short pause, 'I can't answer anything else' (45:31), meaning he has nothing to add to this enigmatic statement. Indeed, in complete contrast to ABA's total control of autistic children's actions, Esthella Solano, another psychoanalyst interviewed in *The Wall*, says the treatment of autistic children requires 'no willingness of control, no educative willingness, no compelling of anything' (41:27).

The Wall is a campaigning documentary and the psychoanalysts certainly do not come over well in their explanations of autism or indeed what seems like an extraordinarily literal and rather reactionary interpretation of the Oedipus complex. The psychoanalysts in the film say that autism is a disorder of language that follows either rejection by the mother, conscious or otherwise, or an inability to separate from the mother leading to a fusion that makes language unnecessary. The analysts in *The Wall* say that all mothers have (literal) incestuous desire for their children that is only interrupted from outside, by the real or symbolic father; that the fathers of autistic children are not allowed to penetrate the bond between the mother and child and so the incestuous desire continues uninterrupted. For Esthella Solano the incest between mother and son leads to psychosis, whereas between father and daughter it's really, she feels, not so bad. For another contributor the infrequency of mother–son sexual abuse (or as they prefer to call it, incest) follows from the fact that there is no need for it since the mother and child are already fused, whereas the father is outside of this circle and his incest, therefore, is necessary. For someone not analytically trained, and perhaps for those who are analytically trained, the narrative offered here seems at best ridiculous and in many ways (a kind of normalization of sexual abuse not the least of them) harmful.

Psychoanalysis does not have the hold over the management of mental health in the UK or the USA that it does in France, but nor has it been entirely discredited in the UK for the treatment of autistic children. Didier Houzel, a French psychoanalyst writing in the *Journal of Child*

Psychotherapy (2004) about a British autistic boy under his analysis, says that 'The century-old experience of psychoanalysts and their patients offers ample proof of the fact that if something is felt in the mind without, for whatever reason, being *represented* in this sense of the word [that is, is given or restored to a 'psychic shape'], it inevitably becomes a source of pain and mental disorder' (2004:227). He then describes what he calls the soft feminine and hard masculine surfaces that children encounter in their infancy and the importance to the child of integrating the masculine and feminine, the child's bisexuality as he calls it. He then illustrates the curative potential of psychoanalysis through a case study of a 3-year-old boy, Cyril, who has ASD. His mother had to rest through most of the pregnancy, having had several prior miscarriages. In the therapy session the child empties his modelling boxes and then asks to leave. Houzel recounts 'I interpreted this to him in terms of the impression he may have had of emptying me of everything ... so that maybe he wanted to leave because he felt I could be dangerous' (2004:232). Clearly, the psychoanalyst finds his interpretation of the boy's actions meaningful, and believes that the child does also, but for those outside of the magic circle of psychoanalysis the interpretation seems overdrawn and unlikely to resonate with a 3-year-old.

Psychoanalysis seems to rely on fanciful interpretations of the child's actions, and the documentary *The Wall* succeeds in its indictment of psychoanalysis. However, although it clearly wants to claim that Julien's failure to recover from autism is a consequence of his being denied appropriate educational interventions such as TEEACH, ABA and PECS, the contrast in Julien's behaviour and that of the children filmed in a promotional documentary for the Elijah School that uses ABA does not seem so significant. In this documentary, for example (https://www.youtube.com/watch?v=FO1W7iXTSQE), three autistic children who find daily tasks such as dressing and cleaning their teeth very difficult, and who have limited language, attend the Elijah School with the highly interventionist, detailed training programme of ABA. Yet their interpersonal relationships seem very similar to those of Julien, and indeed it is hard to feel that the constant up-close surveillance of ABA is not also a kind of assault on the child's senses.

Neurodiversity

The congruence of events and practices that named a collection of behaviours as 'autism' and invented the figure of the autistic child also produced another identity, one that embraced autism as an important facet of selfhood. This is what Foucault means when he says that power is not only repressive but also productive. It produces the forbidden subject out of pre-existing relations and practices (homosexuality, madness, criminality, autism) and in doing so generates new sites of identity from which people resist the conditions laid down for their existence.

Psychoanalysis and ethnographies of autistic children and their families are mostly, if not entirely, the views of those who do not have direct, personal experience of autism. In contrast the neurodiversity movement is made up of autistic people and their allies as a way of being in the world, different to but as valid as the behaviours of neurotypicals (as the movement calls people who are not on the autistic spectrum). They object to the search for a 'cure' for autism on three grounds. Firstly, the search for a cure for autism violates the disability rights slogan, 'nothing about us, without us'. Secondly, to eradicate autism is to eradicate the selfhood of people with autism. Thirdly, they believe that the search for the genetic origins of autism is at least in part, and perhaps entirely, a search for genetic markers that can be identified in foetuses to enable them to be aborted and thereby to permanently eradicate autistic people from the world. Such a claim is far from unlikely. The well-respected child psychiatrist Michael Rutter OBE recently asked in a paper why autism did not simply 'die out' (2011:400).

The neurodiversity movement has attracted some controversy and criticism, particularly about who is in the movement and whom it speaks for. Many people outside of the movement, including some autistic people and some parents of autistic children, have said that the high-functioning autism of the leaders of the movement means that their experience bears no comparison with the difficulties faced by autistic people who do not speak or who need assistance with the tasks of daily living. Activists in the neurodiversity movement argue that even if there is a difference between the daily experiences of people with different levels of autism, people with autism have a better understanding of one another's experience than people without autism do.

Activists in the neurodiversity movement object to the use of person-first labels (that is, speaking of 'people with autism' rather than 'autistic people'). Person-first labels were a demand of the first wave of disability rights activism and the emergence of Disability Studies and the social model of disability. The intention behind using person-first language is to insist on the personhood of a person with a disability and to suggest that what makes a person 'disabled' is not their specific impairment but the social attitudes that prevent their full participation and mobility from being facilitated. Subsequent moves towards what is sometimes called 'the new materialism' insist on the importance of a person's body (including their brain) to their experiences of being in the world, to their social ontology. In this view disability is not an appendage to a person's subjectivity but an integral part of it, and therefore it is more true to people's experiences or sense of self to refer to disabled people rather than people with disabilities.

The rejection of person-first labels when referring to autistic people frequently references Jim Sinclair's assertion, in his 1993 speech 'Don't Mourn for Us', that person-first labels suggest that autism is a 'container' in which the 'real' child is hiding. In other words, person-first terminology implies that autism is an appendage to the person, and suggests that if they could be 'cured' of autism then they would, essentially, remain the same person. In this claim they are extending the social model of disability into the cultural arena in ways similar to the work done by Deaf activists. The term 'D/deaf' (that is, upper-case Deaf or lower-case deaf) was intended to signal that deafness is both hearing impairment and a cornerstone of Deaf culture. If being deaf produces an orientation to the world and a distinctive language, then the eradication of deafness through the use of cochlear implants is thought by Deaf activists to be much more than a simple fix for hearing impairment and instead to be the annihilation of human difference.

Parenting autistic children

The claims of the neurodiversity movement are beginning to impact on how parents think about what it means to raise an autistic child. Parents' memoirs of raising their autistic children are a rapidly expanding field and, as Silverman (2012:93–124) comments, parents are frequently 'expert amateurs' in autism research. In an ethnographic study of mothers of children with ASD, Cascio (2012) discusses the absorption of neurodiversity perspectives into the discourses of parent support groups. An online roundtable organized by *Disability Studies Quarterly* asked parents 'How does a notion of neurodiversity affect caregiving?' (Savarese 2010). One of the participants, Susan Etlinger, poignantly captured a sense of what it means to say that a child *is* a pathology rather than that they have a particular mode of being-in-the-world:

> When my son Isaac was first diagnosed with autism, I had a hard time accepting it. It wasn't so much the notion that he had developmental delays – we knew that – as it was that who he was – playful, mercurial, hyper-focused, intensely internal – could add up to a pathology. If that was true, who was he? And who were we, who prized his *himness* so intensely? (Savarese 2010).

Although research with parents of autistic children and accounts by autistic adults of their childhood come a little closer to giving an account of how autistic children themselves engage with the social world and what their sense of selfhood is, there has been no research so far as I am aware with autistic children asking them what they feel about the claims of the neurodiversity movement. This may be because it would be seen as developmentally inappropriate to ask children whether they are satisfied with who they are in the world, with their modes of dis/engagement, with their sense of self (for exceptions see Madriaga 2010, Winstone et al. 2014); but it is also because most research on autistic children and children with other neurological disabilities continues to be dominated by development psychology, which firmly sees autism as a pathology and rejects the claims of the neurodiversity movement, and of anthropology and psychoanalysis, that autistic modes of communication are culturally signifying.

Conclusion

In her introduction to the edited collection *Re-Thinking Autism*, Katherine Runswick-Cole says that autism 'doesn't exist at the biological level ... [and] can only by understood through examining "it" as a socially/culturally produced phenomenon' (2016:9). This chapter concurs with that argument and has shown how the work of producing this phenomenon has been done and how autistic people and their allies have resisted it. It is important that we resist the view that autistic children are 'basically acultural' because culture (social interaction and symbolic communication) is precisely what makes us human. The production of humanness is an intersubjective achievement; no one becomes human by themselves (this point is developed further in the next chapter), and so it is also for autistic children. It is important to recognize that atypical development, physical and cognitive, shapes children's experiences of the world, of interpersonal relations and their sense of self. However, the intersubjectivity within which children's subjecthood is formed may be different in intensity but not necessarily in kind between children with and without disabilities.

7

Children's Bodies Matter

Introduction

This chapter is about the changing bodies of children. In it I set out a case for thinking of the child as ontologically different to adults, and for attending to children's bodies. Taking seriously what their bodies mean for how they move through, experience and shape the world may involve reorientating Childhood Studies to encompass the differences between children and adults. While I take seriously the claim that childhood is socially constructed and agree that what kinds of people children are understood to be, what competencies, capacities and vulnerabilities we think they have, are socially constructed and culturally shaped, I want to argue that the biological capacities of the child places limits on the social construction of childhood. It is for this reason that Aries (1962) (or at least how he has been interpreted in Childhood Studies) was, to put it simply, wrong. Childhood exists everywhere. There is no culture in the world where physically immature human beings are not thought of as different kinds of people, with different capacities and having different needs, from mature human beings. Of course, the same could be said of gender, but with the exception of reproductive capacities, there are no underlying biological differences between men and women comparable to the differences between children and adults.

Infancy

Let us start at the beginning. How does the infant body experience the world and understand itself as a being in the world? One of the most striking aspects of infant embodiment is that the infant is entirely dependent on the care of others for its survival. As the development psychologist Eva Simms says in her 2001 paper on infant phenomenology, '[a]n infant without adult care is a dead infant, to put it bluntly' (2001:23). Unless the child is brought quickly into a web of social relations, it will not survive (James 2000). This is an irrefutable difference between very young children and adults: that immature humans depend entirely on others for their care. Of course there are adults with disabilities who also depend on others for their care, and in some sense we all depend on others for the literal continuation of our lives. But, unlike non-disabled adults, children cannot exercise agency in making others care for them. Nor can infant children be compared to those disabled adults who depend on others for survival, because it is not a condition of being adult but of being disabled that renders some disabled adults entirely dependent on the care of others. In fact very few disabilities render adults incapable of exercising any agency over their care. While we may speak of 'social death' to refer to the ways that adults are excluded from a social order, often violently and often under the constant threat of actual death, for the infant if nothing is done, she or he will, literally, die.

This intense vulnerability of the infant to death reminds us that the simple fact of a human body is not sufficient to command social personhood. The vulnerability of the child is not always sufficient to guarantee that others will take up its care; infants are sometimes left to die. But many, in fact most, children will be given social recognition and their childishness, their ontological difference to the adults and older children who will care for them, will not be a source of their exclusion; indeed, recognition of their corporeal vulnerability in a sense could be said to compel others, on the whole, to care for them.

In their 2005 paper on neonatal intensive care, Alderson and colleagues think about the care that parents give their preterm and very vulnerable babies as an operationalization of children's rights as set out in the UNCRC. These practices of care include naming their children; speaking about their babies' desires, will and personality; and inviting friends and family to meet their child. Alderson and colleagues want to make the claim that the child's agency is expressed in their apparent recognition of their mothers' voice, or their differential response to another's touch, depending on whether it is the clinical, diagnostic touch of the doctor or the loving touch of the parent or nurse. These writers want to make these claims to protect the figure of the baby from philosophers such as Peter Singer, who argues that babies do not meet the criteria for making claims of humanness and that 'killing a disabled infant is not morally equivalent to killing a person. Very often it is not wrong at all' (Singer 2011:167).

The data that Alderson and her colleagues present, particularly the interview data, upholds their claims, since clearly the infant has someone to speak for them and therefore meets at least one of Singer's criteria for personhood. But is this being spoken for a sign either of child rights as set out in the UNCRC or of a preterm infant's agency? Research in the USA is leading on the development of neonatal care of preterm infants, yet it has not ratified the UNCRC and US law does not recognize child rights. One of the researchers whom Alderson et al. cite focuses her research on what is widely called 'kangaroo care' for preterm infants. She explains the importance of individualized care for preterm infants as arising 'from an evolutionary perspective, [in which] the NICU [neonatal intensive care unit] is a socio-cultural phenomenon engendered by society's desire to preserve the lives of its smallest and most vulnerable members' (Als and McAnulty 2011:3). No mention there of child rights. Nor, despite the fact that Alderson cites Als and McAnulty in support of her contention that babies have 'views' and 'agency', do Als and McAnulty really describe the preterm infant as an agential figure in the way that 'views' implies. These authors say that neurological research shows that foetal babies (that is, very early preterm infants who have not yet completed foetal development) are 'complex, responsive, and active in eliciting social and sensory stimulation, while simultaneously attempting to regulate their own thresholds of reaction and response' (Als and McAnulty 2011:2). This is important and suggests that the preterm infant is much more than a not yet fully formed body; this is a human being, for sure, and one that is already intersubjective – recognizing and responding positively (moving towards) its birth mother's voice.

Why claim that this intersubjective, radically vulnerable infant is expressing, as it turns towards its mother's voice, not an embodied attachment but rather a 'view'? I think Alderson wants to claim this because she thinks that ascribing intentionality to infants in the same kind of terms as we would ascribe intentionality to older children and adults will contribute to their protection by showing that they are human and therefore deserving of rights, including the right to life. Yet we know that other animals display, elicit and respond to social and sensory stimulation and are complex and responsive, including animals that many people kill, cook and eat, such as cows, sheep and goats. Even more controversially, we also know that a foetus aborted at 22 weeks (very few abortions, less than 2 per cent, happen at that stage) would not warrant the social care that would have them in an NICU and make it possible for them to survive and continue their foetal development outside of the womb. It is not their responsiveness and complexity that protect preterm babies; it is both the fact that they *are* human

– regardless of whether or not they have legal rights and regardless of their (in)ability to take a view – and, most crucially, that they have others who advocate for them, who insist on their care.

When the need of the infant for care fails, and the infant is exposed to harm, the ambivalence with which these acts is treated also suggests that cultural work needs to be done before the infant will be recognized as being entitled to the same kinds of protection and recognition conferred on other humans. Even in the examples offered by Alderson, decisions were made to withhold nutrition from babies who could not survive independently of incubators and respirators but whose predicted quality of life was not considered sufficient to justify the continuation of resources to them. Alderson and colleagues claim that even preterm infants are cared for in NICUs because these babies have a right to life under the law, but if they are correct in their statement that 'If the baby survives long enough to breathe independently, a decision to end life alters from "allowing the baby to die" by withdrawing mechanical ventilation into, more controversially, withdrawing fluids and nutrition' (2005:38), then clearly this right is provisional.

The provisional character of the infant's 'right to life' can also be seen in laws on infanticide. In some countries infanticide– that is, the killing of an infant within the first year of life – is distinguished from other kinds of murder or manslaughter. The reason for the distinction is the presumption that the mother's mental state is abnormal because of the disturbance to her hormones from giving birth or lactation. In 2005, judges reviewing the conviction of a woman in the UK who had murdered her 3-month-old son called for the law to be reviewed, to, in effect, include a failure to bond as mitigation for the murder of a child under the age of 12 months (Frith 2005). Crimes of neonaticide (killing a baby within the first 24 hours of life) and infanticide often attract sympathy for the mother, as suggested in the 2005 case just mentioned. The literature on infanticide focuses primarily on the mother's state of mind (and it is predominantly mothers who kill infants) because the child's right to life is in practice, and often in law, provisional until it is secured by its ties to social relationships.

Many of the rituals that attend infancy can be thought of as ways to ensure social recognition for a child, and to extend the web of care and responsibility beyond the infant's immediate kin. The law in itself is insufficient to guarantee life to the infant, and infants' corporeal vulnerability is central to this fact. In religious cultures of all types, various rituals tie the infant to their social-cultural group. Without these protections the infant, particularly if they die, is often hardly thought of as a person at all. These rituals include baptism (Meador and Shuman 2000), infant circumcision, inscriptions on the infant body (Gottlieb 2004:237,

Hannig 2014:299, fn18,), the wearing of amulets and wristbands (Gottlieb 2004:85) and naming ceremonies.

In her research among Orthodox Christian Ethiopians in Amhara Region, Ethiopia, Hannig (2014) says that birth is thought to render both child and mother spiritually vulnerable and dangerous. The peculiar state of pregnancy and birth undoes so much of what we think of as human: our degree of distance from other animals, our distinctness from other humans. Although this may seem like a distinctly religious worldview, the assumption that a woman can be so undone by giving birth and lactating that she should be given special treatment in the case of murder, as in infanticide laws, seems to share a view that pregnancy and birth confound the rules of everyday life. Even as they grow older, children are not bound by the laws that others are bound by; they are frequently believed to be interlocutors for the spirit world and even themselves ghosts or spirits (Allotey and Reidpath 2001, Denham, Adongo, Freydberg and Hodgson 2010) or incarnations of ancestors (Gottlieb 2004), and, similarly, spirits may be thought of as childlike (Sinnott 2014). These differences between how children are thought of arise from the embodied differences between adults and children.

Hannig's respondents said they only felt grief for a child if she or he died 'after having "seen" – that is, having come to know a child grow, eat, or behave *like a human being* in other ways' (Hannig 2014:305, emphasis added). An unbaptized child would not be considered a Christian and therefore not have a Christian burial. Hannig notes that the ethnographic literature indicates a denial of personhood to the newborn child in diverse cultures, citing Stasch (2009) on historical infanticide among the Korowai of West Papua, and Pina-Cabral's (1986) research in Minho.

If being alive is not sufficient in itself to render the vulnerable infant body protected, paradoxically, not being alive does not necessarily erase the infant, or indeed the never born, from social personhood (Shaw 2014). In Japan there is a widespread Buddhist belief that the aborted foetus has spiritual powers that need to be appeased, or the foetus will haunt the 'mother' (Moskowitz 2001). Linda Layne, in her work on pregnancy loss in the USA, speaks of how parents may use material culture to give cultural realness to a baby whose gestation did not come to term or who died after birth (Layne 2000).

Prelinguistic children

Psychoanalysts and many psychologists claim that in the early months of life there is a radical difference in how the body is experienced compared to how it will be experienced later. In particular, the very young child has not yet developed a concept of self and an apprehension of their body as an integrated whole, separate from the bodies of others.

Most people present at a birth or closely involved in the care of newborns respond to the infant as a distinct being separate from other beings. In her review of the book *One: Sons and Daughters* by photographer Edward Mapplethorpe (brother of Robert Mapplethorpe), Aimee Lee Ball says that Andrew Solomon, a professor of clinical psychology who contributed an essay to the book, suggests that: 'Newborns are basically interchangeable and without nuance – we attribute unique characteristics to them rather irrationally because we love them – but at that first birthday, we can start to tell who the child will be' (Ball 2016:10). I remember being very startled when an acquaintance said to me on meeting my then 18-month-old daughter for the second time, 'oh, she is like a real human now!' I had always considered my daughter to be human and long after pondered what this comment might mean. I think what was meant was the same point that Ball says Solomon is making: to people other than their family, infants seem 'interchangeable and without nuance'.

Is the perception of their close family that an infant is someone distinct from all other infants simply wrong? Is it the case that not even the infant themselves feels a distinction between their own and other bodies or between bodies and things? William James famously described the newborn's world as 'one great blooming, buzzing confusion' (James 2013:318, first published 1890). Development psychologists, and even the phenomenologist Maurice Merleau-Ponty, thought that infants had no visual perception (Welsh 2013:46). Increasingly, scientific evidence challenges this view that the infant comes into the world 'a blank slate'.

The study of children's early experiences of the world has been dominated by psychologists. There is very little research in Childhood Studies that addresses the infant experience either culturally, socially, spatially or temporally. (The research of Alderson and her colleagues, already discussed, is an important exception – but it is also noteworthy that most of the sources they cite are neurologists and psychologists.) In any case, we now know that the infant's life before birth was full of sensation, of touch, hearing, sound, sight and taste, but this buzz of sensation is not necessarily confusing. Neuroscience suggests that 'fundamental functions that relate to object perception (detection of color and form) are probably present in some rudimentary form at birth' (Colombo 2001:351) and infants are thought to have facial recognition and be able to distinguish their mothers from strangers at birth, although this facility wanes at age 1 month and returns after age 2 months, perhaps suggesting that the neural structures supporting face recognition are different in newborn infants and in slightly older infants (Nelson 2001:7). It also seems likely that infants understand patterns of sounds many weeks before they understand that these are signs, and months before they themselves articulate even simple words. Infants experience the world through their bodies as an immersion in sensation. They do not have a way of conceptualizing their world and they cannot reflect on their place in the world or their relation to others. They move instinctively towards pleasurable sensations and away from painful sensations. It is in this sense that we can say that infants are immersed in 'the real', an immersion that is interrupted or foreclosed by language.

For those psychoanalysts and psychologists who claim that the newborn infant does not have a capacity for apprehending their bodies as either complete or separate from other objects in the world, the development of a sense of self is largely considered to be a linguistic accomplishment, requiring the development of a theory of mind (see chapter 6). Since young children do not have the cognitive structures to have a theory of (other) mind(s) then, the reasoning goes, they cannot have a sense of self. However, some research on neonates' capacity for imitation challenges this view, and imaging of foetal development substantiates these claims (Lymer 2014). Jane Lymer argues that new research in foetal development shows that the foetus touches itself from as early as 9 weeks' gestation and displays intentional touching from between 22 and 26 weeks' gestation. In the womb the foetus touches its own body and presses its hands on the wall of the uterus. Before birth the foetus is exploring its body and is submerged in sensation that it then develops a capacity to respond to. It seems likely that the neonate already has a sense of its own body, can distinguish familiar sounds from unfamiliar sounds, has a sense of taste and so on.

Further support for the contention that infants do already have an embodied sense of self (not a cognitive sense of self) is offered by research on imitation. This research is highly contested, with challengers asserting that early infant imitation is instinctual or accidental. Lymer (2014) argues, convincingly in my view, that the development of a body schema (as opposed to a body image, which would require a level of cognitive development that the infant does not possess) is accomplished intersubjectively in the womb between the movements of the mother's body and the development of the foetus. She argues what we know is the case for infants: that bodily movement precedes and enables the development of the communicative resources that it anticipates. So imitation in the neonate cannot involve a self-expressive intention to communicate with another, since that would necessitate cognitive structures that the infant does not have. However, a body schema that refers to an embodied sense of self that does not involve a psychological or cognitive 'I' makes sense of neonate imitative behaviour, and indeed that sense one has in the presence of a newborn of being with some *one* in particular, rather than with a body that is substitutable by any other body.

The work that is done on the infant body should not be thought of as entirely making the child from the outside. The infant, like all biological organisms, has a drive towards life. Yet the physical encouragement of others and the availability of things to hold or to suck on are critical in supporting the innate drive of the infant to develop, to sit up, to suckle, to kick and stretch. All of these movements will not only develop the muscularity of the infant but also generate the formation of synapses in the brain that will propel the child into further development, to speech, and to the development of conceptual schemas. As Shai and Belskey note, 'cognition, consciousness, and all mental process are deeply grounded in the interplay between sensorimotor systems of the body, somatosensory regions of the brain, and the environment, which together shape the development of an embodied self' (2011:177).

Despite the intensely embodied, sensory character of the social world of infants, prelinguistic children are nonetheless invited or even compelled to take up social identities. Whether or not we accept the view that infants have an embodied sense of self, or whether we are more convinced of a psychoanalytical account that insists that the infant does not relate to themselves as a coherent entity discrete from other things in the world, others do relate to the infant and the young child as already a social being in the sense of having a gender and belonging to a cultural group. How the infant will be held, comforted, spoken to, moved and dressed will in part respond to the individuality of the infant, but in good part the interaction between the people in the child's world and the child's body will be shaped by gendered and other cultural norms. There is little scope for agency here; the infant cannot conceptualize the cultural work that is being done when her ears are pierced or she is dressed in pink or spoken to softly and rocked gently while her brother may be spoken to loudly and held more confidently. Yet although the cultural work cannot be conceptualized, it works on and through the body and shapes the very muscle tone that the infant develops.

This understanding of the body as the site of subjectivity chimes with Merleau-Ponty's phenomenology (Welsh 2013). Malmqvist and Zeiler, in their paper on embodied being in the world and surgery on intersex infants, note that

> If we are bodily subjects, then subjectivity cannot be understood in terms of a pure and transparent consciousness, a transcendental 'for itself', set apart from and constituting its world as an 'in itself'. We are not primarily knowledge-subjects, and the world around us is not primarily a thought-about or represented world. For Merleau-Ponty,

our basic mode of being in the world is instead practical and prereflec-
tive. (2010: 137)

This is very important for understanding the developing subjectivity of
the child. If I am my body, then who am I, now an adult woman in relation to the 'I' who was an infant girl? If we are persuaded by an account
of subjectivity that takes seriously the body then we also have to also
take seriously the discontinuities between the body as it develops and
changes across the life course.

Changing bodies

Work on the body continues across the life course of the child. In my
own research on army cadets and their body work (Wells 2014), analysing the visual archive of army cadet meetings and training exercises, I
propose that working-class youth may be particularly intensely engaged
in body work. This is in contrast to Chris Shilling's claim that working-
class people think of their bodies as functional or instrumental, as
machine-like. He suggests that to think of the body as a project of self-
cultivation is a particularly middle-class orientation (2012:139). Yet for
working-class people, and perhaps especially for working-class teens
who have few financial resources, the body and its cultivation may be
the main resource that they have control over in projecting their sense
of self into the world. The army cadets and similar organizations give
working-class youth access to body training that will allow them to
project an embodied sense of self into public space (see Wolkowitz
2006:19). The uniform they wear is presented as a sign of the hardness
of the body beneath it, even when that hardness is itself not yet attained.

Menstruation

Much of the work on the body in Childhood Studies and cognate disciplines has been focused on the representational and discursive, including
some of my own contributions. The 'body's presence as a flesh and blood,
thinking, feeling, sentient, species being, a "body with organs" whose
very presence – moving, growing, changing over time – is generative of
a meaning potential to which both the self and others must respond, has
remained rather a shadowy presence' within the sociology of the body
(Evans, Davies and Rich 2016:178).

Girls' first menstruation is one such moment when the changing body
shifts the embodied sense of self in relation to subjectivity. A girl's first

menses often signals an abrupt end to her unambiguous belonging in childhood. For many girls the first period is an event full of shame, for others it is one of anticipation and excitement about becoming a woman, and for others simply an event on the life course – 'no big deal' to cite one of Janet Lee's respondents, whose matter-of-fact attitude to first menstruation was shared by 30 per cent (n = 47) of her sample of girls in the North West USA (Lee 2009:619). In her research on teen attitudes to menstruation, Fingerson (2005) uses the concept of 'body-agency' to capture the ways that girls experience menstruation as something done to them by their bodies. Her respondents used metaphors of being at war and attacked by their periods. At the same time, they expressed many of the same positive feelings about menstruation that Lee's respondents spoke of, particularly in relation to becoming adult and of menstruation as a sign of becoming a woman but also of belonging to a community of women (Jackson and Falmagne 2013). Interestingly, for both Lee's and Fingerson's respondents those girls who did not identity with a feminine self did not value menstruation precisely because it signified belonging to both an individual and a collective sense of womanhood (Fingerson 2005). Transboys have also spoken about the negativity of menstruation as a sign of womanhood that they have no desire to enter into.

Puberty and transgender children

Morgan and Stevens' (2012) narrative research with transgender male-to-female (mtf or m2f) adults identifies early body–mind dissonance as one of three central themes that emerge. Their participants recall very early memories, as young as age 3 or 4 years, of feeling that they were girls and cross-dressing in secret as a way of giving expression to this feeling. The embodied experiences of transgendered children and youth offer an important site for understanding the embodiment of gendered identities and the impossibility of feeling at home with gender norms for many people, both transgender and cisgender. In her paper based on interviews with two trans young men, Jayne Caudwell (2014) tries to get at how this embodied experience of transitioning impacts on her respondents' participation in sport and their being recognized as male. One of her respondents was an active footballer growing up but found that when he declared to his teammates (all girls) his intention to transition in his late teens they felt that he should leave the team. The main focus of Caudwell's paper, as this example highlights, is the difficulty for transgendered bodies of occupying space that is sorted on a gender binary, as it is in sport. Kjaran and Kristinsdóttir's research (2015) on sexualities and gendered bodies in Icelandic schools substantiates a related point: that transgendered youth are expected to deploy stereotypical embodied performances of masculinity or femininity to ground their claims to being male (for ftm or f2m) or female (mtf) youth. One of their respondents, a 19-year-old transgirl, explained that:

> You must have a particular look so people will take you as a transgender woman; accept you as a real woman in a way. I had to change my behaviour, behave in certain ways, to fit in, not be regarded differently. Actually, I am quite a boy inside me, not always behaving in feminine ways. I was brought up on a farm and used to help my parents with the farm work.... I am also active in all kinds of sports, playing football and taking part in paintball. This kind of behaviour is somehow not expected of me. I feel that people cannot grasp it, making them a bit confused. (2015:984, elision in the original)

In her research with twenty-four trans youth in Philadelphia, Sausa (2005) describes the violence that her respondents faced at school, including a boy who had his jaw broken by other students who attacked him with a baseball bat. The students who attacked him were not suspended from the school and the boy, Andrew, dropped out of school soon afterwards, as did three-quarters of Sausa's sample.

Conclusion

Children's changing bodily capacities affect how they experience the world. It is impossible to regard an infant without being aware of their intense vulnerability and dependency on others. The infant and child show very clearly how subject formation is not only about what presses on children from outside but also about relationships between the child and others, the others who care for them but also siblings, peers and even passing strangers. Through thinking about the child's changing body and their increasing capacities for movement and communication, it also seems difficult to maintain the idea that children have agency in the sense of a stable sense of self that is then given external expression in the demands made on others. By taking the body seriously as the site of subjectivity, an embodied subjectivity, we can attend to the specific vulnerabilities and affordances of children and be alert to the difference it makes to their subjectivity, to their experience of and relationship to wider social structures, that they are children and not adults.

8

Development Psychology and Social Identity Theory

Introduction

In the rest of this book I have, for the most part, been discussing how subject positions are pressed onto the child by the governing structures that permeate children's lives from the moment they enter the cultural imaginary, which is often many months before their birth. In chapter 3 on race, I explored through the example of child labour reform in the USA how racism excluded African-American children from the putative benefits of school education and separation from the labour market. The key governing actors here were white philanthropists and white trades unionists. In chapter 4, I showed how girls are harshly disciplined and indeed incarcerated for transgressing the boundaries of femininity, and how while white girls and boys were largely considered redeemable figures, black girls and boys were excluded from the presumption that underlies juvenile justice: that children's involvement with the law should aim for redemption and rehabilitation, not punishment. In these chapters I hinted at the possibility that racism and sexism not only positioned black children and girls as more or less (depending to what extent their exclusions were mitigated by other forms of inclusion) outside of the norms of a liberal, democratic polity but also shaped their sense of self, their interior lives, their psyches. In chapter 5 on class I began to push that idea further, in speaking of respect and recognition, how material exclusions can also feel like symbolic exclusions and how symbolic exclusions shape material exclusions but also shape a sense of self in children. Chapters 6 and 7, on disability and on the body, began to bring that discussion together to think about how the child's body, including their brain, shapes how children interiorize a sense of self or develop an understanding of themselves as particular kinds of subjects.

In this chapter I explore how development and social psychology theorize children's investments in social identities. Psychology as a discipline has a very different approach to the ones that I have drawn on in the writing of the other chapters. It is a discipline that largely takes for granted the existence of the identities that I have been troubling in the rest of the book, especially gender, and ethnicity or race. In general, psychology does not problematize these objects and ask how they came into existence, and it presumes that they can continue to exist without negative effect. This contrasts with my view, and that of many sociologists of race and gender, that racism produces race and sexism produces gender, not the other way around. This is not how psychologists, for the most part, conceptualize race and gender. They want to separate ingroup identity, including ethnic and gender group identity, from the governing structures that (in the view of sociologists) produce these identities.

In general, psychology views racism as a manifestation of a more generic tendency of humans to form themselves into groups and to draw the boundaries of their group partly in opposition to and hostility towards outgroups. Psychologists are interested in the individual motivations that underlie this tendency and less interested in understanding the wider structures that generate racism and sexism. For psychologists, racism or sexism are overgeneralized concepts that are not amenable to empirical testing. In contrast, racial or ethnic identification, negative evaluations and discrimination towards outgroups, and positive evaluations and rewards towards ingroups can be operationalized, tested and measured and the results repeated and generalized. Social psychologists on the whole find that the real-world conditions of racism and discrimination obscure their attempts to get at the underlying psychological processes involved in identifying with one group and being hostile to another. Therefore in psychology the real-world conditions are bracketed out and experiments are designed to establish the minimal conditions for ingroup identity and outgroup derogation. The universalism underlying the discipline of psychology also means that rather than speak of, say, white racism towards black people, psychologists prefer to speak of high-status and low-status groups and the differential effect of status on ingroup belonging and favouritism and outgroup evaluation.

The sub-field of psychology that focuses on children is development psychology. Yet this sub-discipline has played little part in Childhood Studies. Indeed, Childhood Studies partly formed its disciplinary boundaries in opposition to development psychology. Prior to the emergence of Childhood Studies, the two sub-disciplines that were primarily focused on children were development psychology and the sociology of socialization and the family. The exclusion of psychology from Childhood Studies was largely a matter of defining the boundaries of a new discipline by insisting that development psychology was asking fundamentally different kinds of questions and working with a different ontological and epistemological understanding of children and childhood from those of Childhood Studies. There will be mention of Piaget's research in most Childhood Studies textbooks, but only to dismiss him as imposing a universal model on childhood development that takes no account of the cultural context within which children learn. The Soviet psychologist Vygotsky is referenced in more positive terms, since his socio-cultural model of development explicitly acknowledges the role of experience in shaping children's knowledge and the importance of scaffolding between the child and an other to enable new concepts to be grasped, since they can be linked by the child with existing concepts in the child's repertoire.

Although the exclusion of psychology from Childhood Studies makes sense in many ways, it has left something of a gap in our understanding of the connections between cognitive structures and social understanding in children's lives. This chapter explores the contribution of social identity theory from social psychology and development psychology to our understanding of children's perception of their selves and their relationship to social categories, particularly gender and ethnicity, and the formation of prejudice.

There are some prominent exceptions to the general exclusion of psychologists from Childhood Studies. There are three psychologists who are regularly cited in Childhood Studies: Erica Burman, Valerie Walkerdine and Martin Woodhead. Of these three, only Woodhead is a development psychologist. He is Emeritus Professor of Childhood Studies at the Open University and was a member of the *Young Lives* team, a longitudinal study of childhood poverty. Erica Burman is a critical psychologist who has written on the connections between development psychology and Development Studies. Her most widely cited contributions to Childhood Studies are papers on visual representation and the psychic investments that viewers make in representations of 'appealing and appalling' children (Burman 1999). Valerie Walkerdine is also a critical psychologist and has published extensively on subjectivity and neo-liberal economies. Her work that has been taken up in Childhood Studies is in *Growing Up Girl: Psycho-Social Explorations of Gender and Class* (2001, with Helen Lucey and June Melody) and the highly influential volume *Changing the Subject: Psychology, Social Regulation and Subjectivity* (Henriques, Hollway, Urwin, Venn and Walkerdine 1998). All of these authors, with the exception of Martin Woodhead, are critical psychologists and psychosocial theorists; their work is therefore very different to both social psychology and development psychology, and it is probably for this reason that their work has found some purchase within Childhood Studies.

More surprising than the exclusion of child psychology from Childhood Studies is the separation within psychology between development psychology and social psychology. The former has taken as its object cognitive development and the task of establishing the contours of normal and abnormal intellectual development, as discussed in chapter 6, and takes the development of theory of mind as a core concept. The central paradigm of the latter in relation to subjectivity is social identity theory (SIT). SIT posits a hypothesis that humans are naturally predisposed to sort the social world into ingroups and outgroups, and many SIT experiments are interested in understanding what group formation means for people's sense of self in relation to the social. SIT has almost exclusively studied the formation of in/outgroups in adults and has not studied how it applies to, or is different for, children. Indeed, as recently as 2004b Mark Bennett and Fabio Sani could claim that development psychology and social psychology should consider the connections between these two sub-disciplines (implying that it had not yet done so). Beverly Tatum notes that development psychology has paid little attention to racial identity in children and suggests that this is because 'racial identity is not seen as salient for White adolescents' (2003:xv). However, although the broader field of social psychology had not had much cross-fertilization with development psychology, there have been important contributions by development psychologists to the development of SIT.

Social identity theory

Henri Tajfel at Bristol University, England, first formulated SIT in the early 1970s. He designed an experiment around the minimal conditions for identity formation, with the intention of subsequently adding variables until the conditions for group identity formation were found. The so-called minimal conditions experiment found that the conditions for group identity formation were very minimal indeed. Tajfel was surprised to find that group identity quickly cohered even when no social context was in play, when no personal relations existed between participants and their group members, and when participants did not materially benefit from their identification. Participants identified with the group they had been assigned to (the ingroup) and formed negative feelings towards the other group (the outgroup), and withheld resources from them.

The participants in this first study were schoolboys aged 14 to 15 years. In the first of two experiments, they were randomly allocated to one of four groups that they were told were based on their performance in estimating dots on a screen. In the second part of the experiment, they were then randomly sorted into two groups: a group that preferred the artist Klee and a group that preferred the artist Kandinsky. Each participant was then asked to allocate resources to the other participants, using a matrix to justify their decision. This was done in a cubicle so that none of the participants knew anything about any of the other participants. The aim of the experiment was to test the assumption held by previous studies that categorization had to be salient in the social environment for it to be meaningful to individuals.

In contrast to previous identification studies, Tajfel found that ingroup identification occurred even when there were no salient conditions present. He theorized on the basis of this that 'certain societies create, or contribute to, what might be called a "generic" outgroup attitude' (Tajfel 1970):

> [i]n other words, that norms, values and expectations present in their modes of socialization and education foster or reinforce a tendency to behave differentially towards outgroups and ingroups even when such behaviour has no 'utilitarian' value to the individual or to his group, and even when a particular categorization has very little meaning in terms of the emotional investment that it represents and in terms of differences between groups on which it is based. (Tajfel, Billig, Bundy and Flament 1971:151)

The results of the experiment showed that even in these minimal conditions subjects favoured the ingroup, even when no personal advantage accrued to the participant (since rewards were allocated to individuals in the group and not to the group as a whole). Numerous experiments since Tajfel have confirmed the findings of the minimal group experiment.

An additional finding of Tajfel's experiment was that 'another social norm, that of fairness, is also powerful in guiding their choices and that the pattern of data can best be understood as showing a strategy in which a compromise between these two norms is achieved whenever possible' (1971:174). This would seem to suggest that people want to think that their discriminatory behaviour towards the ingroup is based on some principle, rather than on unwarranted hostility or discrimination towards the outgroup. The role of fairness has not been investigated in subsequent social identity minimal group experiments.

It is important to note that, contrary to those who would argue that belonging to ingroups is constructed along so-called naturally occurring social differences (such as ethnicity or gender), the minimal group experiments suggests that the predisposition to connect ourselves with others may be innate but who the others are is not predetermined. It seems that humans want to connect with other people and will use almost any arbitrary basis to do so. This is evident in most people's daily lives. People routinely and often passionately attach themselves to arbitrary groups by mode of transport, workplace, neighbourhood geography, personal style, fandom and other circumstantial groupings. Children are routinely sorted into arbitrary groups, particularly at school where children are assigned to teams, classrooms and sets that they are then encouraged to identify with and to support. There may be little difference between one group and another, but nonetheless these artificial groups inspire a surprising amount of loyalty and commitment.

In fact, people are more identified with groups that they self-attach to than to groups that they are ascribed to (Ellemers, Kortekaas and Ouwerkerk 1999). So these arbitrary but self-selected groups might well generate more sense of identity than identities that are ascribed by others (such as race, gender, class).

One of the questions that is important for SIT is whether or not ingroup identification also involves hostility or negativity towards outgroups (what is known in SIT studies as 'outgroup derogation'). In principle it should be possible for someone to identify with one group while being neutral or even positive about another group. A few studies have used separate measures for ingroup and outgroup attitudes in children. These have found that outgroup derogation does not happen until about 12 years old. Diane Ruble and colleagues cite Brewer, who proposes that outgroup hostilities 'require additional social-structural and motivational conditions that are not inherent in the processes of group formation itself' (Brewer 2001:19 cited in Ruble et al. 2004:61). What these additional conditions are has been little explored in the SIT studies done with children, although recent studies, discussed in what follows, have started to investigate what they might be. The presumption is that family attitudes and school curricula will be significant influences on children's attitudes towards outgroups, in addition to media representation and status differences that are obvious in everyday life. Many SIT theorists propose that either threats or competition over resources are the preconditions for the emergence of outgroup derogation. Threats include real threats, perceived threats and stereotyped threats. The last of these refers to a perception of a threat that emerges from the stereotyped view that the ingroup has about the outgroup, a stereotype that may be based on racist discourse, including media representation.

Social identity theory and social context

Social identification does not only involve naming oneself or being named by others as part of a social category. It also involves feeling that the actions of others within that group somehow reflect on or are relevant to one's self-perception. An example of this might be a child who knows that they are 'British' because others have told them so, or perhaps they have seen their passport or completed a form, but it is unlikely to occur to them in early childhood, if ever, that Britishness might be relevant to how they are expected to behave. Or a child might know that they have the label 'girl' or 'boy' but in order to identify with this label they will have to attach actions and perceptions to it (we girls run, those boys walk). Sani and Bennett (2004) argue that in order to make the connection between labelling and self-perception children will seek out information about group norms and make personal choices about how to act within these norms.

In general, psychologists assume that labelling precedes identification, but some attempts to merge SIT and development theory rebut this assumption. Fabio Sani and Mark Bennett, for example, suggest that individual cognitive constructs are not necessarily the foundation of identity, which is rather more likely to be co-constructed between, as they put it, 'novice and elder' (2004a:87). They cite in support of this contention Jenkins' (1996) statement that 'if identity is a prerequisite for social life, the reverse is also true' (1996:40). In other words, the child's immersion in a social world is a necessary foundation for their construction of identity. It is within an immersive social world that identity is named and made salient.

Further support for the argument that ascription of identity and self-perception about identity are not necessarily congruent with one another is found in research that contrasts belonging in social groups with belonging in minimal condition groups (that is, the artificial groups formed for psychology experiments). Acceptance that one belongs to a particular social category will not necessarily translate into a feeling of commitment to that membership (Ellemers et al. 1999). A sense of belonging may range from being non-existent to contributing to a core sense of self. Displays of ingroup favouritism have not been 'consistently found as a consequence of mere categorization into natural groups (cf. Mullen, Brown, & Smith, 1992)' (Ellemers et al. 1999:372, comparative reference in the original). So although minimal group experiments have repeatedly found that ingroup favouritism quickly coheres, it cannot be presumed that this crosses over into the real world. We cannot therefore assume that, for children, ascription of identity automatically leads to that identity holding salience and meaning.

In Tajfel's original definition there are three elements of SIT, and these need to be separated out in order to trace the relationship between identity categories and ingroup attitudes. The three elements are cognitive, evaluative and emotional (Ellemers, Kortekaas and Ouwerkerk, 1999).

Cognition refers to the knowledge that one is attached to an identity label; evaluation refers to how this identity is evaluated, as good or bad; and emotion refers to the degree of affective connection to an identity. It is the third of these, affective or emotional commitment to an identity, that is assumed to be at the core of social identity if identity is to be understood as an active and salient part of self-concept.

In a study designed to test these three components it was found that people feel more committed to their membership of self-selected than assigned groups; commitment is higher for belonging in minority groups even if the minority group is low-status. Overall, the study found that, the strongest commitment is to high-status, self-selected, minority groups. Belonging to a minority (in the literal sense, of a small group) is, perhaps counter-intuitively, *more attractive* than belonging to a majority group. This is because minority group belonging offers more possibility for coherence between the individual self and the collective self. It is therefore important to assess affective belonging for understanding the formation of social identity, and to make 'a fundamental distinction' (Ellemers et al. 1999:374) between membership of assigned and self-selected groups.

In empirical studies, people in low-status groups have been found to have less ingroup identification than those in high-status groups. However, the link between self-esteem and group identification is contradictory. Not identifying with a group emotionally, even though you acknowledge that most people will label you as being part of that group, does not predict low self-esteem. This may be because there an evaluative component (low social status) has been confounded in analysis with both an affective and a cognitive component (Ellemers et al. 1999).

The presumption of SIT is that members of an ingroup derive self-esteem benefits from belonging to and valuing the group they identify with (with some SIT theorists assessing these as two separate elements of identity, as I have just mentioned). Although this may make sense in minimal condition experiments, it does not necessarily make sense in real-world conditions. If the ingroup has low social status, how can belonging to it contribute to high self-esteem? In general, and again perhaps counter-intuitively, 'low-status groups show heightened in-group favouritism' (Powlishta 2012:118). Both girls and boys show a preference for the company of others of the same gender; being low-status does not lead girls to prefer the company of boys.

In general, outgroup deviants may be liked better than ingroup deviants even if both deviants share the same behaviours and attitudes. This suggests that it is not the norms themselves that children are necessarily invested in, but that ingroup members share practices. So we could imagine that the norms of group A might be that they like dancing; if one of group A does not like dancing they will be disliked for threatening the cohesion of the group. A member of group B who also does not like dancing has no bearing on the boundaries of group A unless dancing is its core or defining practice.

People have a stronger commitment to the group when they belong to minority groups than to majority groups. Children are themselves a (status and numerical) minority group in many communities in the affluent world. We might expect, then, that to belong to an ingroup 'children', although an ascribed identity, might also generate a strong sense of emotional commitment. Similarly, black and ethnic minority children in predominantly white societies might be expected to have a strong attachment to the ascribed but minority group status, while majority group children would be expected to have weak attachment to their white group membership.

On the other hand, attachment to minority group membership might be countered by the evaluation that a group has low status. We know that children are aware by about the age of 3 or 4 years that being white in a majority white, racist society has more status than being black or from another ethnic minority. So although a black child might know that they are black (cognitive categorization), they might evaluate their group negatively or positively, and they might or might not feel an emotional connection to their group. This could account for why in the famous doll studies (Clark and Clark 1958), black children who know they are black say that the 'white' doll is the one most similar to them and that they like the most. This hypothesis is confirmed by some of the studies I discuss later in this chapter.

Gender

In contrast to, say, identifying with a nation or an ethnic group, which are fairly abstract concepts, probably even for many adults, gender identification is commonly assumed to go deep even, or perhaps especially, for children. Numerous studies have shown that children as young as 2 years of age understand that people have a gender and can consistently identify which gender category both adults and children would generally be assigned to. Some studies have suggested that even infants recognize gender. These studies involve showing infants portrait photographs of adults of different genders. Once a pattern is established (say, several photos of women are shown to the infant) the child loses interest until an image of another gender is shown to them.

However, it seems unwarranted to assume that this facility is recognizing gender. It seems more plausible to suggest that what infants see is make-up or beards or un/plucked eyebrows etc. In a similar way when infants respond to a novel voice, if that voice is a woman's when previously they were played men's voices, it is not gender they hear but high or low tonality. Infants simply do not have the cognitive structure to be able to organize characteristics into social body schemas, such as gender.

There are no social psychology studies that I am aware of that consider how children conceptualize people who are/or present as gender-ambiguous. In recent years, at least in the UK and the USA, some young people have rejected gendered labels, referring to themselves as gender non-binary, gender-queer or gender-fluid and using gender-neutral pronouns, such as 'they'. Since these young people articulate their challenge to gender norms in explicitly political ways, appealing to both feminist and queer critiques of gender norms, their conceptualization has not been dismissed as cognitive failure in the way that it might be if it were articulated by younger children. The recent emergence of an active trans-advocacy movement has further challenged a binary conception of gender and the social identities that children and young people recognize, evaluate and connect with. Increasingly, young children's claims to being gender non-binary or transgendered are being accepted by parents and psychologists.

One of the key concepts of gender identity theory within social development psychology is 'constancy'. This is used to mean that children understand both how to allocate a gender to another person or to themselves and that their gender cannot change. Notwithstanding the challenges to gender binaries that I have just mentioned, gender constancy is a useful concept because it helps us to understand why young children often seem to be extraordinarily vigilant about policing gender borders.

In a great example of how psychology fails to problematize gender, in her chapter in Bennett and Sani's *The Development of the Social Self* Kimberley Powlishta claims that the biological difference between 'males and females is perceptually salient. Actual differences between the sexes make gender groupings useful for predicting and monitoring behaviour [the benefit of group categorization]. By definition, males and females play different roles in reproduction. Sex also is a stable, dichotomous, exhaustive, biological, "natural kind" basis for categorisation' (2012:106). This view, I think, is fairly typical of how many people think about gender, as a 'natural kind'; although recent awareness of transgendered individuals may have shifted the common-sense conviction that sex is 'stable, dichotomous, exhaustive, biological'. The fact that 'males and females play different roles in reproduction' is visible to children in that they see women being pregnant, but whether from the women they know who have been pregnant they then theorize that pregnancy defines womanhood seems like quite a cognitive leap. Further, since girls are children (and therefore are not women and cannot reproduce), it is not obvious that they can connect their own identity as girls to adult identities as women. It is also evident that young children often predict (indeed, police) the behaviour of girls and boys and men and women on the basis of their stereotyped knowledge of gender rather than their actual experience in the world.

Young children often display a strong commitment to policing or regularizing the gender behaviours of others, both adults and children. This often mystifies their parents, especially feminist parents, who then reach for theories of innate difference between boys and girls that they had long abandoned to explain why their son is obsessed with trucks and their daughter with dolls. Psychology studies of gender suggest that the explanation is more social than biological. To rehearse the rest of this section, psychological theories of gender identity formation in children suggest that children are aware from a young age that gender is a socially salient category; they are also aware that girls/women are a low-status and boys/men are a high-status group; what they do not know until about the age of 7 years is that their gender cannot change (but see earlier in this section for a discussion on transgendered children and changing gender and on the acquisition of gender constancy). Boys and girls have been told they belong to a group (ascribed social identity) and they then evaluate what it means to belong to the group by identifying group norms (not just parental norms, but the norms of their peer group and wider society). They know from the constant talk about gender that it is highly salient and that not meeting gender norms is considered wrong, but it also takes a while to understand what it signifies to call someone a boy or a girl. The social meaning of these concepts is hard work, not least because it is so arbitrary and far from 'stable, dichotomous, exhaustive'. In addition, before they understand gender constancy, children believe that they can change their gender. For boys this would mean exchanging membership of a high-status group for that of a low-status group. It is hardly surprising, then, that boys are often such enthusiastic gender police.

Psychologists mostly understand children's acquisition of gender identity within the frame of social learning theory and cognitive development theory. Social learning theory has a much more passive view of the child's role in gender socialization than cognitive learning theory does. Social learning theory is derived from Bandura's adaptation of Skinner's behaviourist theories. It says that gender identity is an outcome of social learning (children model their behaviour on similar others). Cognitive development theory, developed out of Kohlberg's theory of moral development (Kohlberg 1981), says that once children grasp that gender does not change (the development of constancy, already mentioned) they fill the label with gender norms.

Discussing the 'gender wars' of the primary school years, Barbara David and colleagues (2012) point out that parents, media and material culture constantly present gender as being a salient category. These writers suggest that this needs to be accounted for within a theory of gender identity, and they propose that social category theory is a useful theoretical framework for integrating gender identity and social norms. They propose that the self is not a 'stable construct' that has a domain within which gender knowledge accumulates and comes to constitute a stable, unitary gender identity. Rather, they suggest that the self is 'a labile, context-dependent process' (David, Grace and Ryan 2012:149) rather than a structure. They derive this view from the self-categorization theory that was developed out of SIT. For David and colleagues the self should be conceptualized as 'whatever an individual means when, at any time, they call themselves or think of themselves as "I", "me", "us", or "we"'. For social categorization theory the self is 'only what is brought into consciousness at any particular time' (2012:142) together with all one's knowledge, memories and understandings.

David and colleagues propose that although gender is highly salient for young children, they do not have the cognitive abilities to understand the complex work involved in attaching a sense of self to the label 'girl' or 'boy'. These authors point out that, without strictly reproducing Piaget's stages of development, there is abundant evidence that suggests that children 'are not born with fully developed cognitive skills and capacities' and that they 'deal with simple and concrete processes before complex and abstract ones' (David et al. 2012:146).

We know from ethnographic studies of gender in schools (Connolly 1998, Thorne 1993) that the daily practices of school constantly make gender salient, from making children line up in boys' lines and girls' lines, to dividing sports by gender, to having different uniforms for boys and girls, and so on. We also know from children's talk about gender that they recognize its importance from early on and that they can evaluate the relative status of being identified as a boy or a girl.

For children who recognize gender (cognitive identity) and believe that their gender cannot change (have acquired constancy), there is some evidence that simply labelling an otherwise gender-neutral activity (say, playing cards) as appropriate for one gender (say, boys) leads to dis/identification and un/improved performance for the in/appropriate child. So, in this example girls who like playing cards on being told that this is a boys' activity would cease to show interest in it and their performance would deteriorate or at least not improve (see Martin and Dinella 2002). Stereotyped knowledge influences behaviour and preferences, and one longitudinal study found that knowledge predicted behaviour one year later (Ruble et al. 2004:58 citing Aubry, Ruble and Silverman 1999). Consistent with that study is the finding that although young children use category membership (I am a boy/I am a girl) to define which groups they belong to and which groups they do not belong to, this does not involve adhering to stereotyped norms until they are about 8 years of age.

Several school ethnographies would contest the view that gender does not become fully or affectively salient until around the age of 7 or 8 years. However, the ethnographies may be focused on the speech rather than other actions of young children. It may be that children's discourse is stereotyped but their behaviour is not; for example, a boy might say that girls cannot play football, while actually playing football with a girl. Until they are about 5 years of age children tend to think of behaviour in terms of actions (girls walk, boys run) and disposition (e.g. girls are nice, boys are mean), with belief (say, girls walk and are nice because they believe it is important to be calm) not becoming important until middle childhood. This suggests that, as chapter 7 on the body discussed, younger children's ideas about the world are grounded in embodied practice that is also temporally and spatially bound, with a sense that these are outward manifestations of an interior state not becoming prominent in children's thinking/feeling until middle childhood. So there is a discrepancy or dissonance between how children talk about social identity and how they perform social identity until they have the cognitive resources to manage the complex work of social identity.

Outgroups and racism

Development psychology, recognizing the importance of understanding how children come to identify with an 'ingroup' and how this correlates with negative outgroup identification, has developed several theoretical paradigms to account for intergroup interactions in children, including socio-cognitive theory (SCT) (Aboud 1988), developmental intergroup theory (Bigler and Liben 2007), subjective group dynamics (Abrams, Rutland and Cameron 2003) and social identity development theory (SIDT; Nesdale 2004). The most influential of these have been SCT, developed by Frances Aboud, and SIDT, developed by Drew Nesdale.

The SIT and SIDT research on ethnicity, race and identification can be broadly divided into two related categories: the impact of ingroup identification on self-esteem, particularly of ethnic minority children; and the development of negativity (hostility, derogation, prejudice) towards outgroups, particularly on the part of white children in the USA, UK and Australia, where most social identity studies have been conducted. In what follows I start by discussing the formation of prejudice in children and then the significance of belonging for low-status ethnic groups.

Social cognitive theory (SCT) proposes that the development of prejudice is connected to cognitive development. SCT draws on Piaget's cognitive development stages and Kohlberg's moral development stages to argue that although young children are aware of ethnic identity, they do not have the cognitive development necessary to form prejudice against others on the basis of identity. In the early years they will attach little or no significance to physiological differences such as skin colour and hair texture that are invested with significance in the wider society. In the concrete operational stage they are more likely to be prejudiced, and prejudice will increase during this stage and subsequently decrease as they develop their capacities for intellectual reasoning congruent with Piaget's formal operational stage. SCT therefore predicts that, other things being equal (which of course, they are not), prejudice will decline from about the age of 10 to 11 years old. Aboud's 1988 study, *Children and Prejudice*, which set out this argument, is widely cited. It argued that children identify with a racial ingroup around the age of 3 years, and that the significance of this increases with age, involves prejudice against the outgroup and then declines into adolescence.

The cognitive basis of prejudice as following Piaget's stages of development is challenged by empirical research that shows that children do not always lose their outgroup prejudice, and in fact it may even increase (Nesdale 2001a, 2001b:197). Drew Nesdale's SIDT, in contrast to SCT, says that ingroup identification and outgroup evaluation can be predicted by social norms and, as SIT is established, by the existence or absence of threats or competition for resources from the outgroup. SIDT therefore builds on SIT specifically in relation to how cognitive development affects the internalization of social norms. Although it accepts that there are developmental changes in how children process social norms, these do not map onto Piaget's schema. SIDT also rejects the theory, posited by SCT, that prejudice is an inevitable aspect of development. The four stages in the development of prejudice according to SIDT are: undifferentiation, ethnic awareness (age 4–5 years), ethnic differentiation (age 5–6 years) and then prejudice (in some children) around the age of 7 years.

Essentially, Aboud's SCT presumes that children get more individualistic as they develop, and Nesdale's SIDT presumes that they become increasingly aware of communal norms. The paper by Nesdale, Lawson, Durkin and Duffy (2010) on their experimental research was intended to test whether change in cognitive function predicts change in attitudes towards ingroup and outgroups, and challenged Aboud's SCT theory. However, although the intention was to test ingroup and outgroup attitudes and the development of ethnic prejudice in children, all of the participants were white, as were all of the images of other children (in the imaginary outgroup).

Although many social scientists would certainly be persuaded by Nesdale's claim that prejudice is not an effect of immature cognition but a response to increasing awareness of communal norms, social scientists would insist on the importance of understanding social interaction in context. In a study in 2005, Nesdale and colleagues address this problem directly (Nesdale, Durkin, Maas and Griffiths 2005) by designing a study in which the ingroup were (as usual) white children but the outgroup were either Pacific Islanders or other white Australian children (so that a comparison could be made about how ethnic identification shaped attitudes to outgroups) rather than arbitrary or minimal condition outgroups. The effects were modest, but confirmed SIDT's prediction that children (like adults) will always favour their ingroup but will not necessarily dislike the outgroup unless they are a threat to the ingroup's standing (in this experiment because the outgroup did not think the ingroup were better at drawing than the outgroup were). However, it also confirmed SCT's findings that cognitive development does impact the formation of prejudice. The threat from the outgroup was more important than their ethnicity in whether the ingroup disliked them. So when the ingroup were told that the outgroup of white Australians thought that they were as good as the ingroup at drawing but the Pacific Islander outgroup did not think they were as good at drawing, then the ingroup would dislike the white Australian outgroup more than the Pacific Islander outgroup. The only effect of ethnicity was on whether a child would elect to join a group of a different ethnicity or the same ethnicity if they left their ingroup. Subsequent research by Nesdale and colleagues (Durkin, Nesdale, Dempsey and McLean, 2012, McGuire, Rutland and Nesdale 2015) supported the contention that norms shaped children's intergroup attitudes and the low salience of ethnicity and high salience of threat in determining ingroup attitudes towards the outgroup. In a study designed to test the impact of media on intergroup attitudes in children, white Scottish children viewed one set of PowerPoint images of Scottish people as white only and another set of images as ethnically diverse. The group who were shown only white images liked the white outgroup more than the multi-ethnic outgroup and the group who had viewed images of Scottish as ethnically diverse liked the multi-ethnic outgroup more than the white group. The point here is that Scottishness forms the parameter of the ingroup and that media have an important role to play in defining national belonging (Durkin et al. 2012).

As Verkuyten (2003) notes, research designs on ingroup bias have tended to use artificial or minimal groups. Even in Nesdale's response to this issue, he chose to use Pacific Islanders as the outgroup to the white Australian ingroup because although they were recognisable in the testing phase as an ethnic group to white children, there was not a strong history of hostility towards Pacific Islanders from white Australians. In other words, the research designs are attempting to develop a kind of abstract model of the development of ingroup ethnic identification and outgroup hostility. Verkuyten sought to address these problems in a study on the effects of a multicultural curriculum on white Dutch and Turkish-Dutch children's assessment of negative behaviours by ingroup and outgroup perpetrators. The study involved 1,593 white Dutch and 598 Turkish-Dutch children in a large cross-section of Netherlands primary schools. Dutch primary schools have been legally required since 1985 to provide a multicultural programme intended to promote positive interaction between ethnic groups and to combat racism and discrimination. Verkuyten's research design aimed to examine the impact of multicultural education on ethnic identification and assessment of ethnic victimization. The design involved children reading four brief stories that involved a child with a classic Dutch or Turkish name telling another child that he or she could not play a game or share a valued object. The implication of the story was that the excluded child was being victimized because of their ethnic identity. The study found that a multicultural curriculum led white Dutch children to assess ethnic victimization of Turkish children negatively. Counter-intuitively, the study also found that children who had experienced ethnic victimization themselves were *less* negative about the perpetrator in the negative story-line than children who had not experienced racist victimization.

Research on self-esteem in ethnic minority children, particularly African-American children, has made important contributions to the legal and policy landscape and to 'common-sense' knowledge about the impacts of racism on children's self-esteem. The studies by Kenneth Clark and Mamie Clark that contributed to the overturning of school segregation in the USA through their expert witness statements to the 1954 case of *Brown v. Board of Education of Topeka* suggest that black children had low self-esteem (Clark and Clark 1958; see Bergner 2009:299). However, since the Clarks were engaged in a politically important strategy to overturn racist laws in the USA it was not of interest to them to investigate separately identification and self-esteem. Other studies have shown that African-American children do not have low self-esteem even when they have negative ingroup evaluation. This may suggest, SIT theorists propose, that identification with a low-status group may lead children to use different criteria to evaluate themselves as individuals and their group. There is also some research that shows that parents' strategies to protect black children's self-esteem and evaluation of themselves and African-Americans as a group against racist threats are often successful, for example by emphasizing the achievements of African culture and of Africans and African-Americans and/or by rejecting the capacity of racists to evaluate black children. Of these two strategies, referred to in the literature as 'racial socialization', parents are more likely to deploy the first (cultural socialization), perhaps concerned that the second (preparation for bias) might upset their children (Hughes 2003; see also Quintana et al. 2006).

A study in the UK (Davis, Leman and Barrett 2007) set out to investigate the relationship between self-esteem, ingroup identification, outgroup negativity and stereotyping. A group of black and white children aged 5, 7 and 9 years completed tasks designed to measure implicit and explicit attitudes, stereotyping and identification of ingroups and outgroups on skin colour and ancestral country. They found that white children did not identify with whiteness and colour could not be used as a basis for ingroup identification with white children. Black characters in the tasks were stereotyped more by black children than by white children in both the implicit and the explicit tasks. At the same time black children's self-esteem scores were comparable to those of white children, suggesting, as other studies have found, that in a racist society black children may separate out ingroup evaluation from personal self-esteem. The study also points to the weakness of the empirical basis of SIDT and SIT, discussed in this chapter, which is that most studies evaluate the attitudes and motivations of ingroup identification of white ethnic majority groups.

Conclusion

SIT, at the point where it meets development psychology, suggests some answers to the question of how children come to understand themselves in relation to social structures such as gender and ethnicity. Certainly, the scientific approach of psychology, which wants to be able to make general predictions about the relationship between the mind or brain and actions and behaviour, is deeply problematic when it comes to understanding what difference it makes to be a boy or a girl, or from an ethnic minority or majority. The conceptualization of identity around 'minimal groups', 'ingroups' and 'outgroups' brackets out some of the most important features of group formation. Specifically, it sets aside the relationship of group formation, evaluation and identity to broader structures of power. In the last ten years or so, development psychologists have paid more attention to these wider structures and to what difference it makes if the ingroup is a low-status group or a high-status group in the wider society. Development psychology has started to consider how ethnic minority children's psychological resilience can be protected in a racist society and to understand empirically how parents and children have sought to protect their self-esteem in the face of racist assessments of the group they are ascribed to. The empirical experimental and survey data that psychology relies on does have some key advantages over other forms of data on the effects of racism and sexism on the internal worlds of children. The ability to replicate experiments and survey instruments means that findings can be tested. For many psychologists the more fuzzy methods of qualitative sociology and anthropology offer little more rigour than anecdote. For some psychologists the acknowledgement that humans are social beings and we attach ourselves to groups does not necessitate the acceptance that racism and sexism are ahistorical, permanent features of human society. Indeed, SIT does not assume that ingroup identification automatically leads to outgroup derogation, and SIDT explicitly rejects the argument that prejudice is an effect of cognitive development, but rather insists that the social context in which children are living will affect how they conceptualize the relationship of ingroups to outgroups.

When Judith Butler (1999:25) claims, following Nietzsche, that there is no 'doer behind the deed' of subject formation, social development psychology suggests otherwise. Children do develop a sense of themselves and others well before they are able to conceptualize social identity. That this self is labile and changing is not at all resisted by at least some strands of development psychology, as we have seen in this chapter. Some rapprochement between Childhood Studies and development psychology seems like a necessary move now if we are to be able to interrogate with some degree of rigour how children come to understand themselves as social subjects.

9

Consuming Childhoods

Introduction

Despite the fact that we think of children as outside of the economy they are in fact deeply involved in it, although increasingly, even on a global scale, more as consumers than producers. Of course most of this consumption gets done for them by their families but that makes it no less significant for understanding how the material world shapes childhood, what resources it offers children for understanding the social world, and how it enables children to be legible social subjects. Dan Cook (2013), in 'Taking Exception with the Child Consumer', argues that consumption has been left out of Childhood Studies because the agential consuming-desiring child is seen as frivolous and as engaging in forms of agency that do not speak to the core agenda of Childhood Studies. There has more generally been a 'notable lack of interest in the symbolic meanings that people, whether adult or child, create around the goods and services they consume' (Martens, Scott and Southerton 2004:193). This chapter aims to take the consuming child seriously and to understand their consumption practices as resources with which they perform and constitute their identities. I analyse how children use material objects and visual representation to explore and perform their social identities.

Children's consumption practices and their aesthetic

Children's consumption practices must be more broadly conceived than the buying of commodities, or the appropriation or remaking of commodities. Children in general, and working-class children in particular, have less access to financial resources than adults do, and this necessarily has implications for their consumption practices. Their separation from employment and, largely as a consequence of this separation, their detachment from decision-making in the household economy mean that children have less economic resources than the adults who share their social world.

If children have less financial resources than the adults who provide for them, this does not mean, of course, that adults have unlimited resources to meet children's consumption desires. The importance of commodities to the presentation of the self, particularly in the Global North, puts particular pressure on working-class families. The sociology of consumption has mainly focused on middle-class lives, but a handful of scholars have explored how poor families in the USA manage their children's involvement in consumer culture. Nonetheless, it is still the case that '[d]espite all the valuable insights gained by a focus on the "production" of children's consumption, relatively little is known about how children engage in practices of consumption or what the significance of this is to their everyday lives and broader issues of social organization' (Martens et al. 2004:161).

An important exception to the lack of academic research on children's consumption is Elizabeth Chin's *Purchasing Power* (2001), whose title invokes how practices of consumption are inseparable from the operations of power. It is an ethnographic study of the consumption practices of poor black children in a small town in the USA. One of her research methods was to give her young participants $20 to spend in the shopping mall. She found that almost all the girls used this money to buy presents for their families, including new shoes. She comments that '[g]ift-giving was a powerful way for children to strengthen, transform, or maintain relationships with those around them' (2001:139). Gift-giving is an intensely social activity that creates webs of obligation between giver and recipient. It is interesting that these children, by using money gifted to them by the ethnographer, then gifted this money back to their families, including their mothers, in commodity form. In doing so they, intentionally or otherwise, created a tie between someone with social capital and financial resources (the ethnographer) and the adults in their lives.

In the example discussed in the previous paragraph, the ethnographer, Elizabeth Chin, gave the children resources so that she could understand what they would do when shopping. For the most part the children in her ethnography did not have resources to go shopping for non-essential commodities. Instead they participated in the work of consumption through bricolage, appropriation and fantasy. This theme of making do but still participating in the symbolic work of consumption is central to another ethnography of children's consumption, Alison Pugh's *Longing and Belonging* (2009). Pugh's respondents were not all working-class, since she wanted to compare working-class and middle-class families' consumption practices and also understand how culture worked across class to shape consumption. Her argument is that consumption is a form of *scrip* that enables people to project themselves into social space and demand recognition, or belonging. For poor working-class families the scope for buying toys or participating in gifting and in social rituals was extremely constrained. Children managed these constraints, Pugh shows, through strategies of fantasy or story-telling, bricolage and appropriation.

Both Pugh and Chin show that children in a consumer-orientated society such as the USA are extremely alert to the social significance of objects. In a study of children's marketing, *Born to Buy*, Judith Schor (2004) demonstrates that this alertness to consumer objects is in part a consequence of marketing strategies. Advertisers, who recognize that children increasingly mobilize household purchases, at least in middle-class US families, target children, using their access to schools (for example in tie-ins with educational software and hardware) to do so, in addition to advertising on children's television. In 2004, for example, about \$15 billion were spent on adverts to children (2004:21). Through this saturation of children's media environments, children have high brand recognition. By the age of 18 months children can recognize logos, and by the age of 6 years they can name 200 brands. Four companies monopolize children's media entertainment market: Disney, Viacom (who own Nickelodeon), Fox and Time Warner. Mattel and Hasbro dominate the toy market, and Sony and Microsoft dominate the games market. It is interesting that the focus of Childhood Studies on the agential child is shared by the advertising industry, which wants to transform 'children into autonomous and empowered consumers ... Today, marketers create direct connections to kids, in isolation from parents and at times against them. The new norm is that kids and marketers join forces to convince adults to spend money' (Schor 2004:17). Advertisers also make use of the ethnographic methods widely used in the sociology of childhood, including focus groups and participant observation; for example, the Girls Intelligence Agency, a marketing research organization, recruits girls for slumber parties both to sell product and to gather market intelligence.

Although we tend to think of children's consumption as being the purchase by or for children of children's commodities, such as toys, games and children's media, children also go shopping for household goods, especially for food, either with or without their parents. The basic presumption of consumer behaviour research is that parents make rational (that is, economic cost–benefit analysis) decisions about their household purchases and that children are irrational, in this economic sense; as Childhood Studies scholars will be aware, neither presumption is safe. Indeed, in her study Chin described how children carefully calculate the value for money of their spending decisions. Others have argued that the separation between rationality and emotion is not so clear-cut and that 'rationality and emotionality can coexist in consumption activities' (Gram 2010:394, citing Hamilton and Catterall 2006).

The beginning of research on children as consumers has been dated to the publication in 1974 of Scott Ward's paper 'Consumer Socialization' in the *Journal of Consumer Research*. Deborah Roeder John's paper (1999) in the same journal reviewing twenty-five years of research on children's consumer socialization takes for granted the kind of age-related stages of development that Childhood Studies contests. The review summarizes the key literature on consumer research with children. Of particular interest for this book is the evidence that children develop quite early on (around age 11 years) a strong sense of the social-symbolic meaning of products and brands. As early as US second grade (UK year 3), children make inferences about people's characters based on their ownership of products, suggesting that, as with gender and race, the social significance of class is understood at a young age. Unsurprisingly, given their understanding that products are linked to prestige, children use products to indicate group identity and belonging. Clothing is a particularly important product for identifying membership of subgroups (John 1999:194).

In 2005 I conducted a study of children's understanding of consumption, specifically how they understood or read the shop signs and commodities in their neighbourhood in relation to the social-spatial character of the area (Wells 2007c). The research was conducted in a neighbourhood in south London that has long been identified with post-war immigration from the Caribbean, specifically Jamaica. In this neighbourhood the local government, sometimes in response to calls for recognition made by activists in the black community or by black artists and intellectuals, has commemorated the flows of people and politics between Africa, the Caribbean and Britain. In addition to two monuments to the struggle against Apartheid in South Africa, the town centre square had recently been landscaped and renamed 'Windrush Square' to commemorate the docking of the *Empire Windrush*, that icon of post-war Caribbean settlement in Britain, in London in 1948. Reflecting the demographic and post-war history of the neighbourhood, the large indoor market that is the commercial hub of the neighbourhood sold, at that time, mostly goods imported from Africa and the Caribbean, including groceries, clothes, music, videos and religious artefacts. A recently growing Latina/o population was reflected in the development of a few Colombian and

Brazilian cafés and shops. The main street that runs through Brixton, and from which the indoor market is entirely concealed, had a number of major high street stores including McDonalds, KFC, Sainsbury's, The Body Shop and WH Smith.

The research involved ten year 6 (USA grade 5) students who attended one of the primary schools closest to central Brixton. During the school day we went to Brixton with a digital camera and took photographs of places that the participants felt reflected the neighbourhood identity and would be used in subsequent focus groups that they were to conduct with year 7 (US grade 6) students on the theme of 'what Brixton means to me'. This was followed by focus groups, three of which were conducted by two of the participants who took part in the photography walk, and one of which I conducted. During the trip the students chose to take photographs of shops that I felt were not all distinctive of Brixton. My assumption was that the indoor market would be thought of as a space that was characteristic of Brixton and therefore would be where most photographs would be taken. In fact, the participants were most interested in spaces that were unmarked. For example, on both trips a good ten minutes were spent discussing whether or not we should include pictures of the supermarket, Tesco. Several participants wanted to go inside the supermarket and photograph the aisles. Although Tesco in Brixton stocks a variety of Indian, African and Caribbean groceries, none of the participants commented on these. The pleasure they took in displaying to me and to each other how well they knew the layout of the store seemed to be precisely in demonstrating their familiarity with something that was not distinctively attached to a Brixton identity. Similarly, they wanted to be photographed outside KFC and McDonalds and spoke in the most abject terms about smaller cafés serving Caribbean and Ethiopian food. In the subsequent focus groups, in response to the question 'How would you describe Brixton to someone who had never been there?', respondents said it was 'nasty', 'busy, dangerous and noisy'. Despite this way of talking about their neighbourhood, on the photography field trip all the children appeared to be quite proud of their knowledge of the area and confident of their occupation of space. They were loud and boisterous. They took up a lot of space on the street and were happy to go into shops by themselves to ask permission of the owners to take photographs. When they encountered people who were drunk (one of the negative points made in focus groups), they displayed a voyeuristic interest, rather than seeming frightened or anxious. This difference between talk and action might be accounted for by the difference between embodied engagement with space and discourse about space, the latter drawing more on media depictions, adult talk and knowledge that outsiders do (or did then) view Brixton as a dangerous space.

What was also evident from the focus groups was that these young participants did not easily read the signs and brands that shops and advertisers use to signify the social symbolism of their products. The unintelligibility of colours and typography as signifiers of place to these participants meant that they could not easily distinguish African from Caribbean stores or, indeed, Ethiopian from Chinese stores (they assumed that all non-Roman script was Chinese and therefore thought that the Ethiopian restaurant, which has Amharic signs on the window, was a Chinese restaurant). Even the naming of the central square as 'Windrush' was lost on these students, many of them the children and grandchildren of Caribbean settlers who were part of the 'Windrush generation'. None of them knew the significance of the name and one suggested, creatively, that it must be called wind-rush because it was an open space and the 'wind rushed through it'.

Shopping and pleasure

Children's unfamiliarity with shopping and the symbolism of shop signs and street names may indicate the exclusion of children from these activities. They may go to the shops on behalf of their parents but they do not 'do the shopping'. In general, the consumption decisions involved in 'doing the shopping' are made by adults, especially when money is constrained. When commodities are bought the child is often not involved in the purchase, either because it is a gift or because they have not taken notice of the financial transaction. In this way, the cost of goods is hidden from the child's view, and the relationship of this cost to other dimensions of the household economy and the wider economy of production is obscured. When children do go shopping on their own behalf, making their own consumption decisions, perhaps spending pocket-money and other gifts, they are in a world of pleasure-seeking. Even when children work for wages, several research studies have shown that they use the money earned, in part, to buy themselves non-essential goods and for the pleasure of consumption. This is the Romantic ethic which Campbell (2005) argues moves along the 'spirit of consumerism'.

The concept of the Romantic ethic is very useful as a description of the idealization of the commodity that characterizes consumption in late modernity. This idealization is accomplished by imbuing commodities, partly through advertising strategies, with the sensual experiences of profoundly pleasurable social moments such as sex, childbirth, parenting, love and friendship. This idealization of the commodity is not limited, of course, to children's consumption. What is distinctive about children's consumption practices, when they are consuming on their own behalf, is that they are *saturated* in the Romantic ethic of hedonistic pleasure-seeking, almost to the exclusion of other dimensions of use-value. The pleasure that children take in hyperreal, idealized and utopian images and objects is evident in the children's market for highly coloured, other-worldly fantasy toys such as My Little Pony, Barbie, the Tweenies or Teletubbies, or television programmes such as *In the Night Garden*; films, videos and PlayStation games directed at child consumers are also marked by unreal and hyperreal images and colours, the easy identification of moral dilemmas and their satisfactory resolution (Seiter 1993).

Children are not themselves involved in the production of the commodities they want to buy, and the extent to which these represent children's culture may be questioned. However, I would concur with Miller's (1995) argument that while the production of goods is not simply a response to consumers' desire, neither can it be seen as simply the effect of advertising strategies. Discussing James' (1979) account of children's own purchases of 'inedible' sweets (strong, artificial colours, modelled on insects, corpses, blood, etc.), Miller comments that these desires reflect 'the emergence, over a considerable period of time of a children's culture' (1995:168). With the development of ethnographic research into children's consumption, we can see children's cultural practices being repackaged as commodities and sold back to them (or their parents). In *Born to Buy*, Schor (2004) recounts how an ethnographic study of children's bath time led to the development of a highly profitable line of shampoo packaged in children's toys which was inspired by children playing with empty household bottles at bath time.

While toys, videos, films and PlayStation games form a core part of children's consumption worlds, children's consumption practices are much broader than buying goods. Other dimensions of buying – choosing, comparison, social/peer advice, knowledge of what counts as 'cultural capital' – may all be brought into play without objects being purchased. If 'What happens to material objects once they have left the retail outlet … is part of the consumption process' (Douglas and Isherwood 1996:36), so is what happens before a purchase is made, or even in the absence of a purchase being made. Given that these are objects of mass consumption, children may even get to work on commodities at other children's houses, at school or in other social settings without themselves owning the object. This expanded conception of consumption acknowledges the ways in which children's (lack of) access to financial resources shapes their practices.

This separation between the world of consumption and that of production is not of course unique to children. The emptying of goods of the human labour and exploitation involved in their production is the essence of the Marxist concept of commodity fetishism that characterizes capitalist consumption. Commodity fetishism refers to the process through which the social relations of production congealed in the commodity are concealed, and the commodity appears as an object with its own autonomous existence.

However, although the division between consumption and production is not unique to children, it takes a particular form in relation to modern childhood. The construction of Western childhood as a time for play and learning in the family and at school involves the ideological, if not always the actual, separation of the child from the world of production and everyday consumption. Adaptations of Piagetian theory to economic socialization suggest that children understand the economy as a series of distinct, unrelated processes and separate out the exchange of money for goods from the exchange of money for labour (Lunt 1995, Leiser et al. 1990). One does not have to subscribe to Piaget's theory of stages of development to acknowledge that children's distance from production is unlikely to generate a clear connection in their minds between production and consumption. This obscuration serves to embolden the Romantic ethic in the child's consumption practices, since there is for the child no external materiality that challenges the idealization of the commodity.

Clothes

Sue Saltmarsh (2009) claims, on the basis of research in early childhood centres in Sydney, Australia, that children use commodity signs, not necessarily attached to commodities as objects, to understand and perform themselves as economic subjects. She illustrates her argument primarily through her analysis of the actions of one boy who repairs the social stigma he experiences when his Spiderman outfit splits by showing a wallet to his class. Her argument is that the economic and social are tied together such that to be a social subject is to be an economic actor who rationally chooses an identity.

In Karen Wohlwend's (2009) ethnographic study of literacy practices in US early childhood classrooms, she claims that '[p]roductive consumption is located in the tension between agency and subjection; children are neither cultural dupes at the mercy of global corporations nor cultural geniuses who shrewdly access and expertly manipulate vast networks of gendered multimedia for their own purposes.' (2009:77). The question of whether consumers are cultural dupes or creative fashioners of their own aesthetic is a central theme in consumer studies. It is not that children are necessarily seen as more likely to be easily duped into buying unwanted goods than are adults. Children may use commodities in very similar ways to adults; for example, in her study of children's interest in fashion Pilcher (2011) suggests that regardless of whether children are knowledgeable about or interested in brands and fashion, they use clothes, as adults do, to fashion the (gendered) self. The 'me-making' (Pilcher 2013) that children engage in is conducted within or, as Pilcher says, determined by the production context of clothes and the discourses of childhood that circulate in the fashion industry and among other institutions and actors. Wærdahl (2005) concurs with the importance for children of deploying knowledge about fashion and trends in identity work. Her interest is in 'anticipatory socialization' in the context of children's transitions to secondary school in rural Norway. Although recognizing the interplay between gender and age in how children construct and project their identities, her central interest is in how children anticipate their move from the category 'child' to the category 'youth' through adopting new sets of cultural practices, including clothes but also in activities. Konig also develops an argument about fashion and the significance of changing clothes to signify the transition to and subsequent occupation of a normative juvenile identity. Her central point, developed from the statements her respondents make about why they choose particular clothes, is that '[t]he claim that one only follows one's own taste, that one presents oneself as authentic, is the most important principle and idea concerning aesthetic action in an individualized society'(2008:227). However, Konig argues, the demand that clothes express an authentic individuality is at the same time one that is necessarily done within the economic constraints and habitus of the child's class position.

Animated film

The research on children's consumption of clothes has mostly been interested in individualization, class, gender and generation (or age). Rather less has been said about how children use commodities as resources for understanding race or racialization. A special issue of *Cultural Studies ↔ Critical Methodologies* (2009) on popular culture, children and race examines how racialization is embedded in dolls (Guerrero 2009), crayons (Roth 2009), television shows (Serrato 2009) and Disney films (Lugo-Lugo and Bloodsworth-Lugo 2009). These papers share an analysis of depictions of race in children's cultural artefacts that masquerade as racelessness and show children the operations of racism in largely uncritical ways.

Surprisingly little attention has been paid to the specific role of popular visual culture in the formation of racial or ethnic identities in young children. Although there is an ethnography of everyday culture (particularly music cultures) and its role in constructing racial and ethnic identities, this has mostly been about older teenagers and young adults. The role of visual culture as race-making resources for children and young people has been neglected. Suki Ali's *Mixed-Race, Post-Race* (2003) is one of the few studies of children that made use of popular visual culture. She uses popular film and television programmes to elicit talk about race and racial identity by her respondents. Since the 1990s the study of children's television and computer games has shown that children are active users/readers (rather than passive consumers/viewers) of media (Kinder 1999, Buckingham 1993, Bazalgette and Buckingham 1995). These studies have made significant contributions to understanding how children use media to construct their identity as children (Mitchell and Reid-Walsh 2002) and as working-class girls (Walkerdine 2007), but the use of media to construct racial identities has been neglected.

If Media Studies have taken children's media seriously the same cannot be said of Film Studies, which has had little to say about children's films. Film Studies has embraced popular films as worthy of serious critical attention, particularly in their representations of race and gender (Willis 1997), but children's films continue to be, with notable exceptions (Wojcik-Andrews 2000, Bazalgatte and Buckingham 1995, Giroux 2001), dismissed as mere entertainment. Disneyland as a physical space has been the subject of studies in social geography (e.g. Zukin 2000, Marling 1997), and there has been some research into the political economy of the Disney studios (Hiaasen 1998, Smoodin 1994), as well as critical assessments of Walt Disney himself (Eliot 2003), but there have been few studies of Disney films or films from other studios that focus on social representation (for a recent exception, see Lacassagne, Nieguth and Dépelteau 2011). The few studies there are have paid significantly more attention to the representation of gender in film than to the representation of race (Bell, Haas and Sells 1995, Giroux 2001). Given that watching film, either at the cinema or on video, is a far from negligible leisure activity for most children in the USA and UK (Livingstone 2002), this critical neglect is undeserved.

Mimesis and alterity: representations of race in children's films

Contemporary animated children's films frequently depict race and gender as performative identities, the competent performance of which is learned through copying the child's intimate others, particularly their mother/maternal figures and, to a lesser extent, their fathers. Race, like gender, is fundamentally performative but the interpellation of children as raced subjects cannot be directly compared with their interpellation as gendered subjects. As I have remarked in earlier chapters, the hailing of children as people with a gender remains normative, notwithstanding shifts in what might be meant by femininity or masculinity. This is not the case for race. Increasingly, the continued pertinence of race to social worlds and the impact of racism on life chances are elided in favour of claims to contemporary racelessness (Goldberg 2001). This claim that contemporary liberal democratic societies are raceless, in the sense that 'race' is no longer a meaningful identity, or is not salient to how resources are distributed or to life chances, is particularly the case in relation to the racialization of children, who are considered to be innocent of race and not to notice skin colour. Children, especially white children, are not hailed as raced subjects directly through language; outside of Apartheid and other segregationist regimes, black children and white children in school are not asked to group themselves racially in the ways that children are constantly asked to group themselves by gender (although see Van Ausdale and Feagin 2001 for how race is deployed in schools). Linguistic references to race are oblique and visual representation – the interpretation of which is more contestable – replaces textual representation (Wells 2010). Notwithstanding discourses of racelessness, children (like adults) are constituted as raced subjects and draw on multiple resources to understand what it means to perform their racial identity conventionally. My contention is that popular culture is one of these resources that present children with representations of the signification and performativity of race (Willis 1997:3, Giroux 2001:1–12).

Notwithstanding the limited scholarly attention that has been paid to children's films, watching animated film is a significant leisure activity for children if the size of the children's animated film market is taken as an indicator of their viewing. Disney's *The Lion King* is in the top ten grossing films at the US box office as at 2016. With Pixar Productions' *Shrek* and *Monsters, Inc.* , it has generated box office receipts of $835 million, unadjusted for inflation (http://www.digitalmediafx.com/special reports/animatedfilms.html).

Representations of race in children's animation

One of the main narrative devices that animated films use to tell this story of how social identities are taken up is that of a displaced child/animal who is rescued by adults of another species, who then more or less willingly protect and nurture the child until she or he can be or is reunited with his or her family. I argue that some very complicated work about the signification of race and gender is done in these films and that they circulate multiple, often contradictory discourses about and representations of 'race'. They propose that species (for which, in children's animated films, read racial) difference is easily transcended or erased by emotional attachment to an other; further, the emotional mother–child attachments that these films set up between different species of animal or animals and people are signified through the child learning to be like the substitute/ adoptive mother, by copying and reproducing the sensibilities and behaviours of the mother and her family (now the orphan's family). Through this trope of mimesis or copying we learn that not only can attachments be made across difference but that difference itself can be dissolved by the infant becoming like the 'mother'.

This discourse of race as a socially constructed identity will be very familiar to readers who have followed the argument of this book, but it is perhaps an unanticipated representation of race from one of the most conservative production companies in the United States (Giroux 2001:91). Although its provenance is contradictory, this representation of race and gender as social and cultural constructions in popular children's films may be welcomed. However, it has not displaced biological discourses of race and gender that insist that the body puts limits on the capacity for mimesis to dissolve alterity, or of a Romantic discourse that essentializes the connection between place and (racial) identity. In contrast to the representation of gender and race as performative accomplishments, heterosexuality is essentialized in these films as an innate, biological drive that finally trumps and undoes the performativity of race and gender by always making the object of sexual desire, as the child comes into adolescence, a character of a different gender and of the same 'race'. These productions attest to and reinforce both the compulsory heterosexuality and the racism that underwrite gendered identities.

Disney's Tarzan   My main object of analysis is the 1999 Disney animation of *Tarzan*. I chose this film because of its particularly clear and sustained use of mimesis for the overcoming or dissolving of alterity. *Tarzan* is a sustained exploration of how children learn to perform their (racial) identity and of the limits that the phenomenology of the body places on the racial roles and scripts that people can successfully deploy. It is also explicitly about the learning of *white* masculinity and the possibility of and limits to being a good person and at the same time being a white man. In this respect, *Tarzan* is an unusual film; the *critical* exploration of the signification of 'race' for white people *qua whites* being almost entirely absent in Western visual culture (Dyer 1997). (Although it could be argued that the uncritical exploration of whiteness is the subject of most of the Western visual canon.) Critical Whiteness Studies has insisted on the importance of rendering the production of whiteness visible in order to undo its social/political/economic power (Ware and

Back 2001). Whatever the merits of that project, it is rather unexpected to find a film from the Disney studios engaging in a critical reading of whiteness.

In the 1999 Disney version of the Tarzan story, Tarzan and his mother and father are shipwrecked off the coast of Africa when he is a baby. Their treetop house is attacked by a tiger that kills both parents. A female ape, whose infant has recently been killed by a tiger, rescues the infant boy. The dead infant ape's father and the head of the extended ape family, Kerchak, objects to her adopting the infant because it is 'not our kind'. She raises the boy and he learns to walk, eats, plays and speaks like the other young gorillas. As he and his peers grow older it is clear that Tarzan believes that he is a gorilla but one that has different capacities to the 'other' gorillas. One of these is his ability to imitate other species and learn their languages; another is that he is physically slower than the gorillas but is able, being human and having a capacity for mimicry, to compensate for his slowness by copying how other animals use the environment as tools or prosthetic extensions of their own capacities.

Kerchak never accepts Tarzan as part of the ape family. He shouts at Tarzan and his mother 'you can't keep defending him. He will never learn. You can't learn to be one of us … look at him, he will never be one of us.' Tarzan runs off, crying and angry. 'Why am I so different?', he asks his mother. 'Kerchak said I don't belong in the family. Look at me.' 'I am', she says 'I see two eyes, like mine, and a nose … two ears. Let's see, what else?' 'Two hands', says Tarzan putting his hand against hers excitedly and then withdrawing them when he sees the difference between his hands and hers. Having failed to establish their physical similarity, she tells him to close his eyes and, putting his hand against his heart, she says: 'forget what you see, what do you feel?' 'My heart.' She puts his face against her chest so he can feel her heart. 'See,' she says, 'They're exactly the same.' For now, Tarzan's fears that the differences between him and his family are unassailable are assuaged, and he ends the conversation determined to be 'the best ape ever'.

It is not long after this moment that the film ends its depiction of Tarzan's childhood and turns to his adolescence/young adulthood. It is at this time that Tarzan meets three other white humans: an elderly explorer and his adult daughter Jane – both gorillaphiles – and a hunter, Clayton, whose sole purpose in being in Africa is to capture gorillas for the profits they will realize him in Europe. Tarzan rescues Jane from an attack by a group of monkeys. She takes him to her camp. Tarzan learns the culture of humans and falls in love with Jane. When the time comes for Jane to leave, still not having found the gorillas they came to observe (or in Clayton's case, capture), Clayton suggests to Tarzan that if Jane could see the gorillas she would stay in Africa. Tarzan, breaking his promise to Kerchak that he will not expose the camp to the humans, takes them to see his family. When Kerchak returns he attacks the humans and they only escape because Tarzan restrains Kerchak. Tarzan, realizing that he has challenged Kerchak's authority before all the family, runs away. His mother finds him and, in response to his despairing comment that he is 'so confused', takes him to the house that he was born in and shows him a picture of himself as a baby with his mother and father. 'Now you know', she says, although what he knows is unclear. Perhaps we are to understand that until this moment Tarzan doesn't realize that he is human, like Jane; or perhaps she means that this explains his confusion about why he defended humans and betrayed his gorilla family to them. In any case, it is at this moment that Tarzan (literally) puts on his father's clothes and leaves 'Africa' to go to England to be with Jane.

Once on the ship Clayton imprisons Tarzan, Jane and her father in the ship's hold before returning to the shore to capture Tarzan's family. Tarzan is furious with himself when he realizes how he has exposed his family to danger. He escapes from the ship and goes to the defence of his family. Kerchak is killed defending Tarzan from Clayton, and in retaliation Tarzan fights Clayton and takes his gun from him. As he puts the muzzle to Clayton's neck, Clayton taunts him 'go ahead, shoot me. Be a man.' 'Not a man like you', retorts Tarzan, flinging the gun away. Clayton and Tarzan's fight ends with Clayton cutting himself free from the hanging branches that Tarzan uses to swing though the jungle. Clayton falls, the branches twisted around his neck, and stops short of the ground: lynched by the forest. Tarzan now goes to his dying father, Kerchak, who asks for Tarzan's forgiveness for 'not understanding that you have always been one of us. Our family will look to you now ... take care, my son.' Tarzan, as the son of the clan's now dead leader, takes up his role as leader of the family, with Jane as his partner.

One of the significant divergences between the books and the early films and this version of Tarzan is the complete absence of Africans. Until Tarzan meets Jane, her father and Clayton, he is not aware that there are others who resemble him. This device of depopulating Africa means that the rendering of Tarzan as alone takes on a different significance from that it has in the books, and would have here were the possibility of Tarzan making a human community with Africans available. In the books, as Torgovnick (1991) points out, Tarzan's first glimpse of another human, an African man who has killed Tarzan's gorilla father, is the first occasion on which he thinks about who he might share being different (from his gorilla family), being human with. The second occasion is when he meets a white woman, Jane. Through Kerchak's murder, which Tarzan is implicated in through his betrayal of the location of the family to

Clayton, Tarzan becomes the leader of the clan with Jane as his partner, establishing himself at the apex of a hierarchy in which all other members are subordinate to him and to Jane.

To understand how race is treated in this film, it is necessary to remind ourselves that this is a children's film that deploys the well-worn convention in books and films for children of anthropomorphizing animals. Filmic and textual representations of animals are then coded through the use of dialect, idiom, actor's voice, gesture and demeanour to signify their 'race' and class location (Byrne and McQuillan 1999). Disney films are replete with instances where these devices are used: the donkey in *Shrek*, the blackbirds in *Dumbo* and the hyenas in *The Lion King* are all examples that readily spring to mind where this sort of coding is used to establish the identity of characters as black or working-class (Giroux 2001:105–6). There is a scene in the animation *Beauty and the Beast* when the curse on the Beast's house ends and all the objects in it are restored to their human form. This is a rare instance where the slipperiness of this kind of coding is fixed. In general these moments of revelation are not available to the viewer and the signification of animals (and talking objects) remains elusive; one can only make a plausible case that a particular set of signs is intended to signify a particular ethnic, national or cultural identification. This slipperiness is not accidental, I suggest; it allows the producers to deal in cultural/racial stereotypes and controversial issues of contemporary identity formation whilst always having the defence that this is *only* a children's film, the figures are *only* cartoons and any resemblance to the real world is unintentional (Bryne and McQuillan 1999:100–1).

Having established that objects and animals in children's animations are racially coded, we can return to the film of *Tarzan* and ask: how are the gorillas coded? There is nothing here, in contrast to, say, *The Lion King*, that codes these animals as human, as Africans. There is no attempt to render their speech in any of the conventional codes Hollywood uses to depict 'African' speech, and there are no attempts to construct a faux African tradition (as there is in *The Lion King*). They are not rendered as human (other than in the capacity for complex language); rather it is Tarzan who is rendered as animal-like. Yet it is Tarzan's human capacity that also allows him to take his up leadership of the clan – it is his combination of human capacities and his intimate knowledge of gorilla life that means he possesses the leadership qualities for this new age of threats from white hunters. My argument is this: the gorillas are intended to be coded as animal and many of the messages of this telling of the Tarzan story speak directly to the environmental/ecological preoccupations of its intended audience, with its sentimental view of animal worlds as more 'humane' than human worlds (as for example in the old trope that only humans kill wantonly). Nonetheless, there is also a racial reading here that is impossible to ignore, because Tarzan's identity crisis in being different to his gorilla family is not so much about what it means to be human as what it means to be a white man. To expose this reading most effectively we might ask: why is the human family that appears in Tarzan's 'Africa' not an African family, why are Jane and her father white, and also what difference would it make to this story and its account of race if they were depicted as black? I suggest that they could not be black because, despite the absence of racial coding, the difference between Tarzan and his (gorilla) family is intended to be read as a story of racial difference, where race is taken as physical difference inscribed on the body which marks the limits to the possibility of dissolving alterity through mimesis. When his gorilla mother takes Tarzan back to his 'birth mother's' house she is affirming her identity as his 'adoptive' mother, in a scene that echoes a familiar narrative of adoption as a crisis of (non-) resemblance between parents and children and purports to establish the limits to the plasticity or constructedness of 'race'. Because the only other humanoid in the film, before Jane and the other white humans make their appearance, is not a racial other but a species other, the limits to mixedness or hybridity that the film establishes can be simultaneously insisted on and disavowed. This, as Torgovnick remarks of the Tarzan books, is 'the threat of miscegenation disguised as species difference' (1991:53).

Learning whiteness   Tarzan's corporeal differences are represented as initially marking the limits of his assimilation into the world of his gorilla family and peers. It is at this point in the film that Jane, her father and Clayton arrive in Tarzan's Africa carrying all the paraphernalia – ideological and material – of Victorian English bourgeois culture with them. It is their camp that becomes the space in which Tarzan will learn to be a white man. Tarzan's lessons in white masculinity are beautifully and comically depicted in Disney's animation. In the original Tarzan stories, he already knows how to read English when he meets Jane, having taught himself from infant readers left in his parents' treehouse. In the animation, Tarzan learns language and from that how to be a white man through mimicking Jane, through Jane's attempts to teach him language, and, brilliantly represented, through his watching and imitating daguerreotypes.

Tarzan's entry into whiteness coincides with his loss of childhood. Only when he has completed his transition to young adulthood does it become imperative that he learns to be a white man; in an entirely related point, it is his whiteness that makes it possible *and* necessary for him to fall in love with a white woman, and it is his love for a white woman that finally undoes his ambivalent species/racial identity. This representation of whiteness as a learned/performed subjectivity is highly unusual. Critical Whiteness Studies has shown how the power of whiteness is partly located in its constant erasure of the acknowledgement of its own existence. Here, in a mainstream film from a production company renowned for its reactionary politics (Giroux 2001), is an exposure of whiteness as a social fact and a denaturalizing of race. How can this be accounted for?

Tarzan does not only learn to be human; he learns to be a white man, and he chooses a particular kind of white man to be. The gaze that the film invites is that of the white boy. This is not, of course, the same as saying that Disney only intends this film to be watched by white boys, any more than in Laura Mulvey's 1975 seminal article she is advancing the argument that Hollywood film is only intended to be looked at by white men. The concept of the gaze draws attention to how a particular kind of audience is conjured up by the representation of gender (and for our purposes 'race') deployed in the film. In the case of Disney's *Tarzan* not only is the central protagonist a white boy/man, he is one of only four human protagonists in the film, all of whom are white. More significant perhaps than this representational erasure (important as that is for an animation ostensibly set in Africa) of black people is that the film is a narrative about finding a liveable, *white, masculine* identity. The struggle that Tarzan goes through invites the identification of a white boy viewer with his screen likeness.

In its address to this imagined audience the film argues for the limits of contact across difference, the limits to the appropriation/incorporation of another's culture, and it establishes those limits through the body and specifically the specular regime of race – it is, after all, by looking at his reflection that Tarzan initially apprehends what he later insists is the incommensurability of himself and his gorilla family. The film then declares that racial identity, although derived from and located in the body, still has to be learned. Finally, it counterpoises 'good' whiteness with 'bad' whiteness, in which the former is situated in the family and with the feminine, and in which the taking up of good whiteness in no way diminishes the social/political authority of whiteness; it is this last point that reconciles a critical deconstruction of whiteness that the film attempts with its provenance from the ideologically conservative world of Disney.

Disney's animation of *Tarzan* might be thought of as a triptych on mimesis. The first panel is Tarzan's imitation of gorilla culture, which ends with the realization that his corporeal difference places limits on the completeness of mimesis and his at-homeness with his gorilla family. The second panel explores the presumption that mimesis rests on physical similarities and, in particular, skin colour. It is this second panel that clarifies the point that, despite the species differences of the first panel, the question or problematic that Tarzan (the character and the film) is dealing with is the fact (or otherwise) of race. The second panel establishes Tarzan's whiteness – the recognition of which is made possible by and necessitates his love for a white woman, Jane – and makes his whiteness/love for Jane drive him into exile from his family and home; which is no longer either family or home. The third panel disrupts this reading/watching, however, because in the last third of the film a theme that has been latent in the second panel is brought to the fore, with great consequences for how the questions of mimesis, alterity and belonging are resolved in the film. This theme is that white masculinity is not monolithic and that there are different ways to take up whiteness.

It is in this third panel that Clayton and Tarzan directly oppose one another as models of white masculinity. Clayton – muscle-bound and violent – is opposed to Tarzan, who is strong, lithe and sympathetic. Tarzan refuses Clayton's challenge to 'be a man' with the response, 'Not a man like you.' Tarzan's determination to be a different kind of white man does not, however, change the relationship between white people and Africa; it merely reformulates it. Here, Tarzan and Jane establish their dominance over Africa not through violence and coercion but through sympathy and a more Gramscian kind of hegemony. Here, reforming whiteness and white masculinity is, for the white man at least, a win-win outcome: he gets to profess his decency without relinquishing power.

Conclusion

Children use the cultural resources around them to play with, perform and explore the meanings of social identities. Through these processes they develop a feeling for how their sense of self is articulated with broader social structures. Consumption of goods and media provide children with the material from which they can fashion their childhood subjectivities. These materials are already saturated with discourses and laden with symbolism; children will not recognize the social significance of all of these to adults and young people. Children may, through new stories about what they watch and play with, and assembling things in novel ways, use these materials to resist their ascribed identities. In whatever way children approach material and visual commercial culture, it will provide the cloth in which they will be able to wrap their embodied subjectivities.

10

Conclusion

This book aims to make a contribution to Childhood Studies through addressing the question of who the child subject is and how they are formed at the intersection of politics, economics, society and culture. I have argued that to understand the formation of the child subject it is necessary to understand what presses on the child from outside (what I call, following Foucault, governing technologies) and to what ends or purposes; and what corporeal and cognitive capacities children themselves bring to these governing technologies. I am suggesting that the child subject is made in the dialectical relationship between these two forces of governing technologies and children's capacities. I hope that this theory of child subject formation will contribute to Childhood Studies by complicating the concept of agency that has been so central to the discipline, and in doing so will bring more clearly into view the structures that shape children's lives in such unequal ways. In this final chapter I want to do two things. Firstly, I summarize the Foucauldian argument on contemporary government and population and what this means for childhood. I then elaborate a theory of childhood subjectivity that recognizes the complex interplay between political economy and socio-cultural forms.

Governing contemporary childhoods

To understand why the figure of the child has become the ideal target of contemporary government, it is necessary to grasp how contemporary government in the developed world differs from classical forms of political rule. In brief, the state can be thought of as an assemblage of practices and institutions that augment its economic wealth in order to secure the power of the ruling class, an economic class which is more or less closely aligned with the governing class. How economic wealth is understood to be generated is therefore crucial to how states govern. If wealth is conceived of as residing in physical stuff (such as gold, or land, or livestock) then the accumulation of wealth and power is based on extraction. In such a mode, territory is of prime importance in amassing both wealth and power. Who lives within the territory is of little interest to the ruler, other than that they submit to demands to give some portion of what they have to the state. The state imposed its rule more or less through violence and the threat of violence. This is why Foucault characterizes this form of governance as governing through taking life (see Foucault 2003:ch. 11); sovereign power has the right to kill or to let live. In contrast to this form of sovereignty, contemporary governance conceives of wealth as an endless process of development in which it is the productive capacities of individuals and not physical capital that are the source of economic growth. Once economic development is conceived in this way, population and increases in the health and welfare of the population become the target of government, and therefore children, as the sine qua non of development, become the ideal target of government. At the level of the general population, government regulates through measuring and intervening in birth rates, infant mortality, management of disease and hygiene; at the level of the individual, it introduces disciplinary mechanisms intended to inculcate the habits of self-governance (Smith 2014).

In his lecture series *The Birth of Biopolitics*, Foucault (2008) explicates the history of liberalism in Western Europe. Whether biopolitics, a politics of life that takes population as its target, is always tied to liberal political economy or not, it is certainly the case that in the Global North it has been so. Liberalism, taking its name from liberty, from freedom, indicates a relationship between the state and society in which that state governs the social in ways that enable the social to govern itself, and distances the state from the governance of the economy.

Children are simultaneously the site of a development potential that must be actualized through schooling, surveillance and social policy, and the figure in whose name government acts (in defence of society, for the defence of the child). Through invoking the necessity and legitimacy of developing the child, government finds its way into civil society and into the private sphere of everyday life, a route which would otherwise be foreclosed to it because of the constraints of governing through freedom. Children provide an ideal target for government that aims to balance intervention to increase productivity against its claim to govern in the name of the people and only to the extent that they need to be governed. This means that far from being a non-political subject, for contemporary liberal governments the child is the ideal political figure. The child's capacities as a developmental subject make government intervention in the lives of children appear to be both legitimate and desirable. The assertion of the principle of liberty requires of government that it has or appears to have limited scope for entering into civil society. It requires the demarcation of a public sphere, which links the population to government, from a private sphere, in which people are at liberty to do what they want. Governing through childhood both preserves the fiction of a division between the private and public sphere and its attendant claim to securing liberty, and enables government to secure the development of the productive forces of the population. The recognition of the child as a developing and vulnerable person allows government to override the principle of liberty in the name of the child's right to development and of the securing of their best interests.

The ideology of modern childhood and the role of government in developing the population and securing its health and welfare make interventions in children's lives a duty of government, rather than an interference in their freedom. This ideological precept makes children available and visible to governing technologies, more so than adults. Schools, and children and family health services, then become sites that are both constituted by and available to government. These governing technologies (police, juvenile justice, the law, schooling, the regulation of family life, the allocation of housing) press onto children from the outside (see chapters 3, 4 and 5), structuring their experiences of childhood and determining their life chances through a highly unequal distribution of resources and of respect and recognition.

This surveillance and intervention are a double-edged sword. On the one hand it can be seen as a force for securing children's wellbeing, but on the other it is also how children become separated into the deserving and the undeserving, and sorted into those who will be governed through biopolitics and those who will be governed through sovereignty. Foucault also insists that with this shift from what he calls sovereignty to biopolitics, modern racism enters into politics and race becomes the caesura, the break or cut, between the population whose health and welfare will be increased and the non-population (non-citizens, foreigners, subaltern minorities) who will be left to die (sometimes literally so, as we are currently witnessing in thousands of deaths of refugees in the Mediterranean). Foucault can seem very prescient here, although his analysis was built partly on explaining the Holocaust and fascism in Europe; his theory explains many of our contemporary political struggles as contests over who gets excluded and who gets included in the category of 'population' within any particular governing formation.

This cut that divides those who benefit from the increase in their health and welfare, and the effort to develop their productive forces, from those who are excluded from this project necessarily enters into childhood. It is not possible for government to stratify the population only for adults; so long as adults experience racism and sexism, children will also. There is, as Walter White, founder of the National Association for the Advancement of Colored People, put it, 'no isolation from life' (White 1995:11, first published 1948, cited in Ritterhouse 2006:108). Childhood innocence, like adulthood naivety, is always an outcome of privilege. It is for this reason that governing through the child is segmented or fragmented by inequality. Governing through childhood simultaneously holds the generic figure of the child as the ideal target of liberal governance and excludes actual black children, immigrant children, girls and working-class children from its full promise. Furthermore, governing children – a category of person not yet entitled to be a free, self-governing subject – involves both punishment (a form associated with classic sovereignty over territory) and discipline (the inculcation of self-governing dispositions). This distribution of different forms of governance of childhood is also gendered and racialized.

Although my argument may appear to parallel those of liberal scholars who argue that the promise of liberalism will not be realized until these excluded children are included within the domain of innocent childhood (Levander 2006), I hope to make a different point. My argument is that political liberalism itself produced these breaks in childhood, rather than liberalism being an as yet to be completed political project. This is so because racism was part of the liberal capitalist project from the outset and remains central to its contemporary form. Racial exclusions allowed government to resolve contradictory claims: on the one hand all men are free and equal, and liberal democracy guarantees their continued freedom and their pursuit of wealth and happiness; on the other hand the unfree labour of black people provided the capital accumulation on which both capitalism and its liberal politics rested. This governing through racism structured the child-saving project, and therefore the ways that children were unequally incorporated into government from the founding of the USA, as I elaborated in chapter 3, and it continues to structure contemporary forms of child rights and child-saving.

Making young subjects

In what is perhaps the most famous line of the Communist Manifesto, Marx and Engels (2008, first published 1848) wrote, 'all that is solid melts into air.' Marshall Berman (1983) took this line for the title of his seminal analysis of how capitalist industrialization and urbanization radically unsettled not only production but also social organization and the cultural mores of the old world. The onset of the modern era in the fifteenth and sixteenth centuries in Western Europe brought with it a 'palpably increasing awareness of the self as something that was not divinely formed and statically placed, but rather changeable and possibly cultivatable through one's own concerted activity' (Hall 2004:17). At the centre of this reformation of life in the modern era was the meaning of personhood and therefore, although it is not often mentioned in the philosophy of subjectivity, of childhood. It is not, as Ariès (or his inter-preters) would have it, that childhood did not exist in the Middle Ages in Europe but that before the modern period children's development was thought to be immanent to them. Children could be cultivated to be stronger or weaker, perhaps, in the same way that plants could be tended, but the fundamental substance of the child and who the child would be were already determined by external forces that were ultimately traceable to a divinely ordered fate.

If who the child was, and who they would come to be, were no longer understood as divinely ordered, then how was the self formed? In *Phe-nomenology of Spirit* Hegel (1977, first published 1807) suggests that the self is formed intersubjectively, that is to say that a person comes to see their self only through the gaze of another (the other). Although the idea of 'the other' has come to be used in much sociological theory to imply a reduction of an other to the status of an object and a mere pro-jection of the subject, this is not what it means in *Phenomenology of Spirit*. Hegel says 'Self-consciousness exists in itself and for itself when, and by the fact that, it so exists for another; that is, it exists only in being acknowledged' (1977:111). This process of recognizing oneself through another is doubled by the fact that the other is also a self to itself: 'for the other is equally independent and self-contained' (1977:112). This recognition of the self in the other inaugurates, according to Hegel, a struggle between the two selves (or two others) that results in the (always temporary) domination of one by the other. Yet the one who dominates and comes to depend on the labour of the other also loses their sense of self, because it depends on the recognition of another who is now sub-jugated and whose recognition therefore counts for little to the subjuga-tor. At the same time the subjugated, compelled by their subjugation to work, find, through their labour, an agency in and on the world that the oppressor, who does not labour but lives off of the labour of another, lacks.

The recognition and negation that Hegel describes in the section on self-consciousness in *Phenomenology of Spirit* may seem like a long way from understanding how children come to self-consciousness, to subjectivity. Hegel's figures are adults. Even if we find his account of the formation of self-consciousness plausible, how does it help us to understand this process in children? A fundamental problem for understanding the subjectivity of infants and children is to know how to think about the child before they know themselves to be a person. If an infant does not have the cognitive tools to think of their self as a person, and yet we want to resist the idea of the child as a blank slate or, to use another common metaphor, an empty vessel, how can we understand their understanding of their selves? In this book I have suggested that the intersubjectivity of subject formation, an intersubjectivity which begins before the child's birth, resolves the problem of how a subject who has not yet come into language can be thought of as a subject in the sense of an agent. Hegel's account of the self/other dialectic is found most intensely in the infant–mother dyad. The infant's selfhood is formed in relation to her immediate caregivers, who, in turn, are reshaped by their relationship to the child. So that when we think of subject formation in relation to children, the profoundly intersubjective nature of subjectivity must be at the centre of our analysis.

Children also bring their own bodily and cognitive capacities to the formation of their subjectivity. Their cognitive development impacts on how they think of themselves in relation to others and how they make sense of the inequalities that they experience. Their changing bodily capacities shape the intensely and unavoidably intersubjective character of their emerging sense of selfhood. Critical points in children's bodily development, especially puberty, make visible the unstable character of young subjectivity and the close connection between the body and selfhood. Their size, the vulnerability of their bodies, and periods of rapid change in brain development during the child's life course, the impact of neurological structures on cognition, and the astonishing plasticity of their brains all impact on how they engage with the social world and on the formation of their own subjectivities. These biological capacities that young humans bring to the social construction of childhood place certain limits on what can be constructed. Children's bodies (including their brains) are, to be sure, adaptable and plastic, but not endlessly so.

Furthermore, subjectivity is not only a sense of an individualized personhood, even one formed intersubjectively and shaped by biological capacities, but organizes humans into kinds of persons in relation to dominant power structures. Marx developed his theory of the dialectic of class formation and class struggle, and his theory of consciousness (as set out in *The German Ideology*), from Hegelian dialectics turned, as Marx puts it in *Capital* (1981, first published 1867), 'right side up again' to 'discover the rational kernel within the mystical shell'. What Marx meant by this is that while Hegel began with an idealist philosophy, Marx began with materialism; with the claim that the material reality of people's lives shapes consciousness (Marx and Engels 1970, first published 1846). For Marx, these material conditions are organized in relation to economic practices and therefore selfhood is not simply a personal self-consciousness but a social consciousness.

This relationship between the material world and consciousness is not only class based, but also structures how racism and sexism place specific material limits on the lives of girls and women and of people of colour, for example in practices such as zoning and policing that limit the spatial freedom of people of colour, or sexual violence and harassment that limit girls' and women's spatial freedoms. The economic effects of racism and sexism can also be seen in unequal access to education, housing, employment and health care. Material conditions in turn shape our ideologies, how we think about the world and our relations to people in it, and how these are expressed in cultural products such as art, religion, music, language, fashion, design and play. So, for example, when Carol Gilligan (1993) argues that girls are concerned with an ethics of care whereas boys are concerned with an ethics of law, she is not being biologically reductive; she is suggesting that because of the material conditions in which girls are raised (taking up less space, resolving conflict through talk rather than force) they develop a particular way of relating to others and thinking about the world. Or when Carol B. Stack (2003, first published 1983) describes how women in a low-income, mostly black neighbourhood look out for one another and share the care of their children, she is not suggesting that black or working-class people are intrinsically more sociable and invested in mutuality than white people, but that the conditions of life produce distinct kinds of social relationships which are then valued. Now of course not all girls share an ethics of care, and not all people living in low-income, densely populated neighbourhoods are invested in mutual aid and daily reciprocity. Nevertheless, these practices become valued and legitimated within a specific socio-cultural field so that it may be possible to speak of girl culture or black culture (although such claims need to guard against essentialism).

Subjects are also relational positions structured through binary oppositions. However, although subject positions are relational, that does not mean that racism and sexism hurt those who derive their social power from these ideologies as much as those that are oppressed by them. Simply put, sexism does not oppress men or boys and racism does not oppress (or 'hurt') white people. Yes, little boys are taught not to cry when they hurt themselves and little girls are taught not to occupy space fully, so both boys and girls are required to shape their selves – or, better, in the process of becoming boys and girls infants are shaped – differently by discourses to accept that 'boys don't cry' or 'you throw like a girl'. The question is not 'are we all shaped by discourse?' (it seems fairly obvious that we are), but 'how are the different subjects constituted through discourse positioned in relation to power?' Those who are subordinate in these oppositional, hierarchical binaries are given less resources (money, space, political power, cultural representation) and are subjected to sanctioned forms of violence. This binary is also spatialized and this spatialization is sometimes codified in law, as for example in Apartheid South Africa or pre-Civil Rights era USA, and applies equally to adults and children, but additionally impacts children in segregated schools and playgrounds or because of children's greater vulnerabilities to environmental risk. Sometimes these spatial orderings are structured economically – in poor and rich neighbourhoods that also often map onto histories of racist exclusions.

Although subject positions have material causes and effects and are relationally structured, they are also arbitrary. That is to say that the range of behaviours, attitudes, dispositions, gestures, even artefacts that are legitimated for boys or girls is arbitrary and oppositional: girls are, or are interpellated as, what boys are not (for example, boys are strong and stoical, girls are weak and emotional). In general these oppositions are also hierarchical (strong and stoical is more valued than weak and emotional) but they are not always so, particularly in moments of cultural transition. So when boys generally got more school qualifications than girls did, and the binary was boys/clever, girls/stupid, being clever was valued. Now that girls are doing better than boys at school (and only marginally so), being clever at school is losing its cultural value. A nice example of this is in the book *Harry Potter and the Philosopher's Stone*: ' "Me!" said Hermione. "Books! And cleverness! There are more important things" ' (Rowling 2000:208).

Subject positions are also naturalized in ways that obscure their social origins and enable their repetition. Identifying children as girls or boys is, for example, widely taken for granted and generally not thought of as negative or as reinforcing sexism. Few people would find it peculiar or offensive if you asked a pregnant woman whether she was expecting a girl or a boy, or suggested that baby girls should not wear blue and baby boys should definitely not wear pink. Having baby girls' ears pierced so that no one mistakes them for a boy is also commonplace. So practices of making gendered young subjects take particular, often quite explicit forms, and are shaped by the intersubjective, relational and material conditions of their formation.

Racism is both more hidden and more explicit than sexism in children's lives. Children know from a fairly young age how ethnicity or race are ascribed and used to structure and legitimate inequalities. In the

Americas and Europe, children know that being black is low-status in dominant discourse (see chapter 9). Parents of black and mixed-race children may try and protect them from racism, as children themselves may do, by both countering and disavowing racist discourse and by positive representations of black culture, but they will not be able to, and may not want to, refuse the identification altogether.

The concept of subjectivity captures several levels of the relationship between a sense of self and the contexts (social, relational, biological) that produce a sense of self. A subject is an 'I' who acts, an agent, but also an 'I' that is asked (but may refuse) to act within a range of legitimate action. This range of legitimate action is prescribed by all kinds of other actors including governing departments (families, children, health, welfare), institutions (schools, families) and bodies of knowledge (child development, neuroscience, Childhood Studies). Subjectivity is related to social identity, but even if a child does not identify with a social identity and its normative contours, others may ascribe that identity to them. Indeed (as discussed in chapters 5–8 on class, disability, the body, and social psychology), young social subjects are often not invested in the identities that are ascribed to them, or may redefine what it means to be interpellated as, say, a girl. Children may refuse these interpellations and the range of action they imply, and that refusal can be thought of as being on a shifting continuum from capacity (can't comply) to resistance (won't comply). Dominant discourses, in this case about what it means to be a raced or gendered person, do not have to map onto the actual, embodied behaviour of the subjects they constitute. All people, but perhaps especially children, do and say things that are not legitimated within the dominant discourses that make subjects up. These oppositional actions (including speech) are sometimes done intentionally, and sometimes unintentionally. Children, not yet fully aware of the discourses that structure their subject positions, perhaps unknowingly challenge the rules of the game.

To be given a gender, a race, a class, a sexuality is to take a place in a recognized social order that, for girls, black children, disabled children and working-class children, is a stigmatized place. Why should we not simply refuse to raise our children in these stigmatized identities that they are offered and say, I am not a girl, I am not black, I am not working-class, I am not queer, I am not disabled, I am not a(n) (im)migrant: I am a human being and I am as entitled to the same respect, recognition, protection from violence, and provision of security as the other humans who call themselves boy, white, straight, middle-class, able and citizen?

The refusal of the first set of labels, the stigmatized labels, as it were, would also involve an erasure of the histories of struggle and resistance that those so labelled have developed and deployed. Gendered and racialized subjects are produced through discourse, but they do not feel themselves to be only an effect of racist and sexist discourses and practices. The social positions available to us may also be felt as sites of self-expression and give us access to histories of resistance and the cultural practices they generated. This is the contradictory ground of subjectivity, that it is both the site of our oppression (or subjection) and the source of our agency. Or, more precisely, to be a subject is to have a position from which to act, and this is the case whether the subject positions that are available are the site of our oppression (as, for example, for girls and black children) or the source of our social power (as, for example, for boys and white children).

Childhood Studies has largely borrowed the language of social constructionism from a version of feminism that takes gender to be a set of cultural practices inscribed on the already sexed body. By way of parallel, then, Childhood Studies appears to claim that childhood is the cultural practices inscribed on the already childish body. Just like gender, childhood is practised in different ways in different times and places. The body itself does not prescribe, shape or limit any particular form to these gendering cultural practices, other than perhaps in relation to reproduction. Women are denied social power, respect and recognition through sexism; children are denied social power, respect and recognition through some parallel mechanism – perhaps we might call it ageism. Ultimately we would hope that gendered orders will end, so in parallel, is the goal of a social constructivist model of childhood, a model that says it is produced by ageism, to end childhood?

Following the logic of these parallels through shows, it seems to me, that it cannot be the intention of Childhood Studies to end childhood, to erase the differences between humans based on age categories. The exclusion of children from political and economic power and even from social personhood is not the same as the exclusion of other groups of humans from full social, political and economic recognition. Children, *qua* children rather than as young members of broader social populations, are ontologically different to adults.

Childhood is a social construction in the sense that what we imagine a good (or indeed, a bad) childhood to be is made at the conjunction of politics, economics, society and culture in specific historical and spatial contexts. By attending to the dialectical relationship between governing technologies and children's immanent and changing bodily (including cognitive) capacities, we can develop a more finely grained understanding of what it means to say that childhood is 'socially constructed'. It is incumbent on us as scholars of Childhood Studies to understand why childhood is unequally structured and to work against that inequality, not simply to show that childhood is socially constructed but to think about what kinds of childhood should be constructed. We need to delineate the inequalities that structure childhoods, account for them in relation to the operation of power, and identify the scope for resistance to their perpetuation. It is my hope that this book makes some contribution to that project.

Bibliography

Abebe, T. (2008). Earning a living on the margins: Begging, street work and the socio-spatial experiences of children in Addis Ababa. *Geografiska Annaler: Series B, Human Geography, 90*(3), 271–84.

Aboud, F. E. (1988). *Children and Prejudice.* Oxford: Blackwell.

Abrams, D., Rutland, A., and Cameron, L. (2003). The development of subjective group dynamics: Children's judgments of normative and deviant in-group and out-group individuals. *Child Development, 74*(6), 1840–56.

Acoca, L. (1999). Investing in girls: A 21st century strategy. *Juvenile Justice, 6*(1), 3–13.

Aderinto, S. (Ed.). (2015). *Children and Childhood in Colonial Nigerian Histories.* New York: Palgrave Macmillan.

Agyepong, T. (2013). Aberrant sexualities and racialised masculinisation: Race, gender and the criminalisation of African American girls at the Illinois Training School for Girls at Geneva, 1893–1945. *Gender & History, 25*(2), 270–93.

Ahmadu, F. (2000). Rites and wrongs: An insider/outsider reflects on power and excision. In B. Shell-Duncan and Y. Hernlund (Eds.), *Female 'Circumcision' in Africa: Culture, Controversy, and Change* (pp. 283–312). Boulder: Lynne Rienner.

Aitken, S. C. (2011). *Young People, Border Spaces and Revolutionary Imaginations.* London/New York: Routledge.

Aitken, S. C., and Plows, V. (2010). Overturning assumptions about young people, border spaces and revolutions. *Children's Geographies, 8*(4), 327–33.

Alanen, L. (1994). Gender and generation: Feminism and the 'child question'. In J. Qvortrup (Ed.), *Childhood Matters: Social Theory, Practice and Politics* (pp. 27–42). Avebury: Aldershot.

Alderson, P., Hawthorne, J., and Killen, M. (2005). The participation rights of premature babies. *International Journal of Children's Rights, 13*(1/2), 31–50.

Ali, S. (2003). *Mixed-Race, Post-Race: Gender, New Ethnicities, and Cultural Practices*. Oxford: Berg.

Allotey, P., and Reidpath, D. (2001). Establishing the causes of childhood mortality in Ghana: The 'spirit child'. *Social Science & Medicine*, 52(7), 1007–12.

Als, H., and McAnulty, G. B. (2011). The Newborn Individualized Developmental Care and Assessment Program (NIDCAP) with Kangaroo Mother Care (KMC): Comprehensive care for preterm infants. *Current Women's Health Reviews*, 7(3), 288–301.

Amendah, D., Grosse, S. D., Peacock, G., and Mandell, D. S. (2011). The economic costs of autism: A review. In D. Amendah, G. Dawson and D. Geschwind (Eds.), *Autism Spectrum Disorders* (pp. 1347–60). Oxford: Oxford University Press.

American Bar Association, and National Bar Association. (2001). *Justice by Gender: The Lack of Appropriate Prevention, Diversion and Treatment Alternatives for Girls in the Justice System*. Washington DC: American Bar Association.

Ansell, N. (2009). Childhood and the politics of scale: Descaling children's geographies? *Progress in Human Geography*, 33(2), 190–209.

Ansell, N., and Van Blerk, L. (2004). Children's migration as a household/family strategy: Coping with AIDS in Lesotho and Malawi. *Journal of Southern African Studies*, 30, 673–90.

Ariès, P. (1962). *Centuries of Childhood: A Social History of Family Life*. New York: Vintage Books.

Asis, M., Huang, S., and Yeoh, B. S. A. (2004). When the light of the home is abroad: Unskilled female migration and the Filipino family. *Singapore Journal of Tropical Geography*, 25,(2), 198–215.

Asperger, H. (1991). 'Autistic psychopathy' in childhood. (Trans. and annotated U. Frith). In U. Frith (Ed.), *Autism and Asperger Syndrome* (pp. 37–92). Cambridge/New York: Cambridge University Press.

Atkinson, W. (2011). From sociological fictions to social fictions: Some Bourdieusian reflections on the concepts of 'institutional habitus' and 'family habitus'. *British Journal of Sociology of Education*, 32(3), 331–47.

Aubry, S., Ruble, D. N., and Silverman, L. B. (1999). The role of gender knowledge in children's gender typed preferences. In L. Balter and Tamis-LeMonda (Eds.), *Child Psychology: A Handbook of Contemporary Issues* (pp. 363–90). Philadelphia: Psychology Press/Taylor & Francis.

Back, L. (1996). *New Ethnicities and Urban Culture: Racisms and Multiculture in Young Lives*. London: UCL Press.

Balagopalan, S. (2014). *Inhabiting 'Childhood': Children, Labour and Schooling in Postcolonial India*. Basingstoke: Palgrave Macmillan.

Ball, A. L. (2016, April 16). The other Mapplethorpe. *New York Times*.

Baron-Cohen, S., and Belmonte, M. K. (2005). Autism: A window onto the development of the social and the analytic brain. *Annual Review of Neuroscience*, 28(1), 109–26.

Baxter, J. E. (2005). *The Archaeology of Childhood: Children, Gender, and Material Culture*. Walnut Creek: AltaMira Press.

Baxter, J. E. (2008). The archaeology of childhood. *Annual Review of Anthropology, 37*(1), 159–75.

Bazalgette, C., and Buckingham, D. (Eds.). (1995). *In Front of the Children: Screen Entertainment and Young Audiences.* London: British Film Institute.

Beazley, H. (2003). Voices from the margins: Street children's subcultures in Indonesia. *Children's Geographies, 1*(2), 181.

Beidelman, T. O. (1997). *The Cool Knife: Imagery of Gender, Sexuality, and Moral Education in Kaguru Initiation Ritual.* Washington: Smithsonian Institution Press.

Belknap, J., Holsinger, K., and Dunn, M. (1997). Understanding incarcerated girls: The results of a focus group study. *Prison Journal, 77*(4), 381–404.

Bell, E., Haas, L., and Sells, L. (1995). *From Mouse to Mermaid: The Politics of Film, Gender, and Culture.* Bloomington: Indiana University Press.

Bennett, M., and Sani, F. (2004a). Social identity processes and children's ethnic prejudice. In M. Bennett and F. Sani (Eds.), *The Development of the Social Self* (pp. 219–46). Hove: Psychology Press.

Bennett, M., and Sani, F. (Eds.). (2004b). *The Development of the Social Self.* Hove: Psychology Press.

Bergner, G. (2009). Black children, white preference: *Brown v. Board*, the doll tests, and the politics of self-esteem. *American Quarterly, 61*(2), 299–332.

Berman, M. (1983). *All That Is Solid Melts Into Air: The Experience of Modernity.* London: Verso.

Bernstein, R. (2011). *Racial Innocence: Performing American Childhood from Slavery to Civil Rights.* New York: New York University Press.

Bettie, J. (2014). *Women without Class: Girls, Race, and Identity.* Oakland: University of California Press.

Bigler, R. S., and Liben, L. S. (2007). Developmental intergroup theory: Explaining and reducing children's social stereotyping and prejudice. *Current Directions in Psychological Science, 16*(3), 162–6.

Blaut, J. M., McCleary, G. S., and Blaut, A. S. (1970). Environmental mapping in young children. *Environment and Behavior, 2*(3), 335–49.

Blaut, J. M., and Stea, D. (1971). Space, structure and maps. *Tijdschrift voor Economische en Sociale Geografie, 62*, 1–4.

Bloch, M. (1986). *From Blessing to Violence: History and Ideology in the Circumcision Ritual of the Merina of Madagascar.* Cambridge: Cambridge University Press.

Bloustien, G. (2003). *Girl Making: A Cross-Cultural Ethnography on the Processes of Growing Up Female.* New York: Berghahn Books.

Bluebond-Langner, M., and Korbin, J. E. (2007). Challenges and opportunities in the anthropology of childhoods: An introduction to 'Children, Childhoods, and Childhood Studies'. *American Anthropologist, 109*(2), 241–6.

Blum, E. J. (2005). *Reforging the White Republic: Race, Religion, and American Nationalism, 1865–1898.* Baton Rouge: Louisiana State University Press.

Blumberg, S., Bramlett, M., Kogan, M., Schieve, L., Jones, J., and Lu, M. (2013). *Changes in Prevalence of Parent-Reported Autism Spectrum Disorder in School-Aged U.S. Children: 2007 to 2011–2012* (National Health Statistics

Report No. 65). US Department of Health and Human Services Centers for Disease Control and Prevention.

Boddy, J. P. (2007). *Civilizing Women: British Crusades in Colonial Sudan.* Princeton: Princeton University Press.

Bogin, B. (2006). Modern human life history: The evolution of human childhood and fertility. In K. Hawkes and R. Paine (Eds.), *The Evolution of Human Life History* (pp. 197–230). Santa Fe: School of American Research Press.

Bourdieu, P. (1986). The forms of capital. In J. Richardson (Ed.), *Handbook of Theory and Research for the Sociology of Education* (pp. 241–58). New York: Greenwood Press.

Bourdieu, P., and Passeron, J. C. (1990). *Reproduction in Education, Society, and Culture.* London: Sage in association with *Theory, Culture & Society.*

Boyden, J., Ling, B., Myers, W. E., UNICEF, International Child Development Centre, and Rädda barnen (Society). (1998). *What Works for Working Children.* Stockholm: UNICEF, International Child Development.

Brewer, M. (2001). Ingroup identification and intergroup conflict. In R. Ashmore, L. Jussim and D. Wilder (Eds.), *Social Identity, Intergroup Conflict. and Conflict Reduction* (pp. 17–41). Oxford: Oxford University Press.

Brown, J. K. (1963). A cross-cultural study of female initiation rites. *American Anthropologist*, 65(4), 837–53.

Brown, L. M., Chesney-Lind, M., and Stein, N. (2007). Patriarchy matters: Toward a gendered theory of teen violence and victimization. *Violence Against Women*, 13, 1249–73.

Brown, L. M., Chesney-Lind, M., and Stein, N. (2013). Patriarchy matters: Toward a gendered theory of teen violence and victimization. In M. Chesney-Lind and L. Pasko (Eds.), *Girls, Women, and Crime: Selected Readings* (2nd edn, pp. 21–38). Los Angeles: Sage.

Buckingham, D. (1993). *Children Talking Television: The Making of Television Literacy.* Abingdon: RoutledgFalmer.

Burman, E. (1999). Appealing and appalling children. *Psychoanalytic Studies*, 1(3), 285–302.

Butchart, R. E. (2010). *Schooling the Freed People: Teaching, Learning, and the Struggle for Black Freedom, 1861–1876.* Chapel Hill: University of North Carolina Press.

Butler, J. (1990). *Gender Trouble: Feminism and the Subversion of Identity.* New York: Routledge.

Butler, J. (1999). *Gender Trouble: Feminism and the Subversion of Identity* (new edn). New York: Routledge.

Butler, J. (1997). *The Psychic Life of Power: Theories in Subjection.* Stanford: Stanford University Press.

Butler, J. (2011). *Bodies That Matter: On the Discursive Limits of 'Sex'.* New York: Routledge.

Buzawa, E. S., and Hotaling, G. T. (2006). The impact of relationship status, gender, and minor status in the police response to domestic assaults. *Victims & Offenders*, 1(4), 323–360.

Byrne, E., and McQuillan, M. (1999). *Deconstructing Disney.* London: Pluto Press.

Campbell, C. (2005). *The Romantic Ethic and the Spirit of Modern Consumerism* (3rd edn). York: Alcuin Academics.

Cascio, M. A. (2012). Neurodiversity: Autism pride among mothers of children with autism spectrum disorders. *Intellectual and Developmental Disabilities, 50*(3), 273–83.

Caudwell, J. (2014). [Transgender] young men: Gendered subjectivities and the physically active body. *Sport, Education and Society, 19*(4), 398–414.

Caughy, M. O., Leonard, T., Beron, K., and Murdoch, J. (2013). Defining neighborhood boundaries in studies of spatial dependence in child behavior problems. *International Journal of Health Geographics, 12*(1), 1–12.

Certeau, M. de. (2013). *The Practice of Everyday Life*. Berkeley: University of California Press.

Chawla, L. (Ed.). (2002). *Growing Up in an Urbanising World*. London: Earthscan/UNESCO.

Chen, X. (2005). *Tending the Gardens of Citizenship: Child Saving in Toronto, 1880s–1920s*. Toronto: University of Toronto Press.

Chesney-Lind, M., and Irwin, K. (2008). *Beyond Bad Girls: Gender, Violence and Hype*. New York: Routledge.

Chin, E. (2001). *Purchasing Power: Black Kids and American Consumer Culture*. Minneapolis: University of Minnesota Press.

Cidell, J. (2006). The place of individuals in the politics of scale. *Area, 38*(2), 196–203.

Clark, K. B., and Clark, M. P. (1958). Racial identification and preference in Negro children. In E. Maccoby, T. Newcomb and E. Hartley (Eds.), *Readings in Social Psychology* (3rd edn) (pp. 169–78). New York: Holt, Rinehart, and Winston.

Collins, D. C. A., and Kearns, R. A. (2001). Under curfew and under siege? Legal geographies of young people. *Geoforum, 32*(3), 389–403.

Collins, P. H. (2015). Intersectionality's definitional dilemmas. *Annual Review of Sociology, 41*(1), 1–20.

Colombo, J. (2001). The development of visual attention in infancy. *Annual Review of Psychology, 52*(1), 337–67.

Connolly, P. (1998). *Racism, Gender Identities, and Young Children: Social Relations in a Multi-Ethnic, Inner-City Primary School*. London: Routledge.

Cook, D. T. (2013). Taking exception with the child consumer. *Childhood, 20*(4), 423–8.

Corsaro, W. A. (2015). *The Sociology of Childhood* (4th edn). Los Angeles: Sage.

Coulter, C. (2009). *Bush Wives and Girl Soldiers: Women's Lives through War and Peace in Sierra Leone*. Ithaca: Cornell University Press.

Curran, T., and Runswick-Cole, K. (Eds.). (2013). *Disabled Children's Childhood Studies: Critical Approaches in a Global Context*. New York: Palgrave Macmillan.

Curran, T., and Runswick-Cole, K. (2014). Disabled children's childhood studies: A distinct approach? *Disability & Society, 29*(10), 1617–30.

David, B., Grace, D., and Ryan, M. K. (2012). The gender wars: A self categorisation theory perspective on the development of gender identity. In M.

Bennett and F. Sani (Eds.), *The Development of the Social Self* (pp. 135–58). Hove: Psychology Press.

Davidson, E. H. (1937). Early development of public opinion against Southern child labor. *North Carolina Historical Review*, 14(3), 230–50.

Davidson, E. H. (1939). *Child Labor Legislation in the Southern Textile States*. Chapel Hill: University of North Carolina Press.

Davis, S. C., Leman, P. J., and Barrett, M. (2007). Children's implicit and explicit ethnic group attitudes, ethnic group identification, and self-esteem. *International Journal of Behavioral Development*, 31(5), 514–25.

De Wolfe, J. (2014). *Parents of Children with Autism: An Ethnography*. New York: Palgrave Macmillan.

Denham, A. R., Adongo, P. B., Freydberg, N., and Hodgson, A. (2010). Chasing spirits: Clarifying the spirit child phenomenon and infanticide in Northern Ghana. *Social Science & Medicine*, 71(3), 608–15.

Dimock, G. (1993). Children of the mills: Re-reading Lewis Hine's child-labour photographs. *Oxford Art Journal*, 16(2), 37–54.

Donzelot, J. (1980). *The Policing of Families* (R. Hurley, Ed.). London: Hutchinson.

Douglas, M., and Isherwood, B. C. (1996). *The World of Goods: Towards an Anthropology of Consumption: With a New Introduction* (rev. edn). London/New York: Routledge.

Du Bois, W. E. B. (1992). *Dusk of Dawn: An Essay Toward an Autobiography of a Race Concept*. New Brunswick: Transaction Books.

Duane, A. M. (2011). *Suffering Childhood in Early America: Violence, Race, and the Making of the Child Victim*. Athens: University of Georgia Press.

Durkin, K., Nesdale, D., Dempsey, G., and McLean, A. (2012). Young children's responses to media representations of intergroup threat and ethnicity: Media representations of ethnicity. *British Journal of Developmental Psychology*, 30(3), 459–76.

Dyer, R. (1997). *White*. London/New York: Routledge.

Eliot, M. (2003). *Walt Disney: Hollywood's Dark Prince*. London: Andre Deutsch.

Ellemers, N., Kortekaas, P., and Ouwerkerk, J. (1999). Self-categorization, commitment to the group and social self-esteem as related but distinct aspects of social identity. *European Journal of Social Psychology*, 28, 371–98.

Evans, B. (2010). Anticipating fatness: Childhood, affect and the pre-emptive 'war on obesity'. *Transactions of the Institute of British Geographers*, 35(1), 21–38.

Evans, B., Colls, R., and Hörschelmann, K. (2011). 'Change4Life for your kids': Embodied collectives and public health pedagogy. *Sport, Education and Society*, 16(3), 323–41.

Evans, G. (2006). *Educational Failure and Working Class White Children in Britain*. Basingstoke/New York: Palgrave Macmillan.

Evans, J., Davies, B., and Rich, E. (2016). Bernstein, body pedagogies and the corporeal device. In G. Ivinson, B. Davies and J. Fitz (Eds.), *Knowledge and Identity: Concepts and Applications in Bernstein's Sociology* (pp. 176–91). Abingdon: Routledge.

Evans-Pritchard, E. E. (1990). *Kinship and Marriage Among the Nuer.* Oxford: Oxford University Press.

Evans-Pritchard, E. E. (2001). *The Nuer: A Description of the Modes of Livelihood and Political Institutions of a Nilotic People* (rpt). New York: Oxford University Press.

Eyal, G., Hart, B., Onculer, E., Oren, N., and Rossi, N. (2010). *The Autism Matrix: The Social Origins of the Autism Epidemic.* Cambridge: Polity.

Farrugia, D. (2009). Exploring stigma: Medical knowledge and the stigmatisation of parents of children diagnosed with autism spectrum disorder. *Sociology of Health & Illness, 31*(7), 1011–1027.

Fauth, R. C., Leventhal, T., and Brooks-Gunn, J. (2007). Welcome to the neighborhood? Long-term impacts of moving to low-poverty neighborhoods on poor children's and adolescents' outcomes. *Journal of Research on Adolescence, 17*(2), 249–84.

Fields, B. J. (2001). Whiteness, racism and identity. *International Labor and Working-Class History, 60,* 48–56.

Fields, K. E., and Fields, B. J. (2014). *Racecraft: The Soul of Inequality in American Life.* London: Verso.

Fingerson, L. (2005). Agency and the body in adolescent menstrual talk. *Childhood, 12*(1), 91–110.

Flouri, E., Midouhas, E., and Tzatzaki, K. (2015). Neighbourhood and own social housing and early problem behaviour trajectories. *Social Psychiatry and Psychiatric Epidemiology, 50*(2), 203–13.

Flynn, C. L. (1983). *White Land, Black Labor: Caste and Class in Late Nineteenth-Century Georgia.* Baton Rouge: Louisiana State University Press.

Fortes, M. (1949). *The Web of Kinship Among the Tallensi.* Oxford: Oxford University Press.

Foucault, M. (2003). *Society Must Be Defended: Lectures at the Collège de France, 1975–76* (rpt). London: Penguin.

Foucault, M., (2008). *The Birth of Biopolitics: Lectures at the Collège de France, 1978–1979* (M. Senellart, Ed.). Basingstoke: Palgrave Macmillan.

Fraser, N. (2003). *Redistribution or recognition? A Political-Philosophical Exchange.* London: Verso.

Freedman, R. (2008). *Kids at Work: Lewis Hine and the Crusade Against Child Labor.* San Diego: Paw Prints.

Freire, P. (1996). *Pedagogy of the Oppressed* (rev. edn). London: Penguin.

Frith, M. (2005, May 4). Scrap outdated infanticide law, say judges. *Independent.*

Frosh, S., Phoenix, A., and Pattman, R. (2004). *Young Masculinities: Understanding Boys in Contemporary Society* (rpt). Basingstoke: Palgrave.

Furber, M., and Pérez-Peña, R. (2016, July 7). After Philando Castile's killing, Obama calls police shootings 'an American issue'. *New York Times.*

Galster, G. C., and Santiago, A. M. (2006). What's the 'hood got to do with it? Parental perceptions about how neighborhood mechanisms affect their children. *Journal of Urban Affairs, 28*(3), 201–26. http://doi.org/10.1111/j.1467-9906.2006.00289.x

Gill, S. (Ed.). (1993). *Gramsci, Historical Materialism and International Relations.* Cambridge: Cambridge University Press.

Gillborn, D., and Kirton, A. (2000). White heat: Racism, under-achievement and white working-class boys. *International Journal of Inclusive Education*, 4(4), 271–88.

Gilligan, C. (1993). *In a Different Voice: Psychological Theory and Women's Development*. Cambridge MA: Harvard University Press.

Giroux, H. (2001). Breaking into the movies: Pedagogy and the politics of film. *JAC*, 21(3), 583–98.

Goldberg, D. T. (2001). *The Racial State*. Malden: Blackwell.

Gosselin, C. (2000). Anthropology and the politics of excision in Mali: Global and local debates in a postcolonial world. *Anthropologica*, 42(1), 43–60.

Gottlieb, A. (2004). *The Afterlife Is Where We Come From: The Culture of Infancy in West Africa*. Chicago: University of Chicago Press.

Graham, E., Jordan, L. P., and Yeoh, B. S. A. (2015). Parental migration and the mental health of those who stay behind to care for children in South-East Asia. *Social Science & Medicine*, 132, 225–35.

Gram, M. (2010). Self-reporting vs. observation: Some cautionary examples from parent/child food shopping behaviour: Self-reporting vs. observation. *International Journal of Consumer Studies*, 34(4), 394–9.

Granpeesheh, D., Tarbox, J., Dixon, D. R., Carr, E., and Herbert, M. (2009). Retrospective analysis of clinical records in 38 cases of recovery from autism. *Annals of Clinical Psychiatry*, 21(4), 195–204.

Grier, B. C. (2006). *Invisible Hands: Child Labor and the State in Colonial Zimbabwe*. Portsmouth: Heinemann.

Guerrero, L. (2009). Can the subaltern shop? The commodification of difference in the Bratz dolls. *Cultural Studies ↔ Critical Methodologies*, 9(2), 186–96.

Haar, M. (1977). Nietzsche and metaphysical language. In D. B. Allison (Ed.), *The New Nietzsche: Contemporary Styles of Interpretation* (pp. 5–36). New York: Dell.

Halberstam, J. (1998). *Female Masculinity*. Durham NC: Duke University Press.

Hall, D. E. (2004). *Subjectivity*. New York: Routledge.

Hall, J. D., Leloudis, J., Korstad, R., Murphy, M., Jones, L. A., and Daly, C. B. (1987). *Like a Family: The Making of a Southern Cotton Mill World*. Chapel Hill: University of North Carolina Press.

Hamilton, K., and Catterall, M. (2006). Consuming love in poor families: Children's influence on consumption decisions. *Journal of Marketing Management*, 22(9–10), 1031–52.

Hannig, A. (2014). Spiritual border crossings: Childbirth, postpartum seclusion and religious alterity in Amhara, Ethiopia. *Africa*, 84(2), 294–313.

Hardman, C. (2001). Can there be an anthropology of children? *Childhood*, 8(4), 501–17.

Harris, A. (Ed.). (2004a). *All About the Girl: Culture, Power, and Identity*. New York: Routledge.

Harris, A. (2004b). *Future Girl: Young Women in the Twenty-First Century*. New York: Routledge.

Hart, R. A. (1997). *Children's Participation: The Theory and Practice of Involving Young Citizens in Community Development and Environmental Care*. London: Earthscan.

Hart, R. A. (2002). *Children's Participation: The Theory and Practice of Involving Young Citizens in Community Development and Environmental Care* (rpt). New York: UNICEF.

Hebdige, D. (1991). *Subculture: The Meaning of Style.* London/New York: Routledge.

Hecht, T. (1998). *At Home in the Street: Street Children of Northeast Brazil.* Cambridge: Cambridge University Press.

Hegel, G. W. F., Miller, A. V., and Findlay, J. N. (1977). *Phenomenology of Spirit* (rpt). Oxford: Oxford University Press.

Henriques, J., Hollway, W., Urwin, C., Venn, C., and Walkerdine, V. (1998). *Changing the Subject: Psychology, Social Regulation and Subjectivity.* London: Routledge.

Hewitt, R., and Wells, K. (2005). *On the Margins? A Qualitative Study of White Camden Households at Risk of Exclusion from Education and Employment.* Camden: Camden Council, Equalities and Exclusion Team.

Hiaasen, C. (1998). *Team Rodent: How Disney Devours the World.* New York: Ballantine Books.

Hoang, L. A., Lam, T., Yeoh, B. S. A., and Graham, E. (2015). Transnational migration, changing care arrangements and left-behind children's responses in South-East Asia. *Children's Geographies*, 13(3), 263–77.

Hoang, L. A., and Yeoh, B. S. A. (2015). Children's agency and its contradictions in the context of transnational labour migration from Vietnam. *Global Networks*, 15(2), 180–97.

Hoffman, D. (2011). *The War Machines: Young Men and Violence in Sierra Leone and Liberia.* Durham NC: Duke University Press.

Holloway, S. L., and Valentine, G. (Eds.). (2000a). *Children's Geographies: Playing, Living, Learning.* London: Routledge.

Holloway, S. L., and Valentine, G. (2000b). The 'street' as thirdspace. In S. L. Holloway and G. Valentine (Eds.), *Children's Geographies: Playing, Living, Learning.* London: Routledge.

Holsinger, K., Belknap, J., and Sutherland, J. (1999). *Assessing the Gender Specific Program and Service Needs for Adolescent Females in the Juvenile Justice System.* Colombus: Office of Criminal Justice Services.

Holt, J. (2013). *Escape from Childhood: The Needs and Rights of Children.* Medford: Author.

Holt, L. (2013). Exploring the emergence of the subject in power: Infant geographies. *Environment and Planning D: Society and Space*, 31(4), 645–63.

Holt, L. (2016). Food, feeding and the material everyday geographies of infants: Possibilities and potentials. *Social & Cultural Geography*, 1–18.

Honneth, A. (1995). *The Struggle for Recognition: The Moral Grammar of Social Conflicts.* Cambridge: Polity.

Hopkins, P. E., and Hill, M. (2008). Pre-flight experiences and migration stories: The accounts of unaccompanied asylum-seeking children. *Children's Geographies*, 6(3), 257–68.

Hörschelmann, K., and Van Blerk, L. (2011). *Children, Youth and the City.* Abingdon: Routledge.

Houzel, D. (2004). The psychoanalysis of infantile autism. *Journal of Child Psychotherapy*, *30*(2), 225–37.

Hughes, D. (2003). Correlates of African American and Latino parents' messages to children about ethnicity and race: A comparative study of racial socialization. *American Journal of Community Psychology*, *31*(1–2), 15–33.

Humphries, J. (2010). *Childhood and Child Labour in the British Industrial Revolution*. Cambridge: Cambridge University Press.

Ingram, N. (2009). Working-class boys, educational success and the misrecognition of working-class culture. *British Journal of Sociology of Education*, *30*(4), 421–34.

Jackson, T. E., and Falmagne, R. J. (2013). Women wearing white: Discourses of menstruation and the experience of menarche. *Feminism & Psychology*, *23*(3), 379–398.

James, A. (1979). Confections, concoctions and conceptions. *Journal of the Anthropological Society of Oxford*, *10*, 83–95.

James, A. (2007). Giving voice to children's voices: Practices and problems, pitfalls and potentials. *American Anthropologist*, *109*(2), 261–72.

James, A., Jenks, C., and Prout, A. (1999). *Theorizing Childhood* (rpt). Cambridge: Polity.

James, A., and Prout, A. (Eds.). (1997). *Constructing and Reconstructing Childhood: Contemporary Issues in the Sociological Study of Childhood*. London: Falmer Press.

James, W. (2013). *Principles of Psychology: Part I*. n.p.: Read Books.

James, W. R. (2000). Placing the unborn: On the social recognition of new life. *Anthropology & Medicine*, *7*(2), 169–89.

Jeffrey, C. (2010). Geographies of children and youth I: Eroding maps of life. *Progress in Human Geography*, *34*(4), 496–505.

Jenkins, R. (1996). *Social Identity* (3rd edn). London: Routledge.

Jenks, C. (Ed.). (1982). *The Sociology of Childhood: Essential Readings*. London: Batsford.

Jenks, C. (2005). *Childhood* (2nd edn). London/New York: Routledge.

John, D. R. (1999). Consumer socialization of children: A retrospective look at twenty-five years of research. *Journal of Consumer Research*, *26*, 183–213.

Jonas, A. E. G. (2006). Pro scale: Further reflections on the 'scale debate' in human geography. *Transactions of the Institute of British Geographers*, *31*(3), 399–406.

Jones, G. A., and Rodgers, D. (Eds.). (2009). *Youth Violence in Latin America: Gangs and Juvenile Justice in Perspective*. Basingstoke: Palgrave Macmillan.

Kane, E. W. (2013). *Rethinking Gender and Sexuality in Childhood*. London: Bloomsbury.

Kanner, L. (1943). Autistic disturbances of affective contact. *Nervous Child*, *2*, 217–50.

Katz, C. (2004). *Growing Up Global: Economic Restructuring and Children's Everyday Lives*. Minneapolis: University of Minnesota Press.

Kelly, P. F. (2000). *Landscapes of Globalization: Human Geographies of Economic Change in the Philippines*. London: Routledge.

Kinder, M. (Ed.). (1999). *Kids' Media Culture*. Durham NC: Duke University Press.

King, W. (1998). *Stolen Childhood: Slave Youth in Nineteenth-Century America* (rpt). Bloomington: Indiana University Press.

King, W. (2005). *African American Childhoods: Historical Perspectives from Slavery to Civil Rights*. New York: Palgrave Macmillan.

Kjaran, J. I., and Kristinsdóttir, G. (2015). Schooling sexualities and gendered bodies: Experiences of LGBT students in Icelandic upper secondary schools. *International Journal of Inclusive Education*, 19(9), 978–93.

Knupfer, A. M. (2001). *Reform and Resistance: Gender, Delinquency, and America's First Juvenile Court*. New York: Routledge.

Kohlberg, L. (1981). *Essays on Moral Development*. San Francisco: Harper & Row.

Konig, A. (2008). Which clothes suit me? The presentation of the juvenile self. *Childhood*, 15(2), 225–37.

Kovats-Bernat, J. (2006). *Sleeping Rough in Port-au-Prince: An Ethnography of Street Children and Violence in Haiti*. Gainesville: University Press of Florida.

Koven, S. (1997). Dr. Barnardo's 'artistic fictions': Photography, sexuality, and the ragged child in Victorian London. *Radical History Review*, 1997(69), 6–45.

Kraftl, P., Horton, J., and Tucker, F. (2014). Children's geographies. In H. Montgomery (Ed.), *Oxford Bibliographies for Childhood Studies*. DOI: 10.1093/obo/9780199791231-0080

Lacassagne, A., Nieguth, T., and Dépelteau, F. (Eds.). (2011). *Investigating Shrek: Power, Identity, and Ideology*. New York: Palgrave Macmillan.

Lancy, D. F. (2008). *The Anthropology of Childhood: Cherubs, Chattel, Changelings*. Cambridge: Cambridge University Press.

Lander, E. M. (1953). Slave labor in South Carolina cotton mills. *Journal of Negro History*, 38(2), 161–73.

Lareau, A. (2011). *Unequal Childhoods: Class, Race, and Family Life* (2nd edn with an update a decade later). Berkeley: University of California Press.

Lavelle, T. A., Weinstein, M. C., Newhouse, J. P., Munir, K., Kuhlthau, K. A., and Prosser, L. A. (2014). Economic burden of childhood autism spectrum disorders. *Pediatrics*, 133(3), e520–9.

Layne, L. L. (2000). 'He was a real baby with baby things': A material culture analysis of personhood, parenthood and pregnancy loss. *Journal of Material Culture*, 5(3), 321–45.

Lee, J. (2009). Bodies at menarche: Stories of shame, concealment, and sexual maturation. *Sex Roles*, 60(9/10), 615–27.

Lee, N. (2005). *Childhood and Society: Growing Up in an Age of Uncertainty* (rpt). Maidenhead: Open University Press.

Leiser, D., Sevon, G., Levy, D., Leiser, D., Sevon, G., and Levy, D. (1990). Children's economic socialization: Summarizing the cross-cultural comparison of ten countries. *Journal of Economic Psychology*, 11(4), 591–614.

Leonard, L. (2000). "We did it for pleasure only": Hearing alternative tales of female circumcision. *Qualitative Inquiry*, 6(2).

Leppik, I. E., Cloyd, J., and Sawchuk, R. J. (1978). Coefficient of variation as measure of compliance. *Lancet*, 2(8094), 849.

Levander, C. F. (2004). 'Let her white progeny offset her dark one': The child and the racial politics of nation making. *American Literature*, 76(2), 221–46.

Levander, C. F. (2006). *Cradle of Liberty: Race, the Child, and National Belonging from Thomas Jefferson to W. E. B. Du Bois.* Durham NC: Duke University Press.

Leventhal, T., and Brooks-Gunn, J. (2003). Children and youth in neighborhood contexts. *Current Directions in Psychological Science*, 12(1), 27–31.

LeVine, R. A. (2007). Ethnographic studies of childhood: A historical overview. *American Anthropologist*, 109, 247–60.

Livingstone, S. M. (2002). *Young People and New Media: Childhood and the Changing Media Environment.* London: Sage.

Locke, J. (1997). *An Essay Concerning Human Understanding.* London: Penguin.

Lovaas, O. I. (1987). Behavioral treatment and normal educational and intellectual functioning in young autistic children. *Journal of Consulting and Clinical Psychology*, 55(1), 3–9.

Lugo-Lugo, C. R., and Bloodsworth-Lugo, M. K. (2009). 'Look out new world, here we come'? Race, racialization, and sexuality in four children's animated films by Disney, Pixar, and DreamWorks. *Cultural Studies ↔ Critical Methodologies*, 9, 166–78.

Lunt, P. (1995). Psychological approaches to consumption. In D. Miller (Ed.), *Acknowledging Consumption: A Review of New Studies* (pp. 238–63). London: Routledge.

Lutkehaus, N., and Roscoe, P. B. (Eds.). (1995). *Gender Rituals: Female Initiation in Melanesia.* New York: Routledge.

Lymer, J. (2014). Infant imitation and the self: A response to Welsh. *Philosophical Psychology*, 27(2), 235–57.

Lynch, K., and Banerjee, T. (Eds.). (1977). *Growing Up in Cities: Studies of the Spatial Environment of Adolescence in Cracow, Melbourne, Mexico City, Salta, Toluca, and Warszawa.* Cambridge MA: MIT Press.

Mabry, W. A. (1940). Reviewed work: *Child Labor Legislation in the Southern Textile States* by Elizabeth H. Davidson. *North Carolina Historical Review*, 17(1), 74–7.

Mac an Ghaill, M. (1988). *Young, Gifted, and Black: Student–Teacher Relations in the Schooling of Black Youth.* Milton Keynes: Open University Press.

Madriaga, M. (2010). 'I avoid pubs and the student union like the plague': Students with Asperger syndrome and their negotiation of university spaces. *Children's Geographies*, 8, 23–34.

Malinowski, B. (2005). *The Sexual Life of Savages in North-Western Melanesia: An Ethnographic Account of Courtship, Marriage, and Family Life among the Natives of the Trobriand Islands, British New Guinea* (H. Ellis, Foreword). Whitefish: Kessinger.

Mallett, R., and Timimi, S. (2016). *Re-Thinking Autism: Diagnosis, Identity and Equality* (K. Runswick-Cole, Ed.). London: Jessica Kingsley.

Malmqvist, E., and Zeiler, K. (2010). Cultural norms, the phenomenology of incorporation, and the experience of having a child born with ambiguous sex. *Social Theory and Practice*, 36(1), 133–56.

Mapplethorpe, E. (2016). *One: Sons and Daughters*. Brooklyn: PowerHouse.

Marling, K. A. (Ed.). (1997). *Designing Disney's Theme Parks: The Architecture of Reassurance*. Montréal: Centre Canadien d'Architecture/Canadian Centre for Architecture.

Marston, S. A., Jones, J. P., and Woodward, K. (2005). Human geography without scale. *Transactions of the Institute of British Geographers*, 30(4), 416–32.

Martens, L., Scott, S., and Southerton, D. (2004). Bringing children (and parents) into the sociology of consumption. *Journal of Consumer Culture*, 4(2), 155–82.

Martens, P. J., Chateau, D. G., Burland, E. M. J., Finlayson, G. S., Smith, M. J., Taylor, C. R., ... Bolton, J. M. (2014). The effect of neighborhood socioeconomic status on education and health outcomes for children living in social housing. *American Journal of Public Health*, 104(11), 2103–13.

Martin, C. L., and Dinella, L. M. (2002). Children's gender cognitions, the social environment and sex differences in cognitive domains. In A. V. McGillicuddy-De Lisi and R. De Lisi (Eds.), *Biology, Society, and Behavior: The Development of Sex Differences in Cognition* (pp. 207–41). Westport: Ablex.

Marx, K., and Engels, F. (1970). *The German Ideology* (C. J. Arthur, Ed.). London: Lawrence & Wishart.

Marx, K. (1981). *Capital: A Critique of Political Economy*, vol. 1. London/New York: Penguin in association with *New Left Review*.

Marx, K., and Engels, F. (2008). *The Communist Manifesto* (S. Moore, Trans.; D. Harvey, Intro.). London: Pluto Press.

Matthews, H., and Limb, M. (1999). Defining an agenda for the geography of children: Review and prospect. *Progress in Human Geography*, 23(1), 61–90.

Matthews, H., Taylor, M., Sherwood, K., Tucker, F., and Limb, M. (2000). Growing-up in the countryside: Children and the rural idyll. *Journal of Rural Studies*, 16(2), 141–53.

Mayall, B. (2002). *Towards a Sociology for Childhood: Thinking from Children's Lives*. Buckingham: Open University Press.

McDonough, P. M. (1997). *Choosing Colleges: How Social Class and Schools Structure Opportunity*. Albany: State University of New York Press.

McDowell, L. (2002). Transitions to work: Masculine identities, youth inequality and labour market change. *Gender, Place & Culture*, 9(1), 39–59.

McDowell, L. (2003). *Redundant Masculinities? Employment Change and White Working Class Youth*. Malden: Blackwell.

McEachin, J. J., Smith, T., and Lovaas, O. I. (1993). Long-term outcome for children with autism who received early intensive behavioral treatment. *American Journal of Mental Retardation*, 97(4), 359–72.

McGee, G. G., Paradis, T., and Feldman, R. S. (1993). Free effects of integration on levels of autistic behavior. *Topics in Early Childhood Special Education*, 13, 57–67.

McGuire, L., Rutland, A., and Nesdale, D. (2015). Peer group norms and accountability moderate the effect of school norms on children's intergroup attitudes. *Child Development*, 86(4), 1290–7.

McRobbie, A. (1991). Settling accounts with subculture: A feminist critique. In A. McRobbie (Ed.), *Feminism and Youth Culture: From 'Jackie' to 'Just Seventeen'* (pp. 16–34). London: Macmillan Education.

Mead, M. (2001). *Coming of Age in Samoa: A Psychological Study of Primitive Youth for Western Civilisation* (1st Perennial Classics edn). New York: Perennial Classics.

Meador, K. G., and Shuman, J. J. (2000). Who/se we are: Baptism as personhood. *Christian Bioethics: Non-Ecumenical Studies in Medical Morality*, 6(1), 71–83.

Miller, D. (1995). *Material Culture and Mass Consumption* (rpt). Oxford: Blackwell.

Miller, S. (2012). *History of Childhood in America*. Retrieved from http://www.oxfordbibliographies.com/display/id/obo-9780199791231-0052

Mills, C. W. (2011). *The Racial Contract* (rpt). Ithaca: Cornell University Press.

Mitchell, C., and Reid-Walsh, J. (2002). *Researching Children's Popular Culture: The Cultural Spaces of Childhood*. London/New York: Routledge.

Mitchell, C., and Rentschler, C. A. (Eds.). (2016). *Girlhood and the Politics of Place*. New York: Berghahn Books.

Mitchell, M. N. (2008). *Raising Freedom's Child: Black Children and Visions of the Future after Slavery*. New York: New York University Press.

Moehling, C. M. (2004). Family structure, school attendance, and child labor in the American South in 1900 and 1910. *Explorations in Economic History*, 41(1), 73–100.

Mohammadzaheri, F., Koegel, L. K., Rezaee, M., and Rafiee, S. M. (2014). A randomized clinical trial comparison between pivotal response treatment (PRT) and structured applied behavior analysis (ABA) intervention for children with autism. *Journal of Autism and Developmental Disorders*, 44(11), 2769–77.

Montgomery, H. (2009). *An Introduction to Childhood: Anthropological Perspectives on Children's Lives*. Chichester: Wiley-Blackwell.

Montgomery, H. (2012). *Anthropology of Childhood*. Retrieved from http://www.oxfordbibliographies.com/display/id/obo-9780199791231-0002

Moore, H. L. (2009). Epistemology and ethics: Perspectives from Africa. *Social Analysis*, 53(2), 207–18.

Morgan, S. W., and Stevens, P. E. (2012). Transgender identity development as represented by a group of transgendered adults. *Issues in Mental Health Nursing*, 33(5), 301–8.

Moskowitz, M. L. (2001). *The Haunting Fetus: Abortion, Sexuality, and the Spirit World in Taiwan*. Honolulu: University of Hawaii Press.

Mukhopadhyay, S. (2008). *Understanding Autism Through Rapid Prompting Method*. Denver: Outskirts Press.

Mullen, B., Brown, R., and Smith, C. (1992). Ingroup bias as a function of salience, relevance, and status: An integration. *European Journal of Social Psychology*, 22(2), 103–22.

Mulvey, L. (1975). Visual pleasure and narrative cinema. *Screen*, 16(3), 6–18.

Nayak, A. (2006). Displaced masculinities: Chavs, youth and class in the post-industrial city. *Sociology*, 40(5), 813–31.

Nayak, A., and Kehily, M. J. (2013). *Gender, Youth, and Culture: Young Masculinities and Femininities* (2nd edn). Basingstoke: Palgrave Macmillan.

Nelson, C. A. (2001). The development and neural bases of face recognition. *Infant and Child Development*, 10(1–2), 3–18.

Nesdale, D. (2001a). The development of prejudice in children. In M. A. Augoustinos and K. J. Reynolds (Eds.), *Understanding Prejudice, Racism, and Social Conflict* (pp. 57–73). London: Sage.

Nesdale, D. (2001b). Language and the development of children's ethnic prejudice. *Journal of Language and Social Psychology*, 20, 90–110.

Nesdale, D. (2004). Social identity processes and children's ethnic prejudice. In M. Bennett and F. Sani (Eds.), *The Development of the Social Self* (pp. 219–46). London: Psychology Press.

Nesdale, D., Durkin, K., Maass, A., and Griffiths, J. (2005). Threat, group identification, and children's ethnic prejudice. *Social Development*, 14(2), 189–205.

Nesdale, D., Lawson, M. J., Durkin, K., and Duffy, A. (2010). Effects of information about group members on young children's attitudes towards the in-group and out-group. *British Journal of Developmental Psychology*, 28(2), 467–82.

Nicholson-Crotty, S., Birchmeier, Z., and Valentine, D. (2009). Exploring the impact of school discipline on racial disproportion in the juvenile justice system. *Social Science Quarterly*, 90(4), 1003–18.

Ochs, E., and Solomon, O. (2010). Autistic sociality. *Ethos*, 38(1), 69–92.

Offit, T. A. (2008). *Conquistadores de la Calle: Child Street Labor in Guatemala City*. Austin: University of Texas Press.

Omi, M., and Winant, H. (2015). *Racial Formation in the United States* (3rd edn). New York: Routledge/Taylor & Francis Group.

Opie, I. A., and Opie, P. (2001). *The Lore and Language of Schoolchildren*. New York: New York Review Books.

Oswell, D. (2013). *The Agency of Children: From Family to Global Human Rights*. Cambridge: Cambridge University Press.

Osypuk, T. L. (2015). Shifting from policy relevance to policy translation: Do housing and neighborhoods affect children's mental health? *Social Psychiatry and Psychiatric Epidemiology*, 50(2), 215–17.

Panelli, R., Punch, S., and Robson, E. (Eds.). (2007). *Global Perspectives on Rural Childhood and Youth: Young Rural Lives*. New York: Routledge.

Panter-Brick, C. (2004). Homelessness, poverty, and risks to health: Beyond at risk categorizations of street children (1). *Children's Geographies*, 2(1), 83–94.

Pasko, L. (2010). Damaged daughters: The history of girls' sexuality and the juvenile justice system. *Journal of Criminal Law and Criminology*, 100, 1009–130.

Peacock, G., Amendah, D., Ouyang, L., and Grosse, S. D. (2012). Autism spectrum disorders and health care expenditures: The effects of co-occurring conditions. *Journal of Developmental & Behavioral Pediatrics*, *33*(1), 2–8. http://doi.org/10.1097/DBP.0b013e31823969de

Perkins, K. L., and Sampson, R. J. (2015). Compounded deprivation in the transition to adulthood: The intersection of racial and economic inequality among Chicagoans, 1995–2013. *RSF: The Russell Sage Foundation Journal of the Social Sciences*, *1*(1), 35–54.

Pettit, B. (2004). Moving and children's social connections: Neighborhood context and the consequences of moving for low-income families. *Sociological Forum*, *19*(2), 285–311.

Piaget, J. (2001). *The Language and Thought of the Child*. London: Routledge.

Pilcher, J. (2011). No logo? Children's consumption of fashion. *Childhood*, *18*(1), 128–41.

Pilcher, J. (2013). 'Small, but very determined': A novel theorization of children's consumption of clothing. *Cultural Sociology*, *7*(1), 86–100.

Pina-Cabral, J. de. (1986). *Sons of Adam, Daughters of Eve: The Peasant Worldview of the Alto Minho*. Oxford: Oxford University Press.

Pipher, M. (1994). *Reviving Ophelia: Saving the Selves of Adolescent Girls*. New York: Ballantine Books.

Pomfret, D. M. (2009). Raising Eurasia: Race, class, and age in French and British colonies. *Comparative Studies in Society and History*, *51*(2), 314–43.

Pomfret, D. M. (2016). *Youth and Empire: Trans-Colonial Childhoods in British and French Asia*. Stanford: Stanford University Press.

Porter, C., and Goyal, R. (2016). Social protection for all ages? Impacts of Ethiopia's Productive Safety Net Program on child nutrition. *Social Science & Medicine*, *159*, 92–9.

Powlishta, K. K. (2012). Gender as a social category: Intergroup processes and gender-role development. In M. Bennett and F. Sani (Eds.), *The Development of the Social Self* (pp. 103–34). Hove: Psychology Press.

Pratt, G. (2012). *Families Apart: Migrant Mothers and the Conflicts of Labor and Love*. Minneapolis: University of Minnesota Press.

Prout, A. (Ed.). (2000). *The Body, Childhood and Society*. Basingstoke: Macmillan.

Pugh, A. (2009). *Longing and Belonging: Parents, Children and Consumer Culture*. Berkeley: University of California Press.

Quintana, S. M., Chao, R. K., Cross Jr., W. E., Hughes, D., Nelson-Le Gall, S., Aboud, F. E., … Vietze, D. L. (2006, October 9). Race, ethnicity, and culture in child development: Contemporary research and future directions. *Child Development*, pp. 1129–41.

Qvortrup, J. (1994). Gender and generation: Feminism and the 'child question'. In J. Qvortrup, M. Bardy, G. Sgritta and H. Wintersberger (Eds.), *Childhood Matters: Social Theory, Practice and Politics* (pp. 27–42). Aldershot: Avebury.

Qvortrup, J., Bardy, M., Sgritta, G., and Wintersberger, H. (Eds.). (1994). *Childhood Matters: Social Theory, Practice and Politics*. Aldershot: Avebury.

Read, M. (1987). *Children of Their Fathers: Growing Up Among the Ngoni of Malawi*. Prospect Heights: Waveland Press.

Reay, D. (2001). Finding or losing yourself? Working-class relationships to education. *Journal of Education Policy*, *16*(4), 333–46.

Richards, A. I. (1995). *Chisungu: A Girls' Initiation Ceremony among the Bemba of Zambia* (rpt). London: Routledge.

Ritterhouse, J. L. (2006). *Growing Up Jim Crow: How Black and White Southern Children Learned Race.* Chapel Hill: University of North Carolina Press.

Robinson, J. V., and James, A. L. (1975). Some observations on the effects produced in white mice following the injection of certain suspensions of corroding bacilli. *British Journal of Experimental Pathology*, 56(1), 14–16.

Rogers, S. J., and Vismara, L. A. (2008). Evidence-based comprehensive treatments for early autism. *Journal of Clinical Child & Adolescent Psychology*, 37, 8–38.

Rose, N. S. (1999). *Governing the Soul: The Shaping of the Private Self.* New York: Free Association Books.

Rose, N. S., and Abi-Rached, J. M. (2013). *Neuro: The New Brain Sciences and the Management of the Mind.* Princeton: Princeton University Press.

Roth, L. (2009). Home on the range: Kids, visual culture, and cognitive equity. *Cultural Studies ↔ Critical Methodologies*, 9(2), 141–8.

Rousseau, J.-J. (1991). *Emile: or, On Education* (A. Bloom, Trans. and Ed.). Harmondsworth: Penguin.

Rowling, J. K. (2000). *Harry Potter and the Philosopher's Stone.* London: Bloomsbury.

Ruble, D. N., Alvarez, J., Bachman, M., Cameron, J., Fuligni, A., Garcia Coll, C., and Rhee, E. (2004). The development of a sense of 'we': The emergence and implications of children's collective identity. In M. Bennett and F. Sani (Eds.), *The Development of the Social Self* (pp. 29–76). Hove: Psychology Press.

Ruddick, S. (2003). The politics of aging: Globalization and the restructuring of youth and childhood. *Antipode*, 35(2), 334–62.

Ruddick, S. M. (1996). *Young and Homeless in Hollywood: Mapping Social Identities.* New York: Routledge.

Runswick-Cole, K. (2016). Understanding this *thing* called autism. In R. Mallett, S. Timimi, and K. Runswick-Cole (Eds.), *Re-Thinking Autism: Diagnosis, Identity and Equality* (pp. 19–29). London: Jessica Kingsley.

Rutter, M. L. (2011). Progress in understanding autism: 2007–2010. *Journal of Autism and Developmental Disorders*, 41(4), 395–404.

Salad, H. (2015). Female genital cutting: Exploring the perspective of Somali women in London on the discourse against FGC. MSc dissertation, Birkbeck, University of London.

Sallee, S. (2004). *The Whiteness of Child Labor Reform in the New South.* Athens: University of Georgia Press.

Saltmarsh, S. (2009). Becoming economic subjects: Agency, consumption and popular culture in early childhood. *Discourse: Studies in the Cultural Politics of Education*, 30(1), 47–59.

Sampson, R., Morenoff, J., and Felton, E. (1999). Beyond social capital: Spatial dynamics of collective efficacy for children. *American Sociological Review*, 64, 633–60.

Sampson, R. J., and Sharkey, P. (2008). Neighborhood selection and the social reproduction of concentrated racial inequality. *Demography*, 45(1), 1–29.

Sani, F., and Bennett, M. (2004). Developmental aspects of social identity. In M. Bennett and F. Sani (Eds.), *The Development of the Social Self* (pp. 77–103). Hove: Psychology Press.

Saunders, F. S. (2016, March 3). Where on Earth are you? *London Review of Books*, pp. 7–12.

Sausa, L. A. (2005). Translating research into practice: Trans youth recommendations for improving school systems. *Journal of Gay & Lesbian Issues in Education*, 3(1), 15–28.

Savage, M., Devine, F., Cunningham, N., Taylor, M., Li, Y., Hjellbrekke, J., Le Roux, B., Friedman, S., and Miles, A. (2013). A new model of social class? Findings from the BBC's Great British Class Survey experiment. *Sociology*, 47, 219–50.

Savarese, R. J. (moderator). (2010). Parent and sibling roundtable: Neurodiversity and caregiving. *Disability Studies Quarterly*, 30(1). Retrieved from http://www.dsq-sds.org/article/view/1061/1236

Schaffner, L. (2006). *Girls in Trouble with the Law*. New Brunswick: Rutgers University Press.

Schor, J. (2004). *Born to Buy: The Commercialized Child and the New Consumer Culture*. New York: Scribner.

Segal, L. (2001). Back to the boys? Temptations of the good gender theorist. *Textual Practice*, 15, 231–50.

Seiter, E. (1993). *Sold Separately: Children and Parents in Consumer Culture*. New Brunswick: Rutgers University Press.

Sennett, R., and Cobb, J. (1973). *The Hidden Injuries of Class*. New York: Vintage Books.

Serrato, P. (2009). 'They are?!': Latino difference vis-à-vis *Dragon Tales*. *Cultural Studies ↔ Critical Methodologies*, 9(2), 149–65.

Shai, D., and Belsky, J. (2011). When words just won't do: Introducing parental embodied mentalizing. *Child Development Perspectives*, 5(3), 173–80.

Shaw, A. (2014). Rituals of infant death: Defining life and Islamic personhood. *Bioethics*, 28(2), 84–95.

Shilling, C. (2012). *The Body and Social Theory* (3rd edn). Los Angeles: Sage.

Sickmund, M., Sladky, A., and Kang, W. (2015). Easy access to juvenile court statistics: 1985–2013. *National Juvenile Court Data Archive: Juvenile Court Case Records 1985–2013*. Pittsburgh, PA: NCJJ Online. http://www.ojjdp.gov/ojstatbb/ezajcs

Silverman, C. (2012). *Understanding Autism: Parents, Doctors, and the History of a Disorder*. Princeton: Princeton University Press.

Silverman, E. K. (2004). Anthropology and circumcision. *Annual Review of Anthropology*, 33, 419–45.

Simkins, S., Hirsch, A. E., Horvat, E. M, and Moss, M. B. (2004). School to prison pipeline for girls: The role of physical and sexual abuse. *Children's Legal Rights Journal*, 24(4), 56–72.

Simmons, D. J., Keane, A. T., Holtzman, R. B., and Marshall, J. H. (1975). Plugged haversian canals and skeletal dose in radium cases. *Health Physics*, 29(5), 767–75.

Simms, E.-M. (2001). Milk and flesh: A phenomenological reflection on infancy and coexistence. *Journal of Phenomenological Psychology, 32*(1), 22–40.

Sinclair, J. (1993). Don't mourn for us. *Our Voice, 1*(3). Retrieved from http://www.autreat.com/dont_mourn.html

Singer, P. (2011). *Practical Ethics* (3rd edn). New York: Cambridge University Press.

Sinnott, M. (2014). Baby ghosts: Child spirits and contemporary conceptions of childhood in Thailand. *TRaNS: Trans-Regional and National Studies of Southeast Asia, 2*(2), 293–317.

Skelton, T. (Ed.-in-chief). (2016–). *Geographies of Children and Young People* (12 vols.). New York: Springer.

Smith, K. (2012). Producing governable subjects: Images of childhood old and new. *Childhood, 19*(1), 24–37.

Smith, K. M. (2014). *The Government of Childhood: Discourse, Power and Subjectivity*. Basingstoke: Palgrave Macmillan.

Smith, T., Lovaas, N. W., and Lovaas, O. I. (2002). Behaviors of children with high-functioning autism when paired with typically developing versus delayed peers. *Behavioral Interventions, 17*, 129–43.

Smoodin, E. L. (Ed.). (1994). *Disney Discourse: Producing the Magic Kingdom*. New York: Routledge.

Sofaer Derevenski, J. S. (2000). *Children and Material Culture*. London: Routledge.

Solomon, O., and Bagatell, N. (2010). Introduction: Autism: Rethinking the possibilities. *Ethos, 38*(1), 1–7.

Sommers, C. H. (1985). *Who Stole Feminism: How Women Have Betrayed Women*. New York: Simon & Schuster.

Stack, C. B. (2003). *All Our Kin: Strategies for Survival in a Black Community* (rpt). New York: Basic Books.

Stasch, R. (2009). *Society of Others: Kinship and Mourning in a West Papuan Place*. Berkeley: University of California Press.

Stea, D. (2005). Jim Blaut's youngest mappers: Children's geography and the geography of children. *Antipode, 37*(5), 990–1002.

Stearns, P. N. (2011). *Childhood in World History* (2nd edn). London: Routledge.

Tajfel, H. (1970). Aspects of national and ethnic loyalty. *Social Science Information, 9*(3), 119–44.

Tajfel, H., Billig, M. G., Bundy, R. P., and Flament, C. (1971). Social categorization and intergroup behaviour. *European Journal of Social Psychology, 1*(2), 149–78.

Tatum, B. D. (2003). *'Why Are All the Black Kids Sitting Together in the Cafeteria?': And Other Conversations about Race*. New York: Basic Books.

Thorne, B. (1993). *Gender Play: Girls and Boys in School*. New Brunswick: Rutgers University Press.

Tomasello, M., Kruger, A., and Ratner, H. (1993). Cultural learning. *Behavioral and Brain Sciences, 16*(3), 495–552.

Torgovnick, M. (1991). *Gone Primitive: Savage Intellects, Modern Lives* (rpt). Chicago: University of Chicago Press.

Tucker, F., and Matthews, H. (2001). 'They don't like girls hanging around there': Conflicts over recreational space in rural Northamptonshire. *Area*, *33*(2), 161–8.

Turner, V. W. (1970). *The Forest of Symbols: Aspects of Ndembu Ritual*. Ithaca: Cornell University Press.

Tustin, F. (1992). *Autistic States in Children* (rev. edn). London: Tavistock/ Routledge.

UNHCR, UNICEF, and IOM. (2016). With growing numbers of child deaths at sea, UN agencies call for enhancing safety for refugees and migrants. *UNHCR*. Retrieved from http://www.unhcr.org/uk/news/press/2016/2/56c6e7676/growing-numbers-child-deaths-sea-un-agencies-call-enhancing-safety-refugees.html

UNICEF (Ed.). (2012). *The State of the World's Children 2012: Children in an Urban World*. New York: UNICEF.

Utas, M. (2003). *Sweet Battlefields: Youth and the Liberian Civil War*. Uppsala Sweden: Uppsala University.

Valentine, G. (1996). Children should be seen and not heard: The production and transgression of adults' public space. *Urban Geography*, *17*(3), 205–20.

Valentine, G., and Holloway, S. L. (Eds.). (2000). *Children's Geographies: Playing, Living, Learning*. Routledge: London.

Van Ausdale, D., and Feagin, J. R. (2001). *The First R: How Children Learn Race and Racism*. Lanham: Rowman & Littlefield.

van Blerk, L. (2006). Diversity and difference in the everyday lives of Ugandan street children: The significance of age and gender for understanding the use of space. *Social Dynamics*, *32*(1), 47–74.

van Blerk, L. (2012). Berg-en-See street boys: Merging street and family relations in Cape Town, South Africa. *Children's Geographies*, *10*, 321–36.

Verkuyten, M. (2003). Ethnic in-group bias among minority and majority early adolescents: The perception of negative peer behaviour. *British Journal of Developmental Psychology*, *21*(4), 543–64.

Vivier, P. M., Hauptman, M., Weitzen, S. H., Bell, S., Quilliam, D. N., and Logan, J. R. (2011). The important health impact of where a child lives: Neighborhood characteristics and the burden of lead poisoning. *Maternal and Child Health Journal*, *15*(8), 1195–202.

Wærdahl, R. (2005). 'May be I'll need a pair of Levi's before junior high?': Child to youth trajectories and anticipatory socialization. *Childhood*, *12*(2), 201–19.

Wald, J. M., and Losen, D. J. (2003). *Deconstructing the School-to-Prison Pipeline*. San Francisco: Jossey-Bass.

Wald, J. M., and Losen, D. J. (2007). 'Out of sight': The journey through the school to prison pipeline. In S. Books (Ed.), *Invisible Children in the Society and its Schools* (3rd edn, pp. 23–38). Mahwah: Lawrence Erlbaum Associates.

Walkerdine, V. (2007). *Children, Gender, Video Games: Towards a Relational Approach to Multimedia*. Basingstoke: Palgrave Macmillan.

Walkerdine, V., Lucey, H., and Melody, J. (2001). *Growing Up Girl: Psycho-Social Explorations of Gender and Class*. Basingstoke: Palgrave Macmillan.

Ward, C. (1990). *The Child in the City*. London: Bedford Square Press.

Ward, G. K. (2012). *The Black Child-Savers: Racial Democracy and Juvenile Justice*. Chicago: University of Chicago Press.

Ward, J. V., and Benjamin, B. C. (2004). Women, girls, and the unfinished work of connection: A critical review of American girls' studies. In A. Harris (Ed.), *All About the Girl: Culture, Power, and Identity* (pp. 15–28). New York: Routledge.

Ward, S. (1974). Consumer socialization. *Journal of Consumer Research*, 1(2), 1–14.

Ware, V., and Back, L. (2001). *Out of Whiteness: Color, Politics, and Culture*. Chicago: University of Chicago Press.

Watras, J. (2014). Historical contributions of Lewis, Willis, and Ogbu to American ethnographic research. *Journal of Ethnographic & Qualitative Research*, 9(1), 55–67.

Wells, K. (2002). Reconfiguring the radical other: Urban children's consumption practices and the nature/culture divide. *Journal of Consumer Culture*, 2(3), 291–315.

Wells, K. (2005). Strange practices: Children's discourses on transgressive unknowns in urban public space. *Childhood*, 12(4), 495–506.

Wells, K. (2007a). Diversity without difference: Modelling 'the real' in the social aesthetic of a London multicultural school. *Visual Studies*, 22(3), 270–82.

Wells, K. (2007b). Symbolic capital and material inequalities: Memorializing class and 'race' in the multicultural city. *Space and Culture*, 10(2), 195–206.

Wells, K. (2007c). On not-reading the signs: Children's social semiotic interpretation of a multicultural neighbourhood. Unpublished paper on request from author.

Wells, K. (2010). Mimesis and alterity: Representations of 'race' in children's film. In K. Hörschelmann and R. Colls (Eds.), *Contested Bodies of Childhood and Youth* (pp. 53–67). Basingstoke: Palgrave Macmillan.

Wells, K. (2011). The strength of weak ties: The social networks of young separated asylum seekers and refugees in London. *Children's Geographies*, 9(3–4), 319–29.

Wells, K. (2012). Making gender and generation: Between the local and the global in Africa. In A. Twum-Danso and R. Ame (Eds.), *Childhoods at the Intersection of the Local and the Global* (pp. 143–59). Basingstoke/New York: Palgrave Macmillan.

Wells, K. (2014). Marching to be somebody: A governmentality analysis of online cadet recruitment. *Children's Geographies*, 12(3), 339–53.

Wells, K. (2015). *Childhood in a Global Perspective* (2nd edn). Cambridge: Polity.

Wells, K. (2016a). Violent lives and peaceful schools: NGO constructions of modern childhood and the role of the state. In J. Parkes (Ed.), *Gender Violence in Poverty Contexts* (pp. 168–82). Abingdon: Routledge.

Wells, K. (2016b). Children's experiences of sexual violence, psychological trauma, death, and injury in war. In C. Harker, K. Hörschelmann and T. Skelton (Eds.), *Conflict, Violence and Peace* (pp. 1–16). Singapore: Springer Singapore.

Wells, K., Burman, E., Montgomery, H., and Watson, A. M. S. (Eds.). (2014). *Childhood, Youth and Violence in Global Contexts*. Basingstoke: Palgrave Macmillan.

Welsh, T. (2013). *The Child as Natural Phenomenologist: Primal and Primary Experience in Merleau-Ponty's Psychology*. Evanston: Northwestern University Press.

White, O. (1999). *Children of the French Empire: Miscegenation and Colonial Society in French West Africa, 1895–1960*. New York: Oxford University Press.

White, W. (1995). *A Man Called White: The Autobiography of Walter White*. Athens: University of Georgia Press.

Whiting, B. B., and Edwards, C. P. (1994). *Children of Different Worlds: The Formation of Social Behavior* (3rd edn). Cambridge MA: Harvard University Press.

Whiting, B. B., and Whiting, J. (1975). *Children of Six Cultures*. Cambridge MA: Harvard University Press.

Willis, P. E. (2006). *Learning to Labour: How Working Class Kids Get Working Class Jobs* (rpt). Aldershot: Ashgate.

Willis, S. (1997). *High Contrast: Race and Gender in Contemporary Hollywood Film*. Durham NC: Duke University Press.

Wing, L. (1981). Asperger's syndrome: A clinical account. *Psychological Medicine*, 11, 115–29.

Winkler, E. N. (2012). *Learning Race, Learning Place: Shaping Racial Identities and Ideas in African American Childhoods*. New Brunswick: Rutgers University Press.

Winstone, N., Huntington, C., Goldsack, L., Kyrou, E., and Millward, L. (2014). Eliciting rich dialogue through the use of activity-oriented interviews: Exploring self-identity in autistic young people. *Childhood*, 21(2), 190–206.

Wohlwend, K. E. (2009). Damsels in discourse: Girls consuming and producing identity texts through Disney princess play. *Reading Research Quarterly*, 44(1), 57–83.

Wojcik-Andrews, I. (2000). *Children's Films: History, Ideology, Pedagogy, Theory*. New York: Garland.

Wolkowitz, C. (2006). *Bodies at Work*. London: Sage.

Young, L., and Barrett, H. (2001). Adapting visual methods: Action research with Kampala street children. *Area*, 33(2), 141–52.

Yousey-Hindes, K. M., and Hadler, J. L. (2011). Neighborhood socioeconomic status and influenza hospitalizations among children: New Haven County, Connecticut, 2003–2010. *American Journal of Public Health*, 101(9), 1785–9.

Zukin, S. (2000). *Landscapes of Power: From Detroit to Disney World* (rpt). Berkeley: University of California Press.

Index

United Nations Convention on the
　Rights of the Child
　(UNCRC)　6, 21, 26, 101–2
urban　10–11, 75–6

Vaincre l'Autisme　86
violence　32, 37–9, 50, 55, 61–6, 77,
　79–80, 110, 153–5
vulnerability　14, 77, 110, 152

War of Independence　8, 35–7
white children　3, 29–31, 33–4,
　41–7, 59–66, 69–74, 139
Whiteness Studies　32, 140, 145
work　3, 7–8, 13, 25, 29, 38, 40–7,
　68–9, 72, 74
writing culture　16, 23

youth (sub)cultures　50–1